"Riveting . . . Lemcke reveals the entire chilling story of an almost perfect husband and an almost perfect killing."
—*Jackson (MS) Advocate*

"A tale of greed, infidelity, and a man who nearly got away with murder . . . Lemcke taps in to the drama and emotion of the case. But he also educates, explaining the ins and outs of the legal system with an easygoing, conversational style that will make readers feel like real insiders. As the twists and turns of the murder plot unfold, Lemcke offers detailed but digestible insights."   —*The Salt Lake Tribune*

"Lemcke . . . comes off as someone who is as honest as the day is long, with a real concern for the parties involved."
—*Publishers Weekly*

IN HER OWN BACKYARD

A Perfect Husband,
A Perfect Marriage,
A Perfect Murder

HOWARD R. LEMCKE

Previously published as
Death in a Fishpond

BERKLEY BOOKS, NEW YORK

THE BERKLEY PUBLISHING GROUP
Published by the Penguin Group
Penguin Group (USA) Inc.
375 Hudson Street, New York, New York 10014, USA
Penguin Group (Canada), 90 Eglinton Avenue East, Suite 700, Toronto, Ontario, M4P 2Y3, Canada
(a division of Pearson Penguin Canada Inc.)
Penguin Books Ltd., 80 Strand, London WC2R 0RL, England
Penguin Group Ireland, 25 St. Stephen's Green, Dublin 2, Ireland (a division of Penguin Books Ltd.)
Penguin Group (Australia), 250 Camberwell Road, Camberwell, Victoria 3124, Australia
(a division of Pearson Australia Group Pty. Ltd.)
Penguin Books India Pvt. Ltd., 11 Community Centre, Panchsheel Park, New Delhi—110 017, India
Penguin Group (NZ), 67 Apollo Drive, Rosedale, North Shore 0745,
Auckland, New Zealand (a division of Pearson New Zealand Ltd.)
Penguin Books (South Africa) (Pty.) Ltd., 24 Sturdee Avenue, Rosebank, Johannesburg 2196,
South Africa

Penguin Books Ltd., Registered Offices: 80 Strand, London WC2R 0RL, England

The publisher does not have any control over and does not assume any responsibility for author or third-party websites or their content.

IN HER OWN BACKYARD

A Berkley Book / published by arrangement with New Horizon Press

PRINTING HISTORY
Previously published as *Death in a Fishpond* by New Horizon Press in June 2005
Berkley mass-market edition / July 2007

Copyright © 2005 by Howard R. Lemcke
Cover design by Pyrographx
Book design by Kristin del Rosario

ISBN: 978-0-425-21646-0

BERKLEY®
Berkley Books are published by The Berkley Publishing Group,
a division of Penguin Group (USA) Inc.,
375 Hudson Street, New York, New York 10014.
BERKLEY is a registered trademark of Penguin Group (USA) Inc.
The "B" design is a trademark belonging to Penguin Group (USA) Inc.

PRINTED IN THE UNITED STATES OF AMERICA

10 9 8 7 6 5 4 3 2 1

For Pam

CONTENTS

AUTHOR'S NOTE

This book is based on the experiences and work of Howard R. Lemcke and reflects his perceptions of the past, present and future. The personalities, events, actions and conversations portrayed within the story have been taken from his memories, extensive court documents, interviews, testimony, research, letters, personal papers, press accounts and the memories of some participants.

In an effort to safeguard the privacy of certain people, some individuals' names and identifying characteristics have been altered. Events involving the characters happened as described. Only details have been changed.

1

The Day Pam Died

August fifteenth was a warm, clear and moonless summer
night in Salt Lake City, Utah. On Capital Hill lights fluttered
on and off. Well-built, early twentieth century houses with
porches, brick and bric-a-brac, that have both individual
character and downtown proximity and are attractive to
young urban professionals with vision, ambition, time and
money, abound. It's one of those places in urban America
where folks of different colors, different accents, different
orientations, different politics, different ages, different means
and different views of the Almighty seem to get along pretty
well. It was not at all surprising that the Meads, a dynamic,
upwardly-mobile interracial couple in their twenties, settled
in and fit in Capital Hill.

The house they bought was a story-and-a-half bungalow
with a front porch. In the yard, a little grass hill humped up a
couple of feet above the front sidewalk and a pretty good-
sized backyard sloped uphill toward an alley. Renovating the
property, the Meads had been involved in several projects
that were in varying stages of completion. The front lawn
was looking good, but the backyard still was a disaster. There
wasn't much except hard-packed dirt, along with those deco-
rations that an eighty-pound dog leaves around. There was
little grass left in the area where Baron, a large and exuber-
ant Chow, was chained to the big tree near a doghouse and a
newly installed pond.

The pond, a metallic blue in the daylight, appeared to be
of black glass in the darkness. About three and a half or four
feet deep, it was etched in the uphill back corner, its opening framed by an inner collar of what masons call common
or construction brick. These were arranged in a spoked fashion

with the long axes focusing toward the center. This bricked collar was in turn surrounded by an outer collar of loose rocks, most of which were a foot or two in diameter. Neither the bricks nor the rocks were cemented down and a black sheet plastic pond liner was easily visible beneath them. Some places in the collar had more rocks than others. A large mound of loose dirt, clear testament that the pool had only been finished four days earlier, was piled a few feet away. The Meads seemed proud of their completed first step in beautifying the yard. Most nights the neighborhood was quiet and peaceful when the couple walked or surveyed their handiwork or talked about their future plans for their new home.

But at about 11:15 that Monday night, neighbors heard shouts and cries from the Meads' backyard. One, Barry Baxter, went to the Meads' and found David in front of his house, soaking wet and in great distress. David led Barry at a run through the home and out to the backyard where Baxter saw David's wife, Pam, laid out alongside the pond. David said that when he got home from his work at the Salt Lake City International Airport, "I found my wife floating facedown in the pond and pulled her out of the water."

Baxter attempted CPR. There was no response. Barry gave David a painfully knowing look. David shrieked, jumped back into the pond and started pulling the rocks and bricks that made up the collar into the water.

The cries that Baxter had heard also drew the attention of other neighbors, who phoned 9-1-1. Two Salt Lake City police officers, Mike Jensen, who would be designated the initial officer, and Sam Tausinga, patrolling in their own cars, took the call and headed for Center Street. The patrolmen arrived to find David in the pond, wailing, punishing the bricks and rocks. Baxter was kneeling by Pam. Jensen first tried sympathy to persuade David to calm down and get out of the water. This was to no avail. Progressively the officer became more firm, moving to request, then demand, once again to no avail. Finally the officer mentioned and displayed a small canister of chemical mace and David allowed Sam Tausinga, a Pacific Islander of enormous strength, to lift him from the pond. As David Mead once again began a torrent of thrashing and wailing, he was secured with handcuffs, wrapped in a blanket and placed in a police car. After he calmed down the handcuffs were removed. Both officers later remembered talking to David Mead in the back of their own police car. It's likely each did take some time to talk to him, but one or the other is confused as to which car. Although both sought to console Mead, neither was able to begin taking a coherent statement.

Soon the paramedics arrived, confirming the obvious. These were followed by a police sergeant, detectives, crime laboratory technicians and the Office of the Medical Examiner. More uniformed officers arrived and helped secure the scene, locate witnesses or physical evidence, take pictures and cordon the area with that yellow tape that shouts "Police Line—Do Not Cross!" They sent for and set up trailer-mounted floodlights. Although the Mead backyard had lights, those didn't work and in any event wouldn't be adequate for the officers' needs.

Jill Candland, a homicide detective, was assigned by the Salt Lake City Police Department to the "unattended" death of Pamela Camille Stokes Mead. Mike Roberts was the sergeant. There is always at least one detective on duty or on call, as well as a supervisor to respond to unattended, unexpected, suspicious or overtly violent deaths. The squad has a coffee mug that sums up, with gallows humor, their mission. It features a smiling skull wearing an SLCPD baseball cap and stereotypical reflecting police sunglasses. Above the skull is the sign, "Salt Lake City Police Department Homicide Squad." Below it another reads, "Our day begins when yours ends. . . ."

If you were casting an actress to play a detective, you probably wouldn't pick Jill Candland. Pretty and petite, she has a friendly face, open smile and easy laugh. Long blond hair pulled back showcases a dramatic silver streak. Intense and attentive, her disarming first impressions of crime scenes often proved useful to experienced cops.

Jill Candland fit neither stereotype nor insider expectation. And Jill Candland did not suffer from those personal insecurities that so often tempt most of us to try to change or disguise who we are to gain only the most shallow of acceptance from those around us—those who, ironically, care so little they're unwilling to accept us for who we are.

Jill started working at SLCPD in 1982, when it wasn't easy to be female in a community of very structured roles and expectations. Ethnic minorities had predated women. Gays may someday be allowed to follow. Police sociology is, after all, a sub-set of society at large.

But all Jill's friends aren't cops. All her interests aren't police work. Her private life is just that. She lives in one of the several beautiful mountain canyon areas that adjoin Salt Lake City. She enjoys, attends and supports the arts and is a passionate golfer. She became active, and later prominent, in the SLCPD union, though Salt Lake, for a number of reasons, is not a hotbed of union activity or sympathy. Jill became a detective in 1988 and moved into homicide in 1990. For a time she was the most senior detective in SLCPD Homicide.

SLCPD, like many other law enforcement institutions and bureaucracies, has its own rituals, history, points of view and assumptions. Police agencies are paramilitary by nature. They are very big—very, very big—into unquestioned loyalty to their people and to their role. The 1960s produced an "us versus them" mentality among many officers and agencies that may never be overcome. It is a well-founded urban stereotype that those without the uniform are untrusted, and untrustable, outsiders in the eyes of cops. Even family, friends, neighbors, "non-sworn" co-workers and, yes, prosecutors are all deemed outsiders.

The area around the Mead home was quickly filled with the concerned and the curious. Some teenagers on their street bikes hung around till well past two in the morning watching the police finish their work, collecting the yellow tape.

David was soaked, shivering, wrapped in a blanket, seated in the backseat of a police car and almost incoherent in his grief. He spent that night at the home of his stepbrother, who lived nearby. Jill Candland was unable to take a statement from the agitated David, but he did tell her he'd been at work at the airport. She sent him off with his relatives and said she'd be in touch.

Pam, who would last leave her Capital Hill home in the gentle care and custody of Ken Farnsworth, an investigator for the State of Utah's Office of the Medical Examiner, lay by the pond, cold to the touch and soaking wet. When Farnsworth, a retired Salt Lake City homicide detective, arrived, he and Detective Candland examined the body. Pam, an attractive, well-built African American woman, was lying faceup alongside the pond. She was wearing a white tee shirt, blue jeans and a pair of open-toed canvas shoes. One of her eyes was open fully, the other partially so. A bloody mucous plug, characteristic of a drowning victim, pushed out of her nose. Although there were no wounds immediately apparent, a closer examination found an injury to the back of her head accompanied by a small amount of blood. Farnsworth inserted the equivalent of a meat thermometer to determine the temperature of Pam's liver, measured the temperature of the air as well as the pond and placed paper bags over her hands. As her body was lifted onto the gurney, it left a wet exaggerated human outline in the grassless dirt. A small stain of blood highlighted where her head last rested.

Candland acquired a high-intensity light, searched around the pond and examined the individual rocks for telltale signs of blood or hair. She found none. She looked in the dirt for signs of a struggle or for those marks indicating that one person dragged another. Again, there were none. All she saw was a paper bag of fish food lying on the ground alongside Pam. She then went into the Mead house.

A bad experience some cases ago emphasized to Jill Candland the need to seek "negative evidence." In that case, also a drowning, relatives later challenged the police, asserting their victim was forcibly drowned in a bathtub and then taken to the location where the body was discovered. Because detectives had not examined that bathtub, they made a very unlikely scenario seemingly possible. So Jill searched the house, bathtubs and showers, and established the absence of such evidence. There was a muddy handprint near the back door and a few other minor instances of disturbance that were consistent with witness accounts.

The detective talked to some of the witnesses and gathered the other officers, wanting to be briefed on their findings. They told her by all accounts the Meads were a happy and well-liked couple with no history of violence or abuse.

David had his own successful company, Valley Ground Service, which performed turn-around services for those airlines that flew into Salt Lake City but didn't have enough daily flights to justify hiring their own ground crews. Pam was a former Continental flight attendant, a "stew," who'd met David through their work and who'd recently become unemployed when Continental discontinued service to Salt Lake. In the past few weeks she had minor surgery on her feet for bunions and was somewhat immobile. Earlier that evening David had helped her walk around the neighborhood. They seemed the perfect match.

When all that could be done had been done, each of the officers was instructed to write a "supp" or supplemental report. The floodlights were folded back onto their trailers and towed away. The yellow tape was taken down and rolled up for its next use. The Mead's home was "secured" by making sure the windows as well as doors were closed and locked. Then everyone went home.

Early the next morning it was Jill Candland's duty to attend the autopsy. At 8:35, the body of Pamela Camille Stokes Mead was before Dr. Todd C. Grey, Chief Medical Examiner for the State of Utah. As Jill drove up to the ME's office, she placed a phone call to Sergeant Chris Ahern of the Salt Lake City Police Department's Airport Detail. She briefly filled Ahern in on the events of the previous night. Ahern had an associate type into a desktop computer the requisite commands to review activity at the airport's security gates. Chris told Jill that David Mead had indeed entered the secured zone of the Salt Lake City Airport by using his pass at Gate #13 at approximately eight thirty the night before. With David's whereabouts at the time of the tragedy now confirmed, no printout was needed of Chris's screen and none was kept. Jill took this information, along with her constant companions, coffee and cigarettes, on the short drive to Dr. Grey's.

The examination protocol defining the process of autopsy is by definition morbid. Todd Grey is not a ghoul. He's a Yale man, tall, dark and handsome, Dartmouth Med, University of California at San Diego internship and residency in pathology. Dr. Grey worked as a medical examiner in New Mexico and Florida before finding his way to Salt Lake, where he worked his way up to Chief Medical Examiner.

Pam was first examined "as received," clothed, wet and muddy. Photographs followed each observation. The temperature probe was kept in place and the time and temperature were noted before it was removed. Next they examined her clothing and found it to be uninjured with some blood staining to the upper back of the tee shirt. The tee shirt, blue jeans, shoes and the normal female undergarments were removed. Rigor mortis and lividity were expected and observed and the pink-white foam coming from the nose and mouth noted. Her eyes remained open. No scars or tattoos were observed. Pam's abdomen had a series of linear abrasions and her right elbow had a small abrasion. The bags were removed from her hands, which had picked up dirt from the backyard but were uninjured. They found her nails long and smooth with no tissue or blood beneath them indicating a struggle. Next they examined the injury to the back of her head. Then her hair, black, thick and wavy, was shaved away and the wound photographed. On about the "hat line" to the right backside of the head they observed a roughly horizontal wound, approximately one and a quarter inches wide and "superiorly undermining." Whatever caused the wound traveled upward, relative to the normal position of the head, intruding underneath the scalp nearly an inch.

Pam's recent surgery was apparent. The great toes on both feet showed swelling and surgical scarring. A metal pin that was inserted into the hollow of the bone extended about a quarter inch beyond the tip of each long, or second, toe.

After that the examination became more gory. Pamela was invaded by the scalpel. Her internal organs and brain were removed, examined and weighed. Her lungs and trachea were congested with the foamy fluids and materials of drowning. It was determined that the rest of her organs were "unremarkable," save for some indication of the potential for uterine cancer had Pam lived. Various fluid samples were collected for submission to the laboratory.

Further examination showed no fracture to the skull beneath the wound nor any epidural or subdural hemorrhaging, bleeding above or beneath the skull. There were no injuries to the neck, brain, brain stem or spinal column. All tests came back negative for the presence of alcohol or drugs.

Dr. Grey restored Pam to what was cosmetically possible and discussed Ken Farnsworth's report and Jill Candland's observations with the detective. Todd announced that he would find this to be a death whose cause was drowning and manner was accident. Detective Candland agreed and left to close her case after an interview with David to tie it up. Todd Grey gave recorded notes to his support staff to type the official report. The next morning, that report was finished, signed and delivered to the Salt Lake City/County Health Department, taking its place as one more vital statistic.

The investigation into the death of Pam Mead was, for all effects and purposes, over. Jill Candland, like any other urban police officer, had a plate full of cases that needed attention. Once David's interview could be put together, SLCPD#94-116932 would be complete.

Although Tausinga, Candland, Grey, Farnsworth and the rest took professional notice of this sad happening, as did Pastor France Davis, and even as the neighbors and friends took shocked notice, the larger world took no notice at all. I didn't. Chief Deputy County Attorney Greg Skordas didn't. Anne Sulton didn't. Roger "Action Jackson" Tinsley didn't. Neither did Patrick Anderson, Wally Bugden, Dave Mack, Kevin Kurumada, Kurt Frankenburg, Jill Dunyon, Vernice Ah Ching, Ron Yengich, Ben Hamilton nor Rich Mauro, attorneys-at-law all. Matt Jenkins, CPA, missed this event, as did the recent SLCPD Sergeant, now Federal Bureau of Investigations Special Agent Jim Bell and FBI Supervising Special Agent Mary Ellen O'Toole. But the others and I would all revisit this night, our original perceptions and misperceptions many times.

2

A Terrible Morning

The awful word came to the Stokes family second- and third-hand. Nobody spoke to David Mead directly. Mary Stokes, Pam's sister, was at work in Atlanta. Her and Pam's parents, Sinie and Garfield, were at work in Colorado Springs. One of David's brothers, all of whom had gathered around the widower, made those calls, along with the many others. Rumors and explanations of how Pam died were incongruous, incomplete and often incorrect. One involved Pam falling in a bird-bath. The Stokeses told the Meads that they were making the necessary arrangements to hurry to Salt Lake so they could see where their daughter's death happened. They were told that David didn't want anyone staying in the house. He was still quite distraught. The Stokeses would have to arrange for a motel room.

I cannot imagine a more terrible thing than losing a child. We come to accept an order of things where our children are there to bury us with the reverse seldom envisioned. A sudden and unexpected death is a traumatic rending of any family or community. When the person is young and vital the void is often filled with those questions directed in pained cries to man and to God: How? Why? Who is to blame? When that person is shared by more than one group and those haven't gotten along, the last question will rise to the fore. With in-laws this approaches a tradition. With this jaded knowledge, Detective Jill Candland picked up the phone to talk to Mary Stokes.

Mary introduced herself, told Jill the funeral had been scheduled for the next Monday, August 22, announced the Stokes family were ill at ease with the idea of Pam's death as an accident and said that the "perfect couple" wasn't.

Mary told Jill of a separation two years before when Pam moved back to Colorado Springs for a few months. On that occasion Pam told Mary she'd overheard a telephone conversation between David and another woman. Mary asked Jill if it would be possible for the Stokes family to meet with the detective. Detective Candland agreed and the two set up a time that next week.

Although Mary's anger and suspicion were not discounted, Candland moved to other pressing cases. Often just being there while others vent is part of a cop's job. Mary's call melded with observations from the scene, the autopsy: they brought reflection but did not convince the detective that David was guilty of anything. They'd have David call when he could function. That was typical for traumatic loss. Everything would be sorted out in due course and Jill would be in a position to talk to the Stokeses, tell them what the investigation showed and commiserate on the reality that sometimes terrible things happen to good people.

Homicide Detective Jill Candland picked up another file, another case that needed work.

Wednesday, August 17 came and went without any event relating to Pam's death landing on the detective's desk. Just another very full day of the details of follow-up investigations on that load of cases every detective carries. A quick trip to court or two for a few minutes of testimony after many minutes of waiting to testify, which resulted as often as not in being told that she didn't have to testify. Even so, there was always coffee and paperwork to fill that time. Her attempts to talk with David led her to his brother who still felt David was too shocked and shaken to give a coherent statement.

That Thursday, though, brought information from other sources.

First, another call to David was intercepted by David's brother John. "Johnny," as his family knows him, told the detective that David was still too upset to give a statement. Jill accepted that and asked if David could call her after the funeral. Johnny said he'd have David do just that.

Then a woman named Angela called.

It's the norm that when someone cold-calls a cop or a prosecutor and has their own story to tell, they'll hem and haw for a while before they either provide their insight or flinch, say "Never mind," and hang up. Conversely, when someone calls to tell what a third person has to say, they come right to the point.

Angela came right to the point. She told Jill, "I have information on the Mead death the police ought to know." According to Angela, Winnie, one of Angela's friends, had been David Mead's mistress for the past few years. Angela said that Winnie was quite distressed, because she put Pam's sudden death into the context of a conversation she'd had with David two weeks prior. Winnie had made a familiar demand "Her or me! Make up your mind!" Angela said Winnie had told her David announced he would just kill Pam and be Winnie's alone, and Winnie now feared for her own safety. Detective Candland suggested "I'd indeed be interested in having you bring Winnie to the police department for a chat." Angela said she'd bring Winnie over the next day.

The Public Safety Building is one of those buildings erected in the late 1950s and early 1960s with the mistaken vision of what the buildings of the 1990s and 2000s would look like. Eight stories of alternating aluminum and once shiny sun-bleached powder blue paint, it originally served as the headquarters of a utility company that had since moved into another building. Now converted into the seat of power for the city's police, fire and parameds, the PSB stands like day-old parfait with awnings and antennas.

The sixth floor—a floor typical of buildings of this period, with several large rooms subdivided into cubicles—houses the PD's detectives. The squads, homicide, burglary, larceny, auto theft and the like, are grouped together around small offices for command-level folks, a conference room and some windowless rooms with hidden video cameras for interviews or short-term detention. It's the sort of crowded, loud, bustling and inelegant environment that breeds camaraderie and wisecracks.

On the morning of the nineteenth, a large and very beautiful flower arrangement arrived for the pretty blond detective, Candland. The only reasonable course of action was to phone up to the squad and have one of the other detectives, one well versed in teasing and wisecrack, come down,

retrieve the flowers and hand deliver them to a loud faux cho-
rus of "Oooh, Jill!" and "What aren't you telling us?" Jill,
looking perplexed, searched for the card. When the greeting
was read aloud, "Jill—Thanks for everything. David Mead."
*Oooh*s stopped and detective juices started flowing. The fishpond case was getting curiouser and curiouser.

Lieutenant Judy Denker and Sergeants Don Bell and Mike
Roberts decided to sit in on Winnie's interview. Although he
was in a position to be detached, that just wasn't Don Bell's
style. Roberts was alongside Bell as a shift commander in
SLCPD Homicide and had been to the scene. Denker was the
next link up the chain of command. It was not lost on this
crew that the business of cleaning regularly scheduled commercial aircraft had some potential for regular inter-city ship-
ment of certain "commodities."

Suddenly Jill's phone rang. There were two women at the
front desk to see Detective Candland. She took the elevator
down and ushered Angela and Winnie in through security so
they could acquire the requisite clip-on visitors' badges
before taking the elevator up to the interview room on six.
The PD was about to hear the first of what would be at least
six accounts, denials and reiterations from Winnetka Walls of
her dealings with David Earl Mead before the death of
David's wife Pam. They would be six incredible accounts.

Incredible is not a word chosen randomly. Although we
use it as an emphatic device, the original use of that word is
to be not credible, not worthy of belief. In the courtroom only
credible evidence possesses the requisite dignity and foundation to be brought before a jury. There are a lot of factors in
credibility, among them motive, bias, any history of the
speaker for crime, truthfulness or untruthfulness and the consistency of prior statements.

Winnetka Walls, a petite, attractive African American
woman, had rounded features. That day she seemed very nervous. Winnie kept either tightening up so that she couldn't
talk or gushing out so that she couldn't seem to stop. During
the ride up in the elevator, Angela pushed Winnie on the areas
Winnie needed to address. One of these caught the cop's
attention. David had a locked room in Winnie's apartment
where he once kept dresses, wigs, makeup, explosives and

strange devices. Winnie insisted Angela remain with her for the interview.

We like to believe that a police interview follows the pattern of the old *Dragnet* TV series: *Just the facts, Ma'am; get to the point*. Unlike Joe Friday's cases, this interview wasn't scripted for a half-hour format. This many people, personalities and shifting disclosures led to a bouncing series of questions and conversations that filled close to two hours and thirty-two pages of single-spaced transcript.

After a bit of background was established, Bell prompted Winnie, who related that a few years back, "I met and started dating David Mead. We were introduced by Dave's brother. After a time we became close and I learned that David Earl Mead was a married man." According to Winnie there were a lot of the stereotypical lines and devices that allowed one side of a triangle to buy time. Meanwhile, Dave and Winnie's relationship became close and ongoing. David bought her presents, found her an apartment and picked up the rent. They took vacations together—nice vacations: Mexico, Catalina, Las Vegas—had Sunday dinner with Winnie's parents and visited a counselor. Pam's job as a flight attendant provided wonderful predictability about when she would be out of town.

Winnie told the detectives her story of how her relationship with David evolved. She loved him, wanted to marry him and have his children. David was an incredibly charming man, an incredibly charming married man. Ultimatums would come and go and it was around Christmas 1993 Winnie first told David to make up his mind, "her or me."

After this ultimatum, David explained his plight: if he left Pam he'd be broke, lose his home and his business.

She said he told her Valley Ground Service was, quite literally, the Mead family business. Some years back Dave's mother had conceptualized, assembled and built the enterprise. The concept was that as an airliner would arrive in Salt Lake as the end point of a route, it would need to be serviced before it could turn around and head out in another direction. In addition to the obvious need for fuel, repairs and aeronautic inspection and adjustment, someone needed to go into the cabin, vacuum, slick up the galley, pick up the trash, fluff up the pillows, fill up the water tanks and empty the lavatory holding tanks. For some carriers, the smaller ones or the large carriers with only a few flights, it made no economic sense to hire and maintain a full-time crew for less than full-time work. This was the niche that VGS filled quite well, according to David.

Oft times the gift that allows someone the genius of ideas does not accompany the strengths of a good manager for an ongoing enterprise. As David learned the business from the ground up, helping his brothers, VGS was having problems with the bookkeeping and the equipment. At one point Dave's mom sold Valley Ground to a man who took over the operations. Some things went well; paying the IRS didn't.

Winnie said David told her how he became the "white knight" of the dream by buying VGS from the successor. Even though David's resources and credit were not up to the task, David's work through Valley Ground Service allowed him to meet a lot of airline personnel and date a Continental flight attendant named Pam Stokes, whose credit was good and whose family had some resources. David got married and his wife took out a personal loan large enough to cover the IRS liens. The bride's sister, Mary Stokes, lent the enterprise enough money to update and obtain equipment sufficient to bid on, and win, a contract to service an additional carrier. The gem of Mom's genius was safe in the Mead family's loving care, subject to certain obligations running to Garfield and Sinie Stokes's daughters. David told Winnie that Mary held a document giving Pam control of the business. This was a matter of the heart, not just the pocketbook, and were the marriage to go the way of divorce, the Mead family dream might prosper in the hands of strangers. Since Dave's mom and brother were working for VGS and others close to that family fire were accruing benefits, the other shoe would fall on his blood family as well. David told Winnie that although the two of them could live on love alone, he couldn't handle the surrender of VGS and he didn't particularly care to be poor. He suggested other options.

Winnie said, "David often used the phrase, 'It will all be resolved.'" She told the officers David spoke of three options. The first was divorce, but that would lead to the problems just related. The second was a variation on "take the money and run": Since Valley Ground Service periodically received checks of up to $17,000 from the airlines it serviced, option two was to grab one of these large checks, cash it and hit the road. The two young lovers with a nest egg could move to Hawaii, California or Mexico and begin life anew. But option two would lead to option one and all those consequences would necessarily fall on the other Meads. Option three was to kill Pam and keep the business and the insurance money.

The insurance money? What insurance money?

According to Winnie, Mr. and Mrs. David Earl Mead took out insurance policies on each other's lives, at Pam's insistence and urging. Winnie told the assembled detectives that these were large policies: she couldn't recall the exact amounts, but two or three hundred thousand dollars sounded right. Oh yes, there was a provision for a bigger payout for an accidental death. Double indemnity? "Yeah, something like that."

Around Christmas David moved Winnie into a two-bedroom apartment in one of those modern, campus-looking complexes a few miles from downtown, put the apartment in Winnie's name, gave her an additional one thousand dollars in startup cash and agreed to go to a session with her counselor.

As Winnie told it, during that session the counselor asked Mead if he was going to leave his wife and he responded, "I can't leave her, because she'll take my business and that's rightfully mine. My mother owned it and I don't want her to take it from me!" The counselor told David he was playing with both women and was dealing with too many lives. She told Winnie that she believed David Mead had a sick mind. She asked Walls if the relationship ever involved violence, but Winnie said no.

"In the spring," Winnie said, "an additional complication occurred when the airline discontinued service to Salt Lake City." Pam found that to be a good occasion to change directions. She was now home all the time and not taking those wonderfully convenient runs out of town or contributing her earnings to the family. Dave would have to pay for those little jaunts with Winnie instead of using an airline employee's ticket privileges.

Then about a month before Pam's death, as Dave and Winnie sat on Winnie's bed, Winnie set a deadline and upped the ante. He had till the end of the month to arrive at a decision or Winnie would mail the videotapes to Pam. Videotapes? Yes, David had made videotapes of the couple's lovemaking in Mexico, California, Park City and Winnie's place. David kept the fifth tape, the one the lovers made in Pam's bed, in a lock box.

"Do you still have them?"

"Yes," she nodded.

"Would you bring them to the police for safekeeping?" She would and she did, along with a cardboard box of photographs of a similar ilk. The tapes and photographs, which were never viewed beyond that glimpse requisite to confirm their existence and character as a substantial threat to David Mead's well-being, were, and are, and are, sealed and stored beyond prying eyes in the police evidence locker.

At this threat David started defining his concept of resolution involving "a rather nasty spill." David would have an alibi and things might be taken from the house to look like a burglary or robbery gone bad.

Jill asked, "Why would it be made to look like a nasty spill and a crime gone bad?" Winnie didn't have a good answer but reiterated that Mead had gone on about steps to "make it look like a robbery."

"And as to the alibi?"

Winnie told Jill that David said "mainly things off the top of his head. He might be at either of two of his brothers' houses or at his mom's or at the airport." He mentioned the airport? Yes, "airport was one of the things mentioned." She was pressed for detail, but little came.

Asked about what followed this conversation, Ms. Walls moved on to "Sunday, two weeks ago." David had Sunday dinner at the home of Winnie's parents, who were aware of David's relationships with both their daughter and Pam. As good parents, they pressed Mead as to how he was going to do right by their child. According to Winnie, David said he'd "kill her. Well he didn't say kill, he said 'murder.'" However, this was in the context of some rather sensational statements David was tossing about.

Winnie's mom mentioned to David that she'd recently seen Pam on crutches. David told the Walls Pam was on crutches because he ran over her feet with a car following an argument. Winnie went on to say that David did say he'd been talking with lawyers and left hope for a future for him and Winnie.

Then Winnie told her version of a phone call she received from David about two thirty on the afternoon of Pam's last day. The officers asked Winnie to reconfirm it several times. Winnie said she'd pushed David: What about the lawyers? He'd insisted, "it won't work out, she'll get the house and business and I'll be poor." She'd pushed further. His next words were chilling: "Don't worry, baby, everything will be resolved. Everything will be resolved by the end of the month."

On Tuesday the sixteenth David's brother called, a strange call, largely stern in tone. Tom told Winnie that David "wouldn't be able to contact" her for a while, nor should she contact David. There had been a terrible accident; Pam was dead, drowned in a birdbath. David would be in touch after the funeral.

Winnie said she was rattled and immediately got hold of Angela, a friend and confidant who knew David. At this point in the interview, Angela interrupted. The two went on, bouncing off of each other, about the next several hours of disbelief, speculation, even panic, telling the detectives it all led to Angela's call to the police department. Angela opined how she translated her shock at the news of Pam into fear for her friend's well-being. In almost every sentence, or conversational sentence fragment, Angela used the word weird. As she spoke of David, David's recent behavior and the whole cloth of the situation, that word seemed apropos. The two women had discussed David's "resolution" of Pam's death. What had been thought a joke now had become a nightmare. As detectives sat listening to the two women they asked themselves, was this woman's story credible? Was she a scorned lover? If it was true, what was David Earl Mead truly capable of?

It may seem somewhat intuitive that when the cops learn bad things about a suspect, for instance, that he has a sick mind, that this would be good evidence in the case against him. But our system has formalized the Rules of Evidence. When evidence makes any disputed question before a judge or jury more or less likely, then this evidence is relevant. But not all relevant evidence is admissible. Evidence may not be admissible if it tends to be overly prejudicial to the defendant. Not prejudicial to his cause in the sense that it proves guilt, but prejudicial to his person in that it would tend to hold him up to hate or ridicule. When evidence is challenged under what we call Rule 404(b), the court must balance the concerns. For instance, the existence and nature of the Winnie tapes as a threat to David and forming his motive is probative, while the specific detailed content, or an extreme of showing the tapes, would be highly prejudicial. If Pam had been killed with a pipe bomb, or by someone appearing to be a "uniquely" dressed and coifed woman, or during a sexual encounter involving several people, Winnie's knowledge might have been probative of David's involvement. But, while interesting, it would be highly prejudicial and not probative of a drowning death with insurance proceeds.

As the interview was concluding, Candland said to Winnie, "Be sure to keep in touch." But Detective Candland, a realist and skeptic by virtue of her profession, knew she had to make some phone calls of her own, the first to Chief Deputy Salt Lake County Attorney Greg Skordas to meet and talk over this strange case. The second was to Utah's Chief Medical Examiner, Dr. Todd Grey. After that call, Dr. Grey did something unusual—not unheard of, but unusual: he amended his finding on the death of Pamela Camille Stokes Mead. The cause of death remained drowning. The manner of death was amended from accident to pending. The fishpond case, which had been so close to being closed and relegated to a curiosity, was off the back burner.

3

A Strange Funeral

The weekend before the funeral passed and that Monday, the twenty-second, Detective Candland received a call from the Denver office of Pennington Insurance. A claims supervisor, Jane Dryer, confirmed Winnie's assertion about the insurance policy. The supervisor said that the Meads had taken out policies on each other's lives less than a year before in the amounts of $250,000 with $250,000 riders for accidental death that cost $137 per month. Dryer noted that Pennington claims had been contacted on the sixteenth by David's younger brother, who had two concerns: payment would be made available quickly and no one else was to know the amounts involved. Ms. Dryer suggested Detective Candland talk to the agent who sold the policy, Gayle Fairfield.

Gayle told Jill that she and Pam became friends working as flight attendants for Continental Airlines. When Gayle's husband started selling insurance and Gayle started thinking about insurance as an on-ground career, she talked casually to co-workers and friends about insurance. Pam had approached Gayle about life insurance and the two talked briefly before turning negotiations over to their respective husbands. Gayle related how "The four of us met at a Denver restaurant, ate dinner and signed the papers." Gayle was a little surprised at the amounts and the accidental death rider, but new to the business. She was pleased with her part in the deal.

According to Gayle, Tuesday morning August 16, the Fairfields were enjoying a little getaway in New Mexico when they got a call from their office in Denver and Gayle learned of her friend Pam's death. After the Fairfields shared tears, she called David Mead's stepbrother, told him how to contact Pennington's claims department and what documentation, including the death certificate, would be required for the claims process to go forward. Gayle didn't share with Jill her distressing thoughts that the policy may have been part of the process of Pam's death.

On Tuesday the twenty-third, the family Stokes kept their promise to meet with the SLCPD. The anger and skepticism expressed by Pam's sister Mary before the funeral was only a hint of the family's emotions after the funeral. Pam's dad, Garfield, was a retired Army NCO, a large man who raised four daughters and a son while he was sent about the world seeing to his nation's needs. His daughter Pam was born in Verdun, France. He had smoked for years, still did; his hip had gone bad and he walked slowly and sadly with the help of a cane. Pam's mom Sinie raised the children and worked in those jobs available to an army wife around this country or this world. Uncle Sam has never paid his troops enough. She defines a picture of quiet dignity; her voice is as soft as her eyes. Of the surviving sisters, Mary, a professional in the competition of the business world, was far more vocal and assertive than Pam's mother.

The Stokeses arrived in tension, their minds made up to bring Pam home to Colorado Springs for burial. When they arrived at David and Pam's house, the greetings were hardly warm or welcoming. They wanted to gather up some of Pam's personal items, but since David didn't want anyone in the house without supervision, they were let in under the watchful eye of a neighbor. The house, according to David, had been burglarized the night after the drowning. Pam's purse and some of her jewelry were gone. They found other things missing: family pictures, a stone menorah-style candelabrum that Pam kept on her mantle and a favorite blanket. The Stokeses had specifically said they wanted to see the pond, but they never saw it because it had been filled.

The Mead family said they were worried about the danger to neighborhood children and, in a collective decision, they went out, cut a bit of a drain on the downhill side, tossed the rocks, the bricks and the black plastic sheeting into the hole and shoveled in the dirt from the adjacent dirt pile. The fate of the fish was not addressed. They hadn't checked in with the police before filling in the pond: the police had abandoned their control of the house, so why not?

David wouldn't hear of having Pam buried anywhere except Salt Lake City. He'd arranged for a mausoleum niche at Mount Calvary Cemetery. Pam attended Pastor France Davis's Calvary Baptist Church, but the fact that Mount Calvary was the Roman Catholic cemetery was lost on the widower. David did tell the Stokeses that he wouldn't be able to help with the $9,000 cost of the funeral. Things were difficult and losing the Continental contract put David in a bind. No one mentioned insurance, but at one point David's mother confided to Sinie that David told his mom she would now be able "to live in a big house on a hill." David was still too outwardly distraught to review the events with his in-laws, but Garfield noticed that Dave's mood was hardly constant.

There are certain routines, rituals and expectations built into a funeral: people gather, commiserate, support one another, share memories and get through the necessary steps. We hug, cry and reminisce about the good memories, and for that short time tend to forgive and forget the wrongs of others. Many will want to see their loved one; some want to view the place where they died and hear some details. I guess that some funerals can go well, but this one didn't.

When Pam's sisters spoke at her funeral, their suspicions were not concealed. Their eulogies closed by swearing, "I promise you, Pam, I will make it my mission in life to find out what really happened," and, "Know that I will give relentless devotion to setting what's wrong, right."

Afterward, at the Stokeses' meeting with the detectives, they had a lot to say. Mary told Detective Candland her views of the history of the perfect couple. According to Pam's sister, when Pam married David, Mary lent them $8,000 for the business on a note that had since been paid and Pam borrowed several thousand dollars to pay off the IRS. Mary had copies of that paperwork and agreed to gather those up and fax them over. Recently Pam had told Mary that losing the Continental contract was a blow and David was back in arrears to the IRS. Mary heard David was supporting his mother through VGS, was maxed out on the couple's credit cards—all in Pam's name due to David's credit history—and once borrowed from a card to meet payroll. There were allegations of a gambling problem within the family Mead.

Mary told about another of David's relationships, this one with a woman named Stormy. Several years before, Pam had walked out on David, come to Colorado Springs and confided to her sister about picking up a telephone extension only to overhear David saying to this Stormy, "I just hate her. Let's just kill her and collect the life insurance." After Pam spent several months on the other side of the Rockies, David convinced his bride to return to Utah. But the relationship had more problems. Pam once more packed and her family headed to Salt Lake City to drive her to the Springs, but David wove his magic and Pam never left home.

"When the airline she worked for decided to stop service to the area, Pam took the opportunity to get out. She wanted to go to school, learn another trade and have elective surgery on her feet." Pam had talked with Mary the year before about David's idea that the couple ought to buy life insurance. Mary's first reaction was shock, particularly after the Stormy call, but Pam responded she wanted to protect her interest in the business were anything to happen to David. The marriage was obviously having good as well as bad days. To Mary's surprise the Meads were now talking about having children. That was only under discussion: some days it sounded wonderful, but on others, Pam opined that David couldn't take care of a wife; how would he ever take care of children?

Recently Pam had told Mary about David's latest attempt to upgrade their property. The pond was one of several projects envisioned for the backyard. There was eventually going to be a deck and maybe a gazebo. The Meads had been working on it for a few months and had just filled it with a garden hose the Thursday before Pam died. Pam put a few goldfish in the pond and kept a sack of fish food in the back room. The couple went out each night to the pool, then sat, cleaned and admired it.

At that point things seemed to be going better. Then came the news of Pam's death. The Stokeses' suspicions about it were fanned when they saw scratches on David's face, neck and body. He said he'd run into tree branches in the backyard and rocks around the pool. But the family had questions.

Couldn't these have really come from a struggling victim? They could, but Pam had neither matching wounds nor tissue under her nails from such a struggle. There clearly wasn't enough here to charge, but there was more than enough to continue to investigate and David still hadn't made a statement.

One of the things that a detective can't do is tell one witness what another has said. It may have been tempting to discuss Angela, Winnie and the Pennington information with the Stokeses, but this wasn't the time. The value of the cards in one's hand is often that only the player knows what they are.

Meanwhile, detectives found out the fishpond had become another stretch of bare ground.

On the morning of the twenty-fourth, the phone rang. It was Patrick Anderson, a Salt Lake attorney in general practice, who had recently concluded his stint with the LDA, Salt Lake's public defenders office formally titled the Salt Lake Legal Defenders Association. Pat is a likeable man, tall, thin, with a pleasant smile, a golfer who has credibility in the community for talent, good humor and integrity. Pat deals with people as a polite, straightforward professional. If he accuses a cop or other witness of poor work or bad motive, it's wise to examine that claim, because, unlike other critics, Pat isn't given to wild accusation. David Earl Mead was sitting in Pat's office ready to be interviewed; Jill Candland grabbed a cassette tape recorder, unfortunately a faulty one, and headed for Anderson's office. Although not unheard of, and clearly within his rights, the way David Mead chose to talk to the cops in the office of a lawyer whose specialty was criminal defense didn't go unnoticed.

Jill walked into Pat's office, was ushered to a small conference room and turned on the recorder, which, unknown to the participants, was only picking up from 40 to 60 percent of the dialogue. The first references to the Meads would be transcribed as the Means. Jill thanked David for the flowers. "You're welcome. I was just . . . You know . . . My family and I just appreciated your—you know—consideration."

Jill spent a while on background, asking about David's family, who everyone was, where they lived, worked and the like. Where was David from? Where had he lived? How long had they been in the house on Center Street? Tell me about the business. What do you do there, David? What hours? What duties? Other family members? Did you start it? It was his mom's and started in 1980. But David bought the company and took it over. Was Pam part of the business? "Yeah, she purchased the company on a loan and I ran it. Basically, both of us owned it."

They talked about the company's finances. Things had not been going well, particularly with the loss of the business of the airline for which Pam worked. David once had a number of employees, at one point mostly family, but was down to just one who helped out on occasion. David never fired anyone, but he talked to them about pay cuts and they all quit. He'd hired a person named Tom a couple of weeks ago who had a full-time job elsewhere, was supposed to clean the planes the evening of the fifteenth but never showed up. The airline only wanted a "quick clean," because they wanted to use their aircraft for some training, so David went to the airport and took care of that chore himself. He saw a few people out there but couldn't remember their names.

Pam had left Continental that spring. The Meads bought into the airline's health insurance program, but it didn't pay for Pam's bunion surgery, which was considered cosmetic. Pam had asked David to get a life insurance policy sometime back—through Pennington.

Pam had had surgery about a month before she died. She'd only been out of a wheelchair and walking for about a week. The Meads went for a walk earlier that evening around their Capital Hill neighborhood. It had been tough on her and she was walking on the outsides of her feet to lessen the pain. They walked slowly, rested frequently when Pam hurt or felt tired and ran into some friends, including Kevin Harris. When they got back from the walk and David realized he'd have to go in to work, he asked Pam to go out, clean the pool and feed the fish. Pam agreed and kissed her loving husband goodbye on his way out the door.

Pam had never cleaned the pond by herself, but David didn't see any problem. Baron did like to jump up on people, but Pam knew this and avoided him. Dave thought it likely she'd have walked wide of Baron and then cut in close to the pool.

According to David, when he returned from the airport the house was dark and Pam nowhere to be found. He called Kevin Harris, other friends and neighbors but couldn't locate her, then decided to walk out into the backyard, pet the dog and admire the fishpond. There were no lights out there, only light from neighbors or distant streetlamps, but he saw Pam in the water. David jumped into the pond and got Pam out. It was a difficult task but at that moment he noticed some of the bricks were displaced. David left Pam on the ground and went for help, ran into a neighbor, ran through the house and into the backyard. While the neighbor was trying to help Pam, David jumped back into the fishpond to destroy the villain by tearing the pond apart until that nice police officer pulled him out.

Did David know who "could have done this" to her? No, she didn't have any enemies.

"If someone did do this . . . who would be above suspicion?"

"Everybody that Pam knew—I mean, she was loved by everybody."

"David, what do you think happened to Pam?"

With a sigh, he said he didn't know, but she might have fallen into the pond. She couldn't swim well and was frightened of having her head under water. He did recall bricks out of place on the pond's edge.

There are interrogation techniques that use questions calculated to gauge reaction as well as answers. Here—no reaction, just answers, including ones to questions not asked, but wasn't this just an interview, with a victim, about a terrible accident?

It was time to talk about the perfect couple and their marriage. David told Jill that he determined, some time ago, they should have kids. He sniffed. He knew he'd betrayed Pam's trust, gone out with someone else, but he was trying to reform. Pam didn't know David had been sleeping around and he didn't believe she'd been unfaithful. About two years ago they had a separation that lasted about three months. David was having a lot of problems, nothing drastic, but pretty soon they started seeing each other again, rejoined their marriage, which had been a lot stronger since.

Of course, recently, David went out with another young woman a few times, nothing serious, he assured Jill. He'd seen her on and off, although there was one time while Pam was out of town—she was a flight attendant—he'd gone out on a date or something: it was unfortunate; he used her, but he was lonely. This girl had given David an ultimatum, told David she'd leave him if he didn't leave his wife in August.

Leave him? Wasn't this just every now and again?

Well, she was saying he couldn't come over anymore, that she was "just going to cut this off." So he told her, "well that's fine" and didn't call her for several weeks. David "never anticipated any kind of separation" from Pam, hadn't seen that other girl for so long he couldn't remember or even guess at a date, but was afraid she might come over, talk to Pam and hurt her. He spoke to this girl the day before the interview and told her he didn't want to even talk anymore. He felt so guilty about cheating on Pam. The girl was angry but pretty much accepted the fact that the affair was over.

Jill asked about a burglary at their house after Pam's death and David said his brother handled the police report. He remembered the Stokeses had been angry, because they thought someone stayed in Pam's house after they were told they couldn't. The Meads were unhappy that the Stokeses went there unsupervised. The cops came over and said the house had been entered and some things taken. It was sort of odd, because they'd taken Pam's purse and jewelry but nothing of David's except a coin jar. Whoever it was picked up and poured out the jar. It weighed about sixty-five pounds. They didn't do any damage, as if they knew exactly where everything was. It occurred to Mr. Mead that "Pam's purse was like a leather backpack and they just poured all the money into that . . . So he reached over and picked it up and threw it in the purse." The broken glass was from a second money jar. Dave's brother was going to hide the jar but dropped it.

Detective Candland wanted to hit two more items and set both up with the same thought: David was going to be asked a lot of questions by family, friends and by the insurance companies and would do well to reflect on everything and everyone he encountered from the time he and Pam woke up on August 15 until he was placed in the police car. Get a little notebook and write down his thoughts. What would David think about taking a polygraph exam, a lie detector? David said of course he'd do that and after some discussion of local personalities who administer those tests, Jill and Patrick Anderson agreed on a general framework of times and folks.

After a day of phone tag over three time zones, Jill got through to Jim Bell at the FBI, who found the fishpond fertile waters for the imagination. The fabled profilers at the National Center for the Analysis of Violent Crime had some materials in the fields of staged homicides that they'd pass along to the SLCPD.

The first was a format for a behavioral analysis interview, a compilation of interrogation techniques for interviews set up as a textbook with analysis of each technique. Most of it was old news to Jill, who'd used a fair amount of the suggested questions and techniques the day before. The analysis segments for some of Dave's responses, however, did raise an eyebrow or two.

Jill:

Listed next are some observations seen at staged homicides. I have also listed some suggestions.

In staged cases it is not unusual for the offender to call somebody prior to reporting the death to law enforcement. Did this happen? If so what did the offender tell the person he called?

Insurance-Related Deaths:

1. *Offender usually has close relationship to victim*
2. *Victim would usually be classified as low risk*
3. *Body usually not concealed*
4. *Organized, has planning involved*
5. *Crime scene orderly*
6. *Little physical evidence*
7. *Weapon brought to and removed from scene*

8. *Often staging is put into effect to make it look like death was an accident or natural causes*
9. *Staged deaths have a high percentage of asphyxia as cause of death*
10. *May be caused by current stressor on offender*
11. *Offender may have solid alibi with selective recall*
12. *Offender may delay reporting so third party may find body*

Staged Domestic Homicide:

1. *Planned*
2. *Crime scene reflects control of offender*
3. *Physical evidence removed or destroyed prior to police arriving. Counts on first responders to destroy evidence. May alter evidence by collapsing, falling, knocking, moving or destroying evidence.*
4. *Body usually not concealed*
5. *Crime scene usually at victim's or offender's residence*
6. *Staged to look like an accident (car, drowning, fall, etc.)*
7. *Offender may start first aid*
8. *To individuals close to offender/victim it may appear that the relationship is improving*
9. *Offender may tell victim's family that victim may have expressed fear over their safety*

Every time a suspect says or does anything, you need to ask yourself: "Why is he doing or telling me this?" He has spent a long time planning this out. There will be a reason for everything.

Keep in mind that you also may be dealing with a criminal, even a bomber. They usually hate face-to-face confrontation. They feel they are much smarter than police officers. Plus they have large egos and are very manipulative.

He will be much smarter than he appears or even acts. Be very careful during your interviews. Even *though he may not act like it, he may be way ahead of you.*

Interviews that make the suspect feel confronted will not convince him that you believe the death is an accident. I wouldn't do the interviews at the police department: too confrontational. Meet with him somewhere else. I suggest that you do all the interviews by yourself. He probably believes that he can manipulate any female.

This is an organized crime. Prior to the murder, he probably already had an alibi in place and knew what he was going to say when anyone questioned him.

*Get a transcript of the 911 and dispatch tapes and listen to **every word.** You should be asking yourself: "Would he really have known that?"*

Interview all first responders to see what he told them.

/s/ Jim Bell

Since drowning is a format of asphyxia, having her case touch twenty out of twenty-one of the FBI's red flags gave Jill something to think about. Too bad these, in and of themselves, aren't admissible evidence. There was a time in American jurisprudence that an officer's hunches and suspicions could go before a jury. Now courts only allow generally accepted scientific principals. DNA has only recently come to be accepted as valid evidence; behavioral profiling is way back on the law's learning curve. Every now and then the FBI reaches a point where they will qualify and provide expert witnesses for exotic investigation techniques, but not until they're ready as an institution to put their method and their reputation on the witness stand. For all his enthusiasm, Jill realized that Jim Bell would not be the one to make that decision.

Winnie was keeping her word to stay in touch and called on Monday the twenty-ninth. David had been to her apartment two nights before, straightforwardly denied killing Pam and, strangely, claimed no memory of discussing the notion of killing his wife as a way to be rid of Pam.

The Stokeses kept in touch as well. Afloat in a crushing cauldron of sorrow, anger and disbelief, they wanted to know of any development however minor. Although the family Stokes was a group she grew to like, Detective Candland knew her cards had to stay hidden.

The Stokeses had news of their own: they'd hired a private investigator to look into Pam's death. Roger "Action Jackson" Tinsley would be in touch with Jill. They were also looking into hiring an attorney, a woman from Denver named Anne Sulton with a reputation in civil rights litigation. Pam's family had no intention of allowing their daughter to go quietly into that terrible night.

The thought of a PI was a mixed message. Of course, it demonstrated their determination to get to the bottom of the matter, but did it evidence a lack of trust in Detective Candland and the SLCPD? If so, was it their skills, their dedication or their fairness in question? There's no way to predict how a detective and a PI will mesh. At best a PI can be a tremendous asset to a police investigation but at worst an obstruction. Since both the PI and the cops will be interviewing the same people and looking at the same evidence, the elements of style and personality of the first investigator will make the work of the second either somewhat easier or much more difficult.

The next two weeks passed with the lack of routine that defines routine police work. Although the fishpond case was pondered and discussed over coffee and cigarettes, it wasn't until Monday, September 12, that Winnie called. She'd spent some time with David over the weekend and David wanted to sell the business, rent the house and live off of the insurance proceeds. He said he'd been seeing a counselor of his own but hadn't told his counselor about Winnie yet. Mead was being followed by a PI and that made him uncomfortable but didn't break Jill's heart.

It was also on the twelfth that Private Investigator Roger Tinsley of Action Jackson Investigations called on the PD to pay his respects. Roger was every bit the model private detective, tall, lean, athletic, clothing off the cover of a fashion magazine. Action Jackson was a young black man, as determined as he was handsome. He hadn't been in town for long, but he had made a strong impression on David Earl Mead, who was upset by Roger's presence and style.

Roger interviewed several of the Meads' friends and neighbors and none sensed anything negative about Pam and Dave's relationship. Roger spoke with David as well and got right to the point. Who was Stormy? Just a friend. David hadn't had any affairs. Did David know Pam told Mary that Pam believed she found Stormy's clothes at the Mead home after their separation? No, those weren't Stormy's clothes. What about that insurance policy? Gayle Fairfield was the driving force on that policy. David didn't enjoy someone in his face, started squirming and the interview deteriorated. Roger noticed David would selectively sob as he spoke of his spouse, but never shed a tear.

Jill got the distinct impression that their two investigations might find parallel and supportive paths. The two hit it off and would stay in touch.

Two days later Pennington's investigator John James stopped by. When someone makes eight $137 monthly payments, then files a claim for half a million dollars, most folks would have a few questions they'd like to ask. Pennington did. James was a pro with the ability to require David to give a detailed statement under oath as a requirement of getting the money David wanted. Candland and James spoke at some length about the progress of their investigations and agreed to keep in touch.

The next day David Earl Mead appeared and took a polygraph examination where the principal examiner and additional scorer were both cops. In the polygraph protocol, a subject is asked a set of relevant questions. David was asked four: Did he intend to tell the truth? He was asked twice if he intentionally caused Pam's death. Did he intentionally cause Pam to fall into the pond? David aced his exam. Polygraphs are scored plus or minus. Scores between plus and minus five are inconclusive, below minus five are "deceptive" and above plus five "truthful." One scorer found David at plus nine, the other at plus twenty-one for a plus fifteen "truthful" average. The truth of the lie detector is that it has never achieved the stature to make it competent or acceptable courtroom evidence. There is also lore that some personalities can fool the poly, but most people and most cops will accept the results of a polygraph given by a good examiner.

Monday the nineteenth, Winnie called again and said David told her about the polygraph results. David said he was asked outright if he'd killed Pam, he said no and passed. Winnie gave Jill the number plus fifteen and wondered aloud if David was telling her the truth.

The nineteenth was the same day Anne Sulton stepped in. In a letter to Police Chief Ruben Ortega and to County Attorney David Yocom, Anne T. Sulton, Ph.D. & J.D., attorney and counselor put them on notice she'd been retained by the Stokeses. It was Sulton's belief, and that of her clients, that the immediate commencement of a formal homicide investigation was well warranted. Formal, informal or otherwise, the fishpond case was vibrating within everyone's thoughts.

4

A Dubious Present

Wade Wayment is a detective with the SLCPD Robbery Squad. A long, lanky man with a distinct and twisted sense of humor, he wandered over to Jill's desk on September 26 with some news. He had just been to the Davis County Jail in Farmington to interview suspects in an aggravated burglary/aggravated robbery that took place in Salt Lake City. One of these, a parolee named James Hendrix, told Wayment he wanted to speak with the detective investigating the death of Pamela Mead. What was Hendrix's connection? Well, the burg took place at the Mead home. The two victims, robbed in their bed, were David Mead and Winnetka Walls. How did Hendrix know that? He says he's David's cousin. One hour later, two appointments summarily canceled, Detective Jill Candland was in Farmington.

There are a number of reasons people tell the cops what they know. First and foremost is the noble duty of citizenship. Most folks in this life are very straightforward, obey the laws and feel others should as well. Others come forward out of various formats of self-interest: reward, revenge, fear or just dumping on someone else are common motives. Some who find themselves in trouble with the law come forward as a device to bargain or deflect responsibility toward others. James Hendrix was unique: he just didn't want to wind up dead and not have anyone else know why or at whose hands. Jack—don't call him Jimmy—was at the time of Pam's death one hard character, an ex-con, cocaine addict and multiply convicted felon. Jack wasn't afraid of much, but he didn't want to be found overdosed and over, his death shrugged off as a junkie's inevitable end. There were some things Hendrix really wanted Jill to know.

One of the features of our system of justice is the first ten amendments to the Constitution of the United States, the Bill of Rights. They take up about half a printed page—the whole Constitution, Preamble through the Twenty-seventh Amendment, requires less than ten—but the case law, treatises and textbooks about the Bill of Rights fill whole buildings. A well-known outgrowth is the *Miranda* decision: "You have the right to remain silent . . ." With Jack facing extremely serious charges out of the aggravated burglary/robbery of David and Winnie, he wasn't going to talk about that without a lawyer. He and Jill agreed to tap-dance around that incident and talk about the rest.

David's and Jack's mothers were sisters; the boys grew up together and at one time of family financial strain even lived in the same household, but they'd never been close. David had generally succeeded; Jack had not. David had successfully dodged trouble; Jack had not. Fair or not, Jack always felt that David looked down on him. As adults they went their separate ways and Jack's way had included the view from behind gray steel bars. With that background, when Jack got out of jail in July and got word from his mom that David had work for Jack and wanted him to call, he was more than a little surprised.

Jack called David and arranged a meeting, came by in his

car, picked Jack up and the two drove off, eventually to stop
behind the Erector-Set football stadium of a local high
school. David turned to Jack, "I've got some work for you."
Pointing to the car seat, David laughed, "I've got a present
for you. I'm sorry, it's not wrapped." Jack's eyes became
saucers. The present was eight grams of cocaine rolled up in
a hundred-dollar bill.

Anyone who has experienced first-, second- or thirdhand
the scourge of addictive hard drugs can start to imagine the
rush of feelings for a self-admitted junkie, broke and fresh
out of jail, in beholding this present. Was David working for
the cops, trying to set Jack up, "narc him off?" Was it "bunk,"
fake drugs, as a cruel joke? *If it's real, how soon can I do it?*
David broke into Jack's careening thoughts.

David told Jack he'd been dealing drugs in kilo-sized
transactions, but there was a person out there named Rob
who'd burned David on a deal. David wanted to know if Jack
would, for the proper price, kill Rob or at least make Rob
suffer substantially. Jack said that he had a friend who'd kill
Rob for proper recompense. David told Jack he'd also like to
hire Jack to follow, to spy on, David's "toy" and went on to
tell Jack about Winnie. Not only would Jack be paid, but
he'd also be given memberships to private clubs to facilitate
the spying. David even wanted to bring Jack into the drug
trade.

The two drove off and went to a bar where David drove
the conversation back to taking human life for compensation.
Would you kill Rob? Or help get Rob killed? Sure. Do you
remember your old girlfriend, Artie? Yeah. Would you kill
her for $250,000? Oh yeah! For $100,000? I guess! The end
point of the exercise questioned whether Jack would kill
Dave's wife Pam for $30,000. The answer, again, was "I have
this friend . . ." The mind of a con with a few bucks and a few
grams was in overdrive: could he possibly get that money up
front, then rip Mead off?

Jack asked about the state of the Meads' marriage. "Word
around the family is that all is going well." David became
quite calm and said he was serious about killing Pam and told
Jack that planning had been underway for nine or ten months
while David had been the perfect loving husband. But the act

was wearing thin and he wanted Pam killed in ten days or two weeks.

The next day the cousins got together. The dope and the money were real, so as Mead drove around, Hendrix wondered what to think. When David produced another fifty-eight grams of coke, $800, in hundreds, and a set of digital scales, Jack listened carefully. Pam would be killed on a day designated by her perfect and loving husband. There was an advantage to this taking place while Pam was still taking medications prescribed after her surgery. Jack couldn't give any more detail about the surgery, beyond Dave's declaration that it took place. Dave would be at work at the airport during Pam's scheduled departure. Pam's death was to appear to be a burglary or robbery gone bad and there should be signs of a struggle. Jack was given a description of where certain items worth stealing were located to bolster the illusion of a burglary.

Jack would get $2,000 up front and the rest thirty days after the killing, from the proceeds of a $250,000 insurance policy Pam insisted on obtaining. The reunited cousins, after a suitable and proper period of mourning, would take a road trip to Las Vegas where they'd party, exchange the funds and explain their changed individual economic circumstances on the whims of the gambling gods. The two agreed that Jack would page David the next day after Jack secured that friend and David defined the detail of when.

But the addict's long-term horizon is not the next windfall, or the next day or anything beyond the next score. Jack had sixty-six grams of cocaine and $900 cash. He'd reached the goal; the journey be damned. As Jack would tell us later, when confronted with that second stash of dope, he was prepared to tell David anything David needed to hear, so Jack could get his hands on that coke. Kill Pam? Hell, yes! When and where?

Jack went off to party. His girl threw him out so he went and found another lady. When you've got lots of dope they're not hard to find. Other newfound friends discovered Jack; that almost always happens too. When the coke was gone, the money went for more. When the money was gone, Jack knew how to steal to get more money and buy more junk. But when

Jack gathered his senses, he reasoned that David was probably furious and called his own mother to see if David had been looking for him. She told Jack that Dave hadn't, but there was awful news, sad news. Pam, Dave's beautiful young wife, was dead in a terrible accident. Jack, being a man of focused ambition, turned to David's accounts of where there were items worth stealing during a staged robbery gone wrong, went over to David's house, found it dark and unoccupied, and broke in. There was the jar full of money and Pam's jewelry as promised. Jack took those and did so carefully. No need to trash Dave's house. But Jack's newfound lady's probation officer paid an unexpected visit, found the lady stoned and with jewelry she couldn't explain. Jack's lady departed in handcuffs and Jack was alone. Some nights later he went back to Pam and David's house and stole some electronic games. By best backtracking estimates, and Jack wasn't too good at retaining detail, the binge went for perhaps fifteen days.

It took a while for Jack to screw up enough courage to confront David Mead. Weeks passed before Hendrix got over to Center Street and found David sitting on the porch. After some initial greetings, Jack put some sarcasm into his voice and opined that it was a shame about Pam. David skated around giving Jack an answer or even a reaction but said, "I feel so shitty that I came to you and asked you to do it. And then it happened. It was a coincidence."

"You can fool some of the people some of the time, but not all of the people all of the time."

"Especially you, Jack."

"That's on you, David. I'll never say anything about what we talked about." With that, they shook hands and smiled. Jack noticed Dave's eyes shift around and, when he saw someone, manage to look sad.

Jack apologized for the break-ins and the thefts. Mead told him not to worry about it; he could always make money on the break-ins. Insurance is wonderful. Jack apologized for the cash and the drugs but David shrugged that off as well. Hendrix found that a little unusual, especially when Dave again raised the notion of Jack helping David sell drugs. David did say that he had an idea for letting Jack work off any debt on the coke and the cash and would detail it later. Jack noticed that what remained of Pam's clothing and personal items had been lovingly gathered up and tossed into a pile on the garage floor.

Mead suggested the two drive off to find a bar. They did so, had a few drinks and were off to a nude bar. In Utah, since nude clubs can't serve booze, they're never the first stop on the tour. David provided Hendrix twenty dollars in one dollar bills to allow Jack to participate in the rituals of tipping the entertainers. Although Jack was appreciative, he saw this as a unique way to mourn the loss of a loved one.

Dave loosened up and bragged to Jack about passing the polygraph and that he'd achieved a plus fifteen. Jack, no stranger to the criminal justice system, wondered aloud if that wasn't too high, something that might engender suspicion. David looked Hendrix in the eye and told how he'd spent weeks obtaining and studying every book and treatise available on lie detectors and the techniques to beat them. How to breathe, how to sit and how to prepare yourself going in. Then David waxed philosophical and said, "Life is just beginning. If I could only get those in-laws off my ass."

David told Jack he needed help to put a wall in the backyard as part of some garage modifications and he'd like Jack to dig a trench for the foundations. Dave would give Hendrix a little cash, but hold most of the pay against the debt. After the trench, Jack could help pour the foundation and build the wall. Jack agreed and met David at the house on Central the next morning. David showed Jack where he wanted the trench, suggested about six feet deep and handed him a shovel. Jack asked if Mead was going to shoot the grade or provide for forms. David said that he knew what he was doing and Jack started to dig. Into that afternoon, Jack's imagination got the best of him, specifically a thought of lying in that trench while concrete covered his corpse. Jack hid his fear and told David he'd come back in the morning. He didn't and the unspecified garage modifications never took place.

At this point the Hendrix narrative was approaching the events of the aggravated burglary/robbery and concluded.

Jack gave the names of his mom, sister and girl, and was returned to his cell.

Although it seems simple logic that charges could be brought against David based on the Hendrix allegations, it's not the legal reality. Although Rule 404(b) and its good friend Rule 403 instruct that the character of a defendant can't be put before the jury to simply show him as a bad person who would commit crime, quite the opposite is true for witnesses. Anyone who takes the stand can, will and should be impeached.

Impeachment in the courtroom is somewhat similar to the political use of the word: it's controlled name-calling where a jury hears about everything bad a witness ever was or did. These are attacks upon credibility; bias and motive to testify are fair game. Jurors see if the witness has the opportunity and ability to witness, recall and relate or if they've been given a benefit. Being a junkie bears directly on those questions. If Jack says yes when the jury learns all about Jack and David says no when the jury learns little about David, guilt beyond a reasonable doubt is well out of reach, unless there is corroboration.

Detective Jill Candland couldn't talk to Hendrix until he had an attorney in place, but she did talk with Jack's mom, who confirmed little more than David's initial efforts to contact Jack and that the two cousins were never close. Jack's sister said Jack told her that David asked him to kill Pam and there was rumor that one of David's brothers quit Valley Ground Service when David asked him to go on a drug run. She felt that David had always been greedy.

Detective Jill Candland couldn't talk with Jack about the burglary/robbery, but she could talk with someone else who was there, Winnetka Walls. Winnie admitted she hadn't been completely forthcoming in keeping the detective informed. She was spending the night with David at the house when in the middle of the night two men she'd never met came knocking on the door. Mead answered the door, seemed to know one of the men and let them in. Although Winnie couldn't make out much of what was said, the discussion got loud and angry, some of it about Pam's death, some about drugs. A handgun was displayed and the man David didn't know said the intruders ought to kill David and Winnie. The man David knew wasn't buying into that, but Winnie was very scared. The men took a few things and left. Winnie was shaken and wanted Dave to call 9-1-1. David was angry but cold. At first he wouldn't call the cops, but after much frantic urging, he did. Before they came Dave said it would be good if he talked to the cops and Winnie didn't.

After Jack had an attorney on board who was aware of the whole situation, Jill interviewed him again. His story was consistent, but Jill wanted to test it further and offered Jack a polygraph of his own, to gauge his reaction to the offer. Jack, not a man of guile, shrugged his shoulders and said, "Sure." The attorney was okay with that, so Jill set up the poly, which Jack took, and passed as a plus seven.

There was a lot of info from the fishpond case to digest. Detective Candland, Sergeants Bell and Roberts, Lt. Denker, Chief Dep. County Attorney Skordas and Chief ME Todd Grey carved out a mutually possible time to meet. It spanned more than one hour and one pot of bad coffee, a very serious discussion that raised as many questions and doubts as it answered, reasonable and otherwise. Were Walls or Hendrix credible witnesses? Whose side would Winnie be on and what version would she give? What would have to be offered to Jack on his aggravated burglary/robbery beef? Might he actually be the one who killed Pam? If not, did David do his own killing? How could they prove that? What other evidence was out there? What other evidence could they hope for? This was a work-in-progress meeting, hardly resolution, and the participants left deep in their own thoughts.

The next morning Todd Grey retrieved case #94-0918 from the Office of the Medical Examiner's files. He dictated a short note; it was typed, then signed:

> OPINION: Pamela Mead, died as a result of drowning. Contributory to death is blunt force injury of the head. Investigation indicates the decedent's death was the result of action(s) by another person(s).
>
> /s/ Todd C. Grey, M.D.
> Chief Medical Examiner

5

A Cleaner Picture

A few days later, October 11, David's stepbrother had his turn on the sixth floor. He knew about the separation and believed that it was over personal differences. The brother introduced David and Winnie, knew they were seeing each other during the Meads' separation, but didn't believe David had any affairs after that. David said he stopped seeing Winnie after Pam returned and never talked about harming Pam. The brother had been at work from six thirty in the evening until ten thirty. His supervisor could verify this. He'd been notified by Kevin Harris about Pam's death.

The stepbrother didn't know about the insurance policy until a couple of days after Pam's death. He remembered that a younger brother had been asking around about insurance to pay for the funeral. David told them the policy was at his airport office, so the stepbrother went out to VGS and retrieved the policy. He had no idea what it was worth and he didn't call Pennington. Instead the younger brother made that call about four or five days after Pam's death, using the stepbrother's name, but he wasn't sure why. The stepbrother spoke to Pennington sometime later and gave them his own Social Security Number.

He talked to David about building the pond and knew that it had just been finished that Saturday night. The day after Pam died, David told his brothers that he couldn't live in the house with the pond. There was a collective family decision to fill in the pond; the stepbrother and another brother went over and did just that.

As the interview ended and they were walking for the door, Jill suggested the stepbrother take a polygraph, he agreed and Jill said that she'd arrange the exam. The next day the stepbrother called and said he'd spoken with a lawyer who'd advised him neither to take a poly, nor speak further to the cops without that lawyer present. Jill said there was no problem bringing a lawyer along, but the stepbrother said he wasn't going to pay for a lawyer and wouldn't be coming in or coming back. Jill asked if that meant he wasn't willing to "eliminate himself from suspicion of any involvement in the murder of Pam," but got no answer.

Later that day Ellen, a friend of Pam's, was interviewed. They'd flown together and been friends for four or five years. According to Ellen, Pam was reluctant to talk about "bad" things in her marriage, but Ellen knew about a problem when Pam learned that David had been in an inappropriate relationship with another woman. Pam said that David assured her that it was just a friendship and wasn't intimate. Pam wasn't going to take David back if it was intimate. He'd merely befriended a single mother of two. Ellen recalled the woman's name was Stormy. Ellen hadn't talked to Pam about the phone call. She had heard about it, though she couldn't recall from whom, but understood that Pam overheard David say, "She's out of the picture," or something like that.

On October 12 Todd Ryan was interviewed at the PSB. Ryan had known Mead for several years, beginning when they lived in the same apartment complex and played tennis. After David Mead married Pam Stokes, Ryan said that Mead "disappeared" and the two saw each other infrequently. Ryan was aware of an affair with a woman named Stormy. He talked to Mead during the separation and Mead talked about the overheard phone call. Asked what was overheard, Mead told him, "We ought to knock the bitch off."

Mead told Ryan about Winnie and her ultimatums but said he wouldn't divorce Pam. Todd spoke to Winnie, who told him about the explosives in the spare bedroom, but Mead said those were just boxes. Mead did talk about insurance some months back and said he had an appointment with an agent.

More and more information, more and more questions filled detectives' heads night and day.

•   •   •

In Utah law, there is a process known as "screening" where a detective presents a case to a prosecutor by setting out the available evidence and discussing the potential criminal charges. A formal screening involves an appointment, assigning a county attorney's case number and a decision where charges are filed, declined, or the case is "FI'ed" and given back to the detective for further investigation. The practice has evolved in Salt Lake to the point that in a complex case there may be a great deal of consultation before a formal screening. Part of the litany of my professional life is "Howie, can I run something by you?" These are good occasions to talk where topics may include other evidence that might be available, credibility of witnesses or principals, balancing the seriousness of the conduct and the resources required to proceed, which jurisdiction may have the best leverage, ongoing conduct and danger, and what the best tactics or directions might be. There are rumors that these informal reviews have aspects of prosecutor shopping by the cops, but more often they occur between people who have developed a level of professional confidence and comfort.

Prosecution in Utah proceeds by information rather than indictment. An indictment is handed down by a grand jury, but an information is a charging document filed directly into court by a prosecutor and containing a sworn statement of probable cause to support any warrants that issue. The person charged then has the right to a preliminary hearing before a magistrate judge, and the State must put on witnesses and evidence subject to cross-examination and courtroom challenge sufficient to convince the magistrate that the offenses have occurred and were probably committed by the accused. Although an accused in Utah has a right to have his prelim— our slang for preliminary hearing—within ten days of his first hearing, most defense attorneys want more time. But one reason for informal consultation is the Ten Day Rule. If a prosecutor files a case, he or she better be prepared, witnesses and evidence in hand, to go to court and put on the major portion of a case less than two weeks after filing. Prosecutors who recklessly file cases can have short careers.

There was also the concept of double jeopardy. Were David Mead to be charged, brought to trial and not proven guilty beyond a reasonable doubt to a unanimous jury duty-bound to presume innocence, he would be found not guilty and be off the hook forever. He could then admit, even brag about, his deeds without further fear of criminal sanction. With no statute of limitations on homicide, caution in filing was clearly the better course. Still, as it was becoming more clear what had happened to Pamela Camille Stokes Mead on August 15, 1994, the question evolved from "Did David Mead really do this?" to "How will we prove David did this?"

Nineteen ninety-four was an election year for Salt Lake County offices and August 15 fell two and a half months before the election. David Yocom, the incumbent officeholder as county attorney, whose office was being renamed district attorney, was running and the election looked to be a piece of cake. Dave had taken over the office eight years earlier and, by the strength of his back and his will, picked up the pieces of a disaster. Dave is neither a perfect person nor a perfect administrator, but he's a damn good one of each. He deserved much credit and awaited the voters' acknowledgement.

However, 1994 was a banner year for the GOP. Dave lost and the bright, open man he'd named chief deputy, Greg Skordas, would also soon leave, but not before he handed me the case of my career.

It was Chief Deputy Salt Lake County Attorney Greg Skordas whom Jill Candland approached when the picture of Pam's death started coming into clearer focus and it was he who would first view the evidence from the somewhat detached perspective of a prosecutor required to convince jurors, unanimously and beyond a reasonable doubt, of the truth of his accusations. As the revelations came forward, Jill and Greg spoke often.

Although there were a lot of other interviews, and although there was a lot of effort, interest and discussion about the fishpond, it was December 12 before Pennington investigator John James could meet with David Mead. Pennington had a half a million bucks at stake and some questions for David.

There is a certain ceremony to this sort of interview: the interviewer brings a tape recorder, sets it up, turns it on, then announces the time, place and participants and anyone else who may be present. The players all recite that they're aware they're being recorded and required oaths are taken. If the tape runs out or the interview is broken by a phone call or rest room break, that's noted along with the time, the tape restarts and the original recitals are re-made. Personal data such as name and date of birth are gathered before the questioning moves to issues of the incident and the insured.

James sat down with Dave Mead late that afternoon and started the interview by asking about how and when the Meads met, when they'd married and where they'd lived. They discussed Pam's work history up to her leaving the airline a few months before her death, Pam's medical history and her recent surgery. David spoke a little about VGS and claimed he had "plenty of insurance" through his company.

James probed the history of the insurance policy and David talked about the Fairfields and the bond between Pam and Gayle. They shared some flights and a growing friendship. Gayle brought up insurance with Pam, then Pam with David who "didn't think too much of it," because "it wasn't one of those major necessities." Gayle "convinced Pam that it would be best" for the Meads to have life insurance. David wasn't entirely convinced and sat on some paperwork for a few months while Pam was pretty adamant about the policy. Gayle and Warren Fairfield each called several times to see how the paperwork was coming and once pushed to the point that David lied and said that the papers were in the mail. But Dave relented, talked to Gayle's husband about questions, forms and procedures and sent off the paperwork. Soon there was a medical checkup and a policy. David wanted it to be adequate to provide for Pam in case of an accident. Mead said he thought that the accidental death rider was just something written into the policy, couldn't really remember the genesis of it.

Next, John brought Mead to the day of his wife's death.

David and Pam's doctor wanted her out and moving, so the Meads went for a walk earlier that evening until Pam tired and needed rest. "At about eight thirty, I was leaving for the airport, asked Pam to feed the fish and she'd agreed."

David got to work, but the person who was supposed to assist him didn't show up. David left for home a little late, about 10:35, and got home close to eleven. He saw some other people, but only knew their first names. There were no logbook entries or trip tickets on the aircraft for David to sign.

David said he thought it unusual that Pam wasn't home when he arrived, since she didn't like to be alone and couldn't get very far because of her recent surgery. David told the investigator he'd called around to friends and neighbors with no results. Then he walked back to the kitchen, saw the fish food and walked out to the backyard to check on the dog. When David got to Baron's territory he looked at the pond, saw Pam floating face down. He screamed, jumped into the pond and struggled with her limp form—he didn't know for how long—and there was a lot of blood, but he finally succeeded in getting Pam out of the pool. He screamed for a while, then made a dash for the house to call 9-1-1. He ran into a tree, scratching himself and fell trying to get into the house. When he dialed 9-1-1, the operator thought David was incoherent.

Then his neighbor Barry Baxter came to the front door. David ran Barry through the house, into the backyard to where Pam lay. Barry tried to start CPR to no avail. David was lying on Pam screaming at Barry, but Barry just looked down and stopped trying to do anything. He didn't have to say anything. David could see that nothing could be done.

James asked Mead to tell him about the fishpond and he described it. David said he built it some months back. "We bought goldfish and koi and poured a ceremonial bottle of mead into the pond." After Pam's death, Mead felt that the pond was a danger for everybody, so he "had the pond buried" for fear that kids or the curious might wander into the yard. By then the police had taken down the crime scene tape and left no indication they needed any more information from or about the pond.

John James then steered the discussion to Pam's family and the allegations David might have caused Pam's death. Mead told James that he was somewhere between hurt and angry with the Stokes family, that he felt abandoned by them and felt it was no longer possible to communicate. He was hurt by what was said during the funeral service about getting to the truth, the implication he was involved, and couldn't understand why the Stokeses, Jill and now the medical examiner though it was a homicide. He was in the dark; no one explained it and they never disclosed why this might be something other than an accident.

"Do you think that it was an accident or a homicide?"

Mead waxed on that it would be easier for him to accept Pam's death were it an accident. As Pam was the single sweetest person he'd ever known, he just couldn't see that anyone would ever want to hurt her. It just made David sick to think about anyone wanting to harm her, but "if you want to get into pointing fingers, there could be a hundred possibilities. There have been kids roaming the neighborhood breaking into cars and Pam had girlfriends who might have become jealous, or potentially psychotic, because of all the nice things Pam had acquired; at least one had a fetish for fine furniture. It could have been racists driven by the fact we were an interracial couple." He paused then his voice rose. "Did I tell you that my cousin, Jack Hendrix, broke into our home five consecutive times after this whole ordeal happened? He took money and jewelry and even robbed me at gunpoint once. His whole family are drug addicts and psychos and his mom is a lost soul who thinks that she talks to God and sends her spirit into outer space. Jack came by some weeks after the accident to offer condolences, but was probably just casing the house. Who knows? Jack might have come by that night, Pam got in the way and he pushed her. He might have hit her. I don't know."

According to Mead, he didn't even know if the detective entertained that possibility. "She's like, per se, going around and talking to everyone else behind my back." David wasn't saying that to discredit Jill or her investigation; when this all blew over he'd hire his own investigators and run his own investigation. He'd pay Jack's friends for the sort of information those people don't give to the police and provide that knowledge to the authorities.

Then, with James's eyes widening, Mead went on. "It could have been the dog. You know, Pam had those pins coming out of her toes and Baron is an eighty-pound Chow who jumped on people. He might have stepped on her toe, causing great pain and making her stumble with the net result of some sort that she wound up in the pond."

James took Mead back to the condition of his marriage. According to David the Meads had endured a brief separation during their first year together. Being married was a new experience, it took a lot of adjustment and they were pretty immature. They occasionally argued over finances, early on, but those conflicts dwindled down. "I let her go shopping when she wanted to; that kind of kept her appeased." They grew a lot and when Pam returned to David the couple was happier and stronger.

David admitted that he had his friends but couldn't see why that was pertinent or had to come out. Friends who were women? Affair type things? Not really. Well, there was one that Pam probably might consider a relationship, but Winnetka Walls was just a friend. "It was never to the extent of ever having kind of a controlling factor on our relationship." He knew the detectives had been talking to Winnie.

Finally, John James got direct and asked David if he'd had anything to do with Pam's death. "No, nothing!"

"Did you ask anyone else to take part in her death?"

"I did not!"

"Is there anything else that you wanted to add?" David was concerned about the insurance policy, because he wanted to make sure that all the arrangements he'd made for Pam would be paid, but realized Pennington's investigation would have to run its course.

At that point, the holidays were almost upon them. The Stokeses were in for that terrible first Christmas without Pam: those close to her would each come across moments, memories or keepsakes that tightened the breath and called forth a tear. Dave Mead also had his first holidays without his wife. Homicide Detective Jill Candland knew that old cases do not disappear with the old year. She focused on the many facets of the death, stared at the ceiling and sorted thoughts long after the lights went out.

One afternoon, close to Christmas, Greg Skordas and Jill Candland stuck their heads inside my office, "Howie, have you got a few minutes to talk about a case?" Greg and Jill walked in. I always have a pot of coffee going. Jill accepted a cup, Greg didn't and Jill handed me a black, shiny three-ring binder labeled, "Pamela Mead." As I reached for it, I was not yet aware that I would be taking on one of the most fascinating cases of my career.

6

Memories of Me

Law is my second career. In 1979 I had a good job as a design engineer in Illinois with a great employer working with good people. Cat stood by me when I was drafted in 1967, wounded in 1968 and went off to finish up my schooling. I passed the exam to become a Registered Professional Engineer and saw my name on patents. A fellow Cat engineer fixed me up on a blind date with a nurse named Nancy around Thanksgiving 1973. We married Columbus Day 1974, bought a house in the suburbs and claimed a dog from the pound. By the summer of '78 I was delighted to learn that I was soon to be a father and perplexed to realize that what I also wanted to be was a lawyer.

I took the LSAT exam and things fell together nicely: the University of Utah accepted me; we could afford to live there; the GI Bill was available; real estate inflation allowed us to sell our house, put a down payment on a new home and bank a nest egg. By October 1982 I was a lawyer, a Deputy Salt Lake County Attorney charged with prosecuting misdemeanors, and the proud father of a son and daughter. In 1985 we had our third child, Lord, help me, a red-headed daughter.

I went into law to compete in the arena of the courtroom. Anyone who wants to practice courtroom law does well starting in a prosecutor's or public defender's office and trying as many cases the first year as classmates will in their careers. When I hired on there was a custom to welcome new lawyers with a file and the announcement that their first trial starts in an hour. You're out of the rowboat; there's the shore: sink or swim. Although a prosecutor correctly starts out trying less serious matters, there is no substitute for the experience and seasoning of taking his or her own cases to court.

I enjoyed my work and I still do. Out of thousands of lawyers in Utah, only about a hundred or so actively practice on the criminal side and they're a good crew. We may get royally worked up in each other's faces within the competition of our cases, but there is collegiality and good humor woven throughout this community. I'd never admit it to their faces, but the defense bar is generally more personable than the prosecution. Our stimulating and entertaining environment extends to the courts' personnel, including the judges, cops, jailers, bailiffs, clerks, interpreters, probation officers, court support agencies and reporters who cover the beat.

Don't look for tons of money or to work in the plushiest digs, only what the county commission will spring for. Our building was a dump, but it was right across Fourth South Street from the courthouse. I had the corner office on the top floor and it was big. Its only window was a narrow strip, almost as wide as a crack in the wall from an old earthquake, that faced a billboard across an alley. Family pictures and personal knick-knacks filled U-assemble bookshelves. It wasn't elegant, but it was comfortably mine.

Prosecuting is also a platform with a huge amount of discretion and an enormous opportunity to accomplish some real good. There are the obvious occasions to safeguard the hometown, putting away those who would do it harm, or seek society's revenge upon those who already have. For each one of those there are many others where proportionality in charging, disposition and sentencing enhance the greater good of the community with out-of-prison sanctions with future expectations imposed and enforced.

There are two rules in this field: every defendant and

incident stands alone as unique; your work is singularly important at work, but you, your family and friends are singularly important away from work.

By New Year's Eve of 1994, I was a well-established felony prosecutor with long stints in the misdemeanor division and drug team before moving to arson/fraud where those around me felt some professional respect and personal comfort. My strengths were some common sense and the fact I enjoyed my job and almost all the people I dealt with. I'm approachable, I like to talk and I try to treat people with the good humor and dignity to which they're entitled.

I get along well with cops by recognizing our separate roles in the process and our common humanity. I had a dream job, a wife I loved and three lovely children. Then I was given the fishpond case.

7

To Charge or Not to Charge

Todd changed his mind; Winnie kept changing her story; Jack was a junkie—the slang verb and descriptive noun "con" take origin in "convict"; a big insurance policy, but no larger than my own, was at stake; the suspect had an alibi and a plus fifteen polygraph: though there was little doubt how Jill Candland saw the fishpond case and I might have been quickly won over to the David-Did-It Camp, I still had a lot of questions and, in my opinion, we still needed to answer them and get more evidence before charging David Mead with murder.

Jill reminded me of Jack's poly, all David's behaviors and lies to Tinsley, James, herself, et al: no blood in the pond, certainly not everywhere, and dead people don't float immediately to the surface. For months we'd meet, talk, joust and leave holding the same ground. Then Anne Sulton filed the lawsuit.

I don't know if it was Roger or the Stokeses who first got in touch with Anne, but together the Stokeses, Anne T. Sulton and "Action Jackson" were about to sweep across the Rockies like a mighty army. Some might discount their resolve or abilities, but Detective Jill Candland eagerly anticipated the onslaught.

Garfield Stokes, Jr. and Sinie Stokes vs. Pennington Life Insurance Company and David Earl Mead, #95-S-752, was originally filed in Denver, in the United States Court for the District of Colorado as a civil tort action in wrongful death against David. Pennington was named as a defendant to preclude them from distributing the insurance proceeds to David, who the Stokeses contended murdered Pam and foreclosed from being her insurance beneficiary. The cause of action against David was the tort of wrongful death alleging David caused Pam's death, depriving the Stokeses of their daughter, brought in Colorado where Pennington sold the policies. David still had Patrick Anderson on board.

Were you ever to walk into a room where Anne T. Sulton, Ph.D., Esq. was present, you would know that Anne was there. Neither a tall nor a physically large person, she nonetheless commands a room by her presence. Attorney Sulton has intelligent, piercing eyes, a large open laugh, a wide smile with a little gap between her front teeth, an occasional concession to reading glasses and a ton of talent. Anne is a person without pretense, guile or fraud who is a formidable advocate. If she's on your side, stand back and watch her go after it; if she's on the other side, just stand back. If she likes you, you'll know it, and if she doesn't, she won't pretend she does.

Anne has appeared on some of those cable talk shows where attorneys of every stripe come together to dissect and analyze high profile crimes and incidents. Since most of these programs seem to seek a cacophony rather than discourse and generate heat not light, they stick with self-promoters who cheerlead their side and name-call the other. Thoughtful lawyers like Anne T. Sulton who bring genuine insight aren't asked to become regular panelists. The traits of a shrill voice, wild gesturing and accusation without forethought might create a television personality, but not a trial lawyer.

Trial lawyers are different creatures. This world is overrun with lawyers, but most lawyers seldom go to court. Over half the people who graduate from law school will never stand in front of a jury, present evidence and argument in a contested matter and wait out the verdict. Most live to draft and exchange documents. Living in and for courtrooms, prosecutors, criminal defense attorneys and the Anne T. Sultons of this world are trial lawyers.

She evolved as a plaintiff's attorney, the one who files the lawsuit. Her cases are often civil rights violations, torts of injury to person, property or reputation, or the all-too-common combinations of the above. Her success provided quite a bit of visibility, particularly in her home state of Colorado, and with visibility come clients. Anne had a successful and visible practice, an extremely visible gold Excalibur convertible and the well-earned luxury to choose the cases she would take. She met the Stokes family, heard their story and knew that the Mead case and Anne T. Sulton were made for each other.

A criminal case is a distant cousin of a civil lawsuit. Instead of being arraigned on charges, a civil defendant files an answer, denying all allegations, and occasionally a counter-suit. Instead of a preliminary hearing and open file examination of the State's evidence, there is civil discovery. In civil practice discovery is two-way, very broad and very complex. Both sides are required to provide their opponents all potential evidence and both are required to submit to interrogatories, written questions one side sends the other, and depositions, formal, sit-down, sworn, recorded questioning of their witnesses. A party might refuse to give answers, but at the peril of summarily losing the lawsuit. Witnesses and parties are held to their answers and it is perjury to lie in a deposition or interrogatory. Some lawyers constantly run back and forth to the judge for rulings on objections to individual questions even though these discovery devices were created so the parties and attorneys could educate themselves on the facts, limit the issues in dispute and not waste the court's valuable time. Lawyers are clever people and evolved complex rituals that allow unchecked civil discovery to drag on for years and a judge may impose a discovery cutoff ordering lawyers to ask their questions within a fixed period of time. Contrary to popular fiction, the process does not allow for a dramatic surprise witness or piece of evidence: if you hide it during discovery, don't bring it to court. It's a process that can generate tons of potential evidence.

Over the Presidents' Day holiday I cross-country skied, felt energized and enjoyed the picturesque scenery. Mountain cabins away from the ski resorts are remarkably peaceful and beautiful in the winter and the quiet is stunning. The wind blew through cracks in the floor of our cabin, but an old wood stove kept us comfortable, solar panels with batteries powered the lights, blender and car stereo and a propane kitchen stove allowed cooking and baking. Even if I were ever so foolish as to own one, no cell phone will reach into the little side canyon nicknamed "Valhalla." Skiing down is a rush, dodging rocks, trees, deer and occasional moose in a weekend for friends, beer and steaks, not the cares of the office.

When I became involved in the fishpond case, weekends had a tendency to become workweeks that started with a voice message from Jill, who kept in close touch with Anne, Roger and Mary Stokes. We'd find a time for coffee or lunch where my detective briefed me and gave me existing evidence to contemplate more fully.

The folks from Colorado were not in a contemplative mood. They were acting and moving forward. Roger "Action Jackson" Tinsley was making an impression. No shrinking violet, he was asking direct questions and comparing notes with Jill, who brought him by my office. We sat down, poured some coffee and talked about what was coming to light. Right in the middle of some small talk, Roger asked me, straight up and out of the blue, what role Pam's race played in the fact we hadn't filed charges. "If she was white, would you file it?" Jill was sitting off to the side and behind Roger with one of those grins that not only said she wondered how I was going to react, but also affirmed a fair question. I was taken aback for a moment, "I don't know, Roger. I hope not. I don't think I work that way. If I get the evidence,

I'll file it. If I don't, I won't. I don't believe that this is a black/white case. It's murder and insurance fraud." There was no sense getting angry. Black people and others in the modern American experience have a real foundation from which to pose such questions.

Utah is a strange and wonderful place. I live here because I want to, because I love it. We have mountains and deserts and red rock and Mormons. A whole lot of my friends, neighbors, co-workers and most of the folks in Utah are Latter-day Saints, or Mormons, genuinely great people whose faith means a great deal to them and who work hard living that faith.

Although the norm for suspicion of motive in Utah is "You're only doing this because I am (or because I am not) Mormon!" I've heard accusations of racial bias. I suspect that in today's world it'd be almost impossible to partake of public life and not have the accusation tossed your way at some point.

But Roger's question reminded me this was a time to numb my personal sensitivities in favor of the sensitivities and assumptions of the Stokeses, whom I'd spoken with but not met. We poured another cup and talked about evidence, strengths and weaknesses that evidence carried. Roger went off to make David Mead, among others, very uncomfortable and find out more, a task of which Roger was very capable.

A short time after the filing of the civil case *Stokes v. Pennington & Mead* several things changed: Patrick and David had a parting of the ways for reasons only known to those two; Pennington put half a million dollars on the table to be contested by the Stokeses and David Mead and walked away; the case was "removed" to the Federal District of Utah where most of the witnesses, evidence and events were. Pennington wasn't contesting the fact of the death, the appearance of accident or their liability. Wally Bugden, a private practitioner with a reputation for both substance and eccentricity—he always wears mismatching socks—came on board. Tall and gangly, he likes to stand so close that I have to look up into his broom straw moustache. On first impression Wally can be a bit much and tends to come off as loud and in-your-face, but if you hang around long enough you will discover his sense of humor, humanity, well-concealed kindness and charm. Lacking that necessary buffer, Wally and Anne did not hit it off.

Candland, markedly more reluctant, and I elected to wait out the civil suit. We'd still investigate, still talk, but wait and keep an appropriate distance between our work and the civil suit. I wanted to stand back and see what surfaced.

The civil case took off into the expected process of interrogatories, motions and depositions. Roger was off defining witnesses and questions and Anne was doing the questioning. One witness not handling this well was Winnetka Walls. Despite admonitions about influencing other witnesses, it became very obvious that David was working Winnie pretty hard. She moved to California, with David's help, did her best to avoid Roger Tinsley, handwrote a note saying that everything she told the Salt Lake Police was a lie, got it notarized and into David's hands. Called for deposition, Winnie took the Fifth. It was more and more apparent that at this point her sympathy/loyalty pendulum had swung all the way back to David and she would do all she could to avoid doing anything to hurt his cause.

So Anne sued her, added Winnetka Walls as a defendant in the civil suit. Since Winnie had been David's mistress, she stood directly to benefit from Pam's death and indirectly from the insurance proceeds. If she refused to cooperate with the plaintiffs and didn't want to "incriminate" herself, wasn't that evidence of guilt, perhaps complicity in the wrongful death itself? It had the intended effect: Anne got Winnie's attention.

Winnie needed an attorney and hired Kevin Kurumada, a great guy and former legal defender with a solid, low-key practice not exclusively in criminal defense. Kev has a ton of common sense and an ability to calm people and situations. He got hold of Anne, got some definition of the situation and the needs of the parties. Then he got Winnie to see the light, even if Kevin had gently to lift her eyelids, but the damage was already done to her value as a witness. Any party was now entitled to know about her old statements as well as the new ones. It also was apparent it was in her self-interest to get out from under the lawsuit. For reasons that I'm not privy to, Winnie replaced Kevin with Kurt Frankenburg, another solid lawyer in general practice.

Somewhere along the road Anne Sulton, Esq., Ph.D. started asking questions of David Earl Mead. She sent interrogatories, held depositions and subpoenaed personal and business records, obtaining the tax filings he actually made. The fact he hadn't made them all wasn't lost on the IRS: all officers of the court have an obligation to report crime to the proper authorities.

Somewhere in this process, and to the best of my knowledge no one knows quite where, the great myth/urban legend of the fishpond case came into being: The woman from the overheard call assumed the identity of an exotic dancer working in the local strip clubs who danced under the *nom de plume* of Stormy. When Anne examined David about Stormy's identity, David was vague, never providing a last name or place of employment. He did come up with a few details, but none involved dancing or strip clubs. Nonetheless, the Stormy legend acquired a life of its own and over a period of two years many SLCPD officers visited the clubs, identified and interviewed approximately fifty young women who performed under some variation of the stage name Stormy.

A year to the day after Pamela's death, a videotaped deposition was taken of Kevin Harris. It had to be done quickly, because Kevin was dying. Kevin, a slight, gay black man, was a neighbor of the Meads and a friend of Pam's. Kevin Harris was from all reports a sweet and nice person who also happened to be one of Pam's best friends. They shopped, lunched and discussed all facets of fashion. In August 1995 Kevin, who had AIDS, and little time, put on a gray mock turtle sweater with a matched set of hematite jewelry and came forth to be deposed before he joined his friend Pamela.

With Pennington's half million safely under the supervision of the court, out of David's reach, and the widower's attention somewhat distracted, the decline of Valley Ground Service became precipitous. Soon it was a memory and David filed for the protections of the laws of bankruptcy and eventually sold the Mead house. The downside of Mead's maneuver was that a bankruptcy filing requires the petitioner to bring to the court and the assigned bankruptcy referee all sorts of documentation and records assembled in one place where a wise practitioner of the civil law, not representing a government entity, like, say, Anne Sulton, could locate and serve a single subpoena for copies of each and every one, a gold mine of information on the financial affairs of VGS and Mead.

Roger Tinsley was doing his thing as well, so well Wally Bugden was filing motions with the court to back "Action Jackson" off. The motions weren't successful and Roger didn't back off. When I saw Wally on the street he railed about Roger, Anne, the case and the poor set-upon widower. Wally and I get along just fine and I like him, but Wally and Anne hit a point where each was regularly suggesting that the court sanction the other for their tactics. The traffic in motions, responses, counter-motions and vitriol became truly astonishing. Wally always ended our encounters with a thought that it would be "crazy" or "insane" to "even think about filing criminal charges." I always responded with a smile and a glance between my eyebrows and reading glasses. As I watched him tromp away railing, I said to myself, "You go, Roger! You go, Anne!"

8

Arguing the Civil Case

Every court system has its own routines, procedures and the like. In the civil courts the Motion for Summary Judgment, a sorting procedure courts use to ensure that there are triable issues for a jury to hear, takes place after discovery has been exhausted. Each side makes its case to the judge, lays out what discovery has brought forth and argues that the opponent's claims are unsupportable. Wally argued the evidence uncovered by the Stokeses could not make a *prima facie* case of wrongful death against his client, David Mead, and therefore Judge Dee Benson ought to dismiss the lawsuit. Anne's burden was to show there were triable issues, genuine questions of fact and sufficient evidence to support a claim of wrongful death.

Utah federal procedure has the written motions and supporting documentation submitted to a magistrate judge for consideration and recommendations to the trial judge, who hears oral arguments and makes a decision. If the decision is to dismiss, it's all over. The United States Magistrate Judge, Ronald N. Boyce, taught me Crim Law, Crim Procedure and Evidence in law school and was still teaching at the U with a proper gallows sense of humor. An old military guy, a former prosecutor, onetime Mister Utah bodybuilder well-aged into a jovial bulldog and a walking set of law books, he has more detailed recollection of case law than any six combined persons you'll ever meet. Once when he spoke at the prosecutors' annual conference in southern Utah's beautiful red rock country, the organizers put together some evening entertainment, "Prosecutor Trivia." Ron Boyce would be one team, everyone else the other. For all you lawyers out there, the first question was "Completely identify all the parties in *M'Naghten's Case*." One hand went up, Ron's. We didn't stand a chance.

Judge Boyce reviewed the pleadings and evidence and recommended Judge Benson dismiss the lawsuit. It was up to Anne Sulton, and Anne alone, to clear this enormous hurdle and have Judge Benson rule against the advice of the most respected jurist in recent Utah history. Jill and I went over to the federal courthouse to show our support and see if Anne could pull it off. If the civil case were "non-suited" at summary judgment, no criminal case would ever be filed.

In late 1996, the hearing commenced before His Honor Benson, a tall, blonde-haired, bright and personable man who at first blush seemed too young to be a federal judge but whose talent and depth quickly became apparent. Wally saw that Jill and I were there and made a point of declaring, rather than asking, while shaking his head, that we couldn't possibly be considering filing criminal charges. As the moving party in this hearing, Wally laid out the facts he felt arose from discovery and, with an edge of frustration and indignation in his voice, told the court there was just no way this evidence even facially supported the contention David killed the wife he loved. He was terribly sorry the Stokeses' understandable grief turned into a vindictive rage and, although unsaid, into an ever so slightly implied motive of greed or, dare we hint, racism now unfairly directed at Wally Bugden's widowed client, David Mead. It was a good, solid, effective presentation. Jill and I exchanged glances in fear that Wally would carry the day. We underestimated Anne.

She took the podium, but she used the whole floor, that entire space between counsel tables and the bench known as the well. Moving deliberately about the well, using her hands in large gestures, but not frenetically, Anne crafted her case out of the facts in evidence and missing from evidence. She made her case that the Stokeses deserved their day in court, in format and syntax alternating between plea and demand, instruction and question. She made the point that some pretty well-paid and experienced attorneys from Pennington elected to put half a million dollars of their client's money on this table and get out of the way. Wally tensed; Jill and I nodded demonstrably to add any support we might as Anne finished her presentation.

Afterward Judge Benson was quiet. Then he leaned back in his tall chair. The courtroom, which held only its own personnel and the few already mentioned in its cavernous majesty, sat in silent tension. Finally, finally His Honor moved ever so slightly, then sat up, turned forward and told Anne that although he really, based on objective criteria, shouldn't let this case go forward, his instincts were to allow Anne Sulton to take this shot for the Stokes family. Anne was to prepare the order.

We stood while the judge returned to chambers, but by the time we got before the bar to congratulate Anne, Wally was gone. He wasn't happy and Wally knew he should not go into his feelings then and there. Anne, Jill and I knew the bullet dodged came very close and we walked out of the federal courthouse feeling satisfaction, not reassurance. The trial was set for late January. The parties went off to their camps to prepare for battle.

Following a final flurry of motions, jurors reported to the former downtown post office building now named the Frank E. Moss United States Courthouse on Tuesday, January 21, the day after the "Human Rights Day" weekend that Utah might celebrate, but wouldn't name after Dr. King for another three years. The Lemckes had an HSA meeting that evening, Utah-speak for what most call PTA.

With my own court schedule, I was only going to be able to watch a few portions of the federal trial. Some lawyers enjoy watching others do their thing, but I don't. I've got my own style and it makes me antsy to watch someone else. It's like watching and second guessing the actor in a school play in the part you had the year before. I was going to watch the defense's main expert, Dr. Kris Sperry, the Chief Medical Examiner of the State of Georgia, who held a national reputation for his work and his opinions. What he had to say and how well he presented it might decide the outcome of the federal civil case and the very existence of a state criminal matter.

Jill briefed me and the other police witnesses, who felt things were "going well" and that Anne was doing a fine job. I went over to watch Dr. Sperry testify. I gave Wally my best knowing smile and heard how it was insane even to think about bringing criminal charges.

Kris Sperry is very much the pro and Wally handled him well. Dr. Sperry conveyed his disagreement with Dr. Grey without being arrogant, condescending or accusatory. The only opening that I saw was that Wally repeatedly asked the witness if he was convinced "to a reasonable scientific certainty." It's a requisite term of art in scientific testimony for bringing in an expert's conclusion that must be used sparingly and limited to conclusions. Although I thought Wally was painting with too wide a brush, it wasn't much of an opening. Still, it might be all I had. Anne did a good job on cross, managing to touch on the existence of FBI "red flags" on staged homicides, while I squirmed watching someone else try a case, wishing I had the internal mechanisms to relax, observe, learn and enjoy.

One genuinely odd thing happened during the federal trial when a gentleman named Bill Morgan walked into the courthouse and asked when he was going to testify. After the natural question of "who are you?" he told them he was the VGS employee who cleaned the aircraft on August 15 and David Mead wasn't there. Wally howled that it was a plot, Anne indignantly asked why Morgan hadn't been identified in discovery and, after a flurry of argument, Morgan was called out of order by the court and he said he was there, didn't see Mead and couldn't say why.

Everyone who attended the closing was thunderstruck. Wally can be emotional but, unlike many inexperienced practitioners, is effective when emotional. He conveyed frustration and anger that anyone could even think these terrible things of his client. But when she spoke, Anne owned the courtroom, anything within sight of the jurors her stage. I saw this during the motion for summary judgment, but it was only a hint of her prowess. Sometimes a preacher, sometimes a conscience, sometimes a teacher of logic, sometimes a proponent of the human condition and always the lawyer, Anne Sulton moved about the well using the podium as a mere pylon, hands, inflection, volume, emotion the well-employed tools of a craftsman. Spent, Anne handed the jury back to Judge Benson. The jurors exited to deliberation and spectators for each side came forward to express thanks and admiration to their champion. Anne was exhausted, Wally remained tense and any niceties between the combatants at having fought the good fight were ceremonial at best as each retired to await the findings of twelve citizens.

Awaiting a jury decision is a time of painful tension. The partisan backslapping, compliments and reassurances at the end of closing argument have a short half-life. Occupied with my own cases, I waited as well.

Through whatever scheme of law was in place when this case was transferred from Denver, the federal case was structured to require all twelve jurors in this matter to come to a unanimous decision. Although His Honor Benson had calmly, clearly and professionally set before the panel that their required burden of proof was a preponderance of the evidence for either side and even though eleven of the members of that body not only understood, but found the Stokeses as plaintiffs met that burden, there were twelve jurors to be won. The last juror felt, deep in his heart of hearts, the Stokeses were accusing David Mead of murdering their daughter Pam and murder required proof beyond a reasonable doubt. Admitting the plaintiffs had satisfied a burden of preponderance, he would not be swayed and *Stokes v. Mead* was a hung jury. At 4:30 PM February 5, Judge Dee Benson declared a mistrial, thanked and excused the jurors.

When we got word of the verdict in the civil case, it felt like the air had been punched out of all of us. After Anne's mesmerizing close, Jill came out very pumped and spread optimism through her office and mine. But when juries stay out tension and disquiet build as hours, then days pass and bravado bleeds away. I didn't see Anne after the verdict, although we talked briefly over the phone. For the most part we communicated through Jill and there wasn't a lot to say. Anne was so intense and she'd built her presentation into such a package of emotional focus, she'd be in adrenaline deficit for some time. But Anne's a pro: at the right time she and Wally would talk and tell Judge Benson what they wanted to do about bringing *Stokes v. Mead* back for round two.

People from my office and the city PD just looked at me, shook their heads and let out breath, generally conceding the criminal case was over before it started. Those who knew how I felt said they were sorry. Jill told me about the rogue juror and was all for just filing and winning the criminal case, but the difference in the civil and criminal burdens of proof, presumptions of innocence and rules of procedure left us staring out of an enormous hole. I fell into the refuge of waiting out the retrial. With the normal scheduling difficulties setting up a multi-week federal jury trial, I'd have at least another year to decide.

Then Jill learned there were discussions between the parties looking to settle. When that came to pass, there was no more cover. It was time for a long, long lunch.

Cops know where to go to get the best food without paying too much and Jill chose a little Japanese restaurant downtown with probably eight tables. Per our custom we took Jill's police car with all her communications and gear and knew we wouldn't be ticketed if the meter ran out. I was wishing that the evidence was as substantial as the *donburi* and we spent the next several hours of a pretty July day going over what evidence we had, how well the witnesses came across in the civil case, the emergence of Bill Morgan, his effect on David's alibi and the mysterious Stormy.

All lawyers have healthy egos and I'm no exception. A lawyer does this work with an underlying belief that he or she's at least as good as every other practitioner. I had a lot of respect for Anne and admiration for the case she put on, but it's just that I'm a lawyer, and lawyers have professional credentials in disagreeing and ego.

Beyond Anne and Wally there was another law-trained individual who sat through the civil case, saw the evidence and heard the witnesses, His Honor United States District Judge Dee Benson. Since we were already in the process of going over to the federal court to withdraw the plaintiff's exhibits from the civil trial, we might as well see if we could get an appointment, talk to the judge and see if he'd share his impressions. With the civil case settled, no longer a case or controversy before him, he was free to discuss it. I phoned his clerk who put me on hold, came back and asked if we could be there at about quarter to five.

His Honor, United States Magistrate Judge Ronald Boyce and offers of soda pop were waiting for us. It was an interesting meeting. Ron was his normal open, jovial and unique self, an easy man to be around even when he deals with the minutiae of the law, because he has a wonderful common-sense, non-academic sense of real world facts. Both jurists agreed on several matters: the civil case barely survived the motion for summary judgment; they were glad it did; each felt David did it, but the evidence they saw wouldn't support guilt beyond a reasonable doubt; each of the pivotal witnesses had serious flaws; they didn't know if I could get a conviction but I ought to try. The clerk brought us the exhibits, I thanked everyone and walked out. Jill and I drove back without words, sorting our own thoughts, and we agreed to think it over.

9

A High Hurdle

In August the questions for me no longer revolved around David Mead's guilt or innocence but on whether we had enough evidence to find him guilty in our court system and how that guilty verdict could be achieved by the prosecution. Nevertheless, I was as ready as possible. It was never going to get any better; Bill Morgan was undoubtedly the last evidence we'd ever find. I met with Jill Candland in an empty conference room and spread everything on the table. We knew we could subpoena all the trial transcripts, exhibits, depositions and interrogatories, knew how witnesses would come across on the stand, but so did David and his lawyers.

With Bill Morgan's testimony that Mead's alibi was contrived, we had to show that it was possible for someone to log in at Salt Lake International Airport Gate #13, get back to his home, conduct the cruel business and return to the airport within given time limits. The urgency arose out of the otherwise good news that Salt Lake City had been awarded the 2002 Winter Olympic Games, an honor that brought a civic determination for large-scale urban upgrade. The largest and most disruptive of these projects was the total reconstruction of the Interstate 15 North/South corridor through the county. The shortest, most logical route from the Mead house to the airport involved crossing the Sixth North Street bridge over I-15 and the demolition of that bridge was the project's kick-off three days in the future. Jill accompanied another police officer driving a plain car who made and timed a series of runs in both directions, under normal traffic conditions at the appropriate time of night, obeying all laws, and wrote a "sup" to the initial report.

The next hurdle was to file the case, a higher hurdle than

it might appear. Procedurally, a homicide filing, a prosecutor's most serious case, must be approved at the highest levels of administration. So I sat down to craft my statement of probable cause as a device to review and organize the evidence we had, writing and rewriting it a few times to see where we were. The PC statement can be a useful device to educate a defense attorney, or the press, to the nature and strength of the case. In this case I needed to use it to sell the boss, Neal Gunnarson, the new DA.

I'd had casual discussions with Neal and the top-level supervision to let them know I was still looking at the fishpond case, but it was time to sit down and tell him I wanted to file. Neal talked it over with some of his advisors and got back to me with conditions. He wanted Jill and me to present our evidence to the office leadership in a formal setting. If I could convince the crew, I could file the case. We didn't set any artificial parameters like unanimous agreement, but we set a date a week out, the afternoon of Wednesday, August 13.

There's a ploy prosecutors sometimes use with charges or jury instructions: in a case with good arguments on both sides of the aisle we'll try to define a line where a jury can comfortably "split the baby." Jurors often want to give something to each side, so if they're provided a group of charges to decide or a lesser-included offense they can reach, they'll seize the opening and cut on the dotted line. I drafted two Informations, each charging David Earl Mead with murder for intentionally and unlawfully causing the death of Pamela Camille Stokes Mead and solicitation of murder for hiring James Hendrix to intentionally and unlawfully cause the death of Pamela Camille Stokes Mead, one quite boldly charging aggravated murder, a capital felony, the other with no fanfare charging murder, a first degree felony.

It's a perfectly valid question to ask why a prosecutor wouldn't go straight to the highest charge available. If David killed Pam or had her killed, it was for the money and would qualify as a "Cap," but a capital case is a creature all its own. The resource input and the consequence output, win or lose, are like nothing else in criminal law practice, and rightly so. The civil trial got regular coverage in the local press that included open speculation that the verdict killed any chance of criminal prosecution, and our office had just been hit with an acquittal on a very high-profile, high-emotion Cap involving the death of an entire family. What first appeared to be a slam-dunk winner wasn't and emotions still ran high, especially because Ron Yengich, Salt Lake's highest profile defense attorney, came out on top.

Ron and I are friends and go back a way. The deliberately unkempt and wild hair of Ron's earlier years is now limited to a great mustache, in part by Ron's choice. We've tried a bunch and got after each other with every resource, emotion and device within our grasp, but when we walk out of the courtroom we're fine; we've settled many more than we've tried. There are others within the DA's Office who don't view Ron in the same light and prefer to hold on to bitter tastes. There was grumbling that Ron's fee structure just ballooned, but I doubt this was true. In a tee shirt motto from one of the several charity events Ron sponsors each year, "A reasonable doubt for a reasonable fee." The visibility of the case undoubtedly brought him more business and the cops reported that more arrested folks announced, "I'm hiring Yengich." Some actually did.

Jill and I got together frequently that week, talked on the phone a lot more, went over her "Homicide Book" with all the police reports, witness statements, laboratory results and photos. We talked about how the witnesses did in the civil case. We reviewed the defense's experts, what they brought to the table, how we ought to organize the case and the presentation to the office. We went to lunch, made the final decisions on who'd say what, came back and carried our gear down from my office to the conference room.

Lawyer by lawyer the leadership filed on in. We got going about five minutes later than planned, well within tolerance, when Neal opened the meeting up by asking, "Do you really want to do this?"

"Yes."

"Do you think you stand a chance of pulling this off?"

"Yeah, Neal, I really do!"

Every set of arms other than mine and Jill's was folded on top of the tummies that emerge as people, showing discomfort in body language, lean back in their chairs as if this will move them out of the line of fire. Slowly letting out a briefly held breath he said, "Okay! Tell us how. And tell us how, if they couldn't get a verdict in the civil case, you think you can get one in a criminal case."

I handed out photocopies of the capital murder Information and addressed the death, the autopsy, the sequence of manners of death, Winnie and her stories, Jack and his history, Bill Morgan and the alibi, Kevin Harris alive only in a videotaped deposition, the missing, mysterious Stormy and the implications of what little physical evidence we had. For about an hour questions came from the troops before we took a break. Jill and I exchanged glances begging the question of success.

As the meeting re-opened body language was more relaxed, until someone broke in with the obvious: if there was no jury win in a civil case with no presumption of innocence and a lower burden of proof, what do you have beyond enthusiasm and ego that makes you think that we have a reasonable likelihood of getting a conviction?

"Fair enough!" First I reminded the crew that everyone involved believed that David killed Pam and was getting away with murder. They responded as I'd hoped, nodded in agreement but brought me back to the question. I announced I had two other units of evidence I believed would carry the day: Anne Sulton and Matt Jenkins.

During the civil case Anne had luxuries of which a prosecutor can only dream. There may be those who damn the Bill of Rights, particularly the Fifth Amendment with its stepchild *Miranda*. I'm not one of those, but I know these only apply in criminal cases. A civil plaintiff's lawyer can depose, submit to interrogatories and even call their defendant to the stand. Anne had and all those answers, many of them contradictory, were recorded. We'd gone over them with no small effort of arranging and cataloguing and I had something that wasn't available to Anne: I had Anne. Where Anne had to bring in David's many statements one witness, one source, at a time and then try to tie in both sides of each individual contradiction during close, I could call Anne, who was witness to all of David's statements, and move from contradiction to contradiction without the extraneous material or regard to sequence, laying out Mead's lies naked to the world.

Anne had also gathered little less than a ton of David's and Valley Ground Service's financial records, box after box after box. We knew from what Winnie, Jack and others said that David's company and lifestyle were in decline. If we could confirm this from the financial records, it would corroborate their testimony and show that their knowledge could have come only through David; none had any other access to that information.

Over my years as a deputy DA, I'd had several occasions to work with the State of Utah's Division of Securities, a very strong office under the direction of one Michael Hines. Given Utah's history of Ponzi schemes and other scams, it needs to be. One of Mike's great internal resources is Matt Jenkins, a CPA who understands forensic accounting. He not only has the skill to go through voluminous records and recognize when and where things literally don't add up, he has the talent to explain things in terms understandable to jurors. Anne had an expert in financial analysis who came at the high price of a well-credentialed expert. I might be able to sell the DA's office on filing the case, but not if we had to hire someone in that price range. I had a personal comfort level with Matt and wanted to take the analysis in a different direction.

There's a certain political checklist in such matters. Even though we'd talked about the fishpond case for three years, I set a meeting formally to request the help Matt could provide. In a good warm-up for the presentation to my own administration, I laid out the case to Mike and Matt, with particular emphasis on what I wanted from financial analysis. Matt eyed the volume of documents and gave Mike an estimate on how much work it would entail and how it would fit into his schedule. I'd have understood if Mike turned me down, but he said okay with some necessary definition of Matt's priorities. Securities is only two blocks from the DA's office, but I used my pickup truck to deliver the goods.

I told the leadership meeting that Matt discerned in a first cursory look at the finances that David's business and personal life were spiraling toward disaster. When Continental pulled out of Salt Lake City and Pam left their employment, David lost a contract, Pam's second income and his predictable calendar of social availability, and was falling behind everywhere, including taxes. Pam after surgery was an economic liability rather than an asset and David didn't get to fly for cheap.

There was probably another half hour of questions and discussion and almost everyone was now leaning forward over the conference table. They were sold on the notion David killed Pam, using the phrase "but a Cap?" in almost every sentence. Active opposition to the fishpond case remained at the table.

Our office has prosecuted people on consumer complaints of "bait and switch," which occurs when an advertised product is suddenly unavailable to a customer who is then sold an alternate product the salesman just happens to have. I won't come out and say it was B&S, but I used this moment to have Jill hand out photocopies of the first degree murder Information. There were several knowing and sly smiles and glances out of the corners of eyes recognizing a well-defined line drawn straight down this baby. At least one other set of eyes, against this from the beginning, flashed panic.

Neal looked over the second Information, set it down, looked over the Cap, put it down, picked up the first degree and broke the silence. "Well, what do you guys think?"

"Yeah!"

"Sure! Go for it!"

"Okay. I can see it."

"Howie, it's your neck."

"Why not? Yeah!"

"You know, Neal, I still don't think that . . ."

"Howie."

"Yeah, Neal?"

"Okay. It's yours! Pick out a second chair. Edit up the PC statement. Keep me advised. Go get 'em! Do you know when you'll file it?"

"Friday. It's the third anniversary of Pam's death."

"Okay. Thanks, everyone! That's all."

Jill and I looked at each other, knowing the die was cast. As we walked out of the conference room, my cohorts gave me knowing looks, smiles and pats on the back: no words were needed; no words were spoken.

Office policy provides that in homicides, high profile or complex cases a second attorney is assigned to serve as the "second chair" and help the lead attorney with the busywork, give the lead someone to bounce ideas off of and season a younger attorney in big cases. Cy Castle, an attorney of proper wit, work ethic and personality, approached me about working as second chair. Unknown to us, later events and assignments would conspire to prevent Cy from ever being able to participate in the fishpond case.

I gave the Information to my team's secretary Michelle to edit and prepare for court. It's almost impossible to overstate how important a good secretary is in a business like mine, so far beyond typing and filing. The DA's office is organized into teams of four to six attorneys bunched by category of crime. Michelle and I had been on the drug team together for a number of years until we each separately moved to arson/fraud. Her desk sat in a large lobby or common area outside my corner office door. Meesh made sure I got out the door to all the proper hearings, handled the requisite marshalling or coddling of witnesses, brought good humor and common sense to a sometimes angry or overly analytical atmosphere and was a friend.

The Information was drafted, assigned DAO#97014022, processed into our records in an orange, officially salmon, folder designating a case with inter-personal violence or a vulnerable victim. The reports were all duplicated for file boxes that would hold the bulk of our case. Another set was made to be given to the defense as discovery.

One issue came up about the PC statement: when Jill discussed the fishpond case with Jim Bell of the FBI, he'd been in a position to give us help, but not FBI backing. That wasn't yet his level within the agency, so if we were going to name the Bureau as a resource, it would have to be under someone else's title. I had Jill ask around and eventually I was given the name of Agent Larry Anchor, I believe from the civil trial when Dr. Sperry was cross-examined about the list of red flags. I'd never spoken to Agent Anchor but thought I was on solid ground to use his name. We'd never be able to get into evidence an FBI opinion that *Mead* fit the firm and fixed profile of a staged homicide, but Dr. Sperry's testimony might give an opening to let our jurors know what the FBI felt were indicia of a staged or insurance fraud homicide. We elected to include this as the last item in the PC statement, if for nothing else the flinch factor.

DOMESTIC VIOLENCE INFORMATION

COUNT I

CRIMINAL HOMICIDE, MURDER, a First Degree Felony, at 582 North Center Street, in Salt Lake County, State of Utah, on or about August 15, 1994, in violation of Title 76, Chapter 5, Section 203, Utah Code Annotated 1953, as amended, in that the defendant, DAVID E. MEAD, a party to the offense, intentionally or knowingly caused the death of Pamela Camille Stokes Mead.

COUNT II

SOLICITATION OF CRIMINAL HOMICIDE, a Second Degree Felony, at 700 East 3300 South, in Salt Lake County, State of Utah, on or about July, 1994, in violation of Title 76, Chapter 5, Section 203, Utah Code Annotated 1953, as amended, in that the defendant, DAVID E. MEAD, a party to the offense, intentionally or knowingly with the intention that a felony be committed, solicited, requested, commanded, offered to hire, or importuned another person to engage in specific conduct that under the circumstances as the actor believes them to be, would be a felony or would cause the other person to be a party to the commission of a felony by causing the death of Pamela Camille Stokes Mead.

Your Affiant bases the above upon the following:

1. The observations of your affiant and the statements of Officers Jensen, Ramonas and Tausinga that on August 15, 1994, after 11:00 PM one Pamela Camille Stokes Mead was found dead at 582 N.

Center Street, Salt Lake City. The body was soaking wet and lying alongside a backyard fishpond. With the body was the defendant herein, David Mead, Pamela's husband. David Mead told officers that he had removed the body from the pond where he stated he found the body floating facedown. When officers arrived, David Mead was in the fishpond, dismantling it. The defendant told officers he had left home and last seen Pamela alive at 8:30 PM.

2. The statement of Dr. Todd Grey, Chief Medical Examiner for the State of Utah, that Pamela Mead died from drowning, that she had a mark showing a blow to the back of her head and scraping to the abdomen. Dr. Grey found the death to be a homicide.

3. The statement of James Hendrix that in late July, 1994, the defendant had asked Hendrix to kill Pamela and make the killing appear to be a burglary or an accident. That the defendant said that he would pay Hendrix $30,000 from the $250,000 he expected to receive shortly after Pamela's death. That the defendant wanted the killing to take place while David was at work and while Pamela was still on medications from recent foot surgery. That the defendant then gave Hendrix money and cocaine as an initial payment, but that Hendrix consumed both during a binge, and that by the time Hendrix regained sobriety, Hendrix learned that Pamela had died.

4. The statement of Winnetka Walls, the defendant's mistress before and after Pamela's death, that Walls had given the defendant an ultimatum to choose around Christmas, and that the defendant told Walls that the defendant had obtained a large insurance policy on Pamela. Later, less than a month before Pamela's death, Walls gave the defendant another ultimatum, and was told by the defendant that the problem would end within a month, that Pamela would have a "nasty spill,"

David would have an alibi, and that it would be a "perfect murder."

5. The statement of Todd Ryan, a friend of the defendant, that David Mead had told Ryan that Pamela had previously left the defendant, on an occasion when Pamela overheard the defendant talking to his mistress previous to Walls, saying "I really hate her. We ought to just knock the bitch off."

6. The records of the Pennington Life Insurance Company that in December 1993, the defendant took out a $250,000 policy on Pamela's life. That inquiries toward collections were made the morning after the death.

7. The statement of Sgt. Ahern and the records of the Salt Lake City Airport that the defendant checked in at the airport at 8:51 PM at a location that would record his comings and goings.

8. The statement of Bill Morgan, an employee of Valley Ground Service, an aircraft cleaning service owned by Pamela, that the check station David used to come and go from the airport was very seldom used by David, as it was well out of the way from Valley Ground Service. That the defendant and other workers normally used a different, more convenient entrance that didn't record comings and goings. That the portion of the shift David worked was one the defendant historically avoided, involved work the defendant seldom performed, and that the total work performed by David, a "quick clean" of an airliner, would only take fifteen to twenty minutes.

9. Your affiant's observation, in driving tests performed before the demolition of the Sixth North overpass, that the drive time between the North Center address and Valley Ground Service was thirteen minutes each way.

10. The statements of Peter Maxwell, Kevin Harris, and James & Janet Acton that after 11:00 PM the evening of August 15, each received a call from David Mead announcing the time and asking if

each knew the whereabouts of Pamela. This was something none can remember David Mead ever doing before.

11. *The statement of Dr. Gregory Anderson that he had performed surgery on both of Pamela's feet, which she was recovering from at the time of her death, and that walking would have been labored and painful.*

12. *The statement of the defendant, to your affiant, that the fishpond had been completed four days before the death, and dismantled the day after the death.*

13. *Your affiant's observations that the backyard had no landscaping or improvements, except the fishpond, it was dirt rather than grass, was covered with dog droppings, there was no functioning backyard light, and at least a fifty-foot slightly uphill walk from the backdoor to the pond.*

14. *The statement of financial analyst Dr. Jerry Boswell, MBA, DBA, that after analyzing the financial documents of David Mead, Pamela Mead and Valley Ground Service, a company owned by Pamela and employing David, that the defendant was in great financial distress at the time of Pamela's death.*

15. *The statement of Dr. David Smith, an expert in hypothermia and still water drowning, that a drowning victim typically sinks after drowning, and normally does not float for many hours. This situation is even more pronounced in lean black females.*

16. *The statement of Agent Larry Anchor of the FBI Violent Criminal Apprehension Program, Behavioral Science Unit, that many of the facts, including David Mead's behaviors fall into categories of indicia of a "staged crime." Particularly of interest, other than the above facts, was the defendant's selective histrionics when undergoing substantive questioning, and that David Mead sent roses to your affiant before Pamela Camille Stokes Mead's funeral.*

/s/ Det. Jill Candland, Affiant

I took a deep breath. This was an entirely circumstantial case. I needed to lay those circumstances out. We'd never found Stormy, and the Hearsay Rule would keep us from getting in Pam's conversation with Mary, although Mead's mouthing off to Todd Ryan would allow us to get in the existence, and a piece of the substance, of the Stormy call. I knew I wouldn't use either Doctors Smith or Boswell, but they each participated in the federal proceedings, so their opinions were a part of that record and properly mentioned in the PC. I could use Dr. Grey or Dr. Maureen Frikke from the ME's office to handle the drowning and floating issues and I was much more comfortable with Matt Jenkins doing the financial analysis.

The paperwork was done and Thursday ended quietly.

Friday, August 15, the third anniversary of Pam's death found Cy, Meesh, Jill and me by the coffee pot that sits on the mini-fridge in my office. Michelle brought in the original Information, which Cy and I signed, and the proposed Warrant of Arrest requesting the judge to set bail at $250,000. Michelle made copies for everyone and Jill walked the originals across the street to the courthouse. There wasn't much conversation and none of the jocularity so common to this crowd.

The Third Judicial District Court was directly across Fourth South Street from our office, a tired old building in its last year of life, part of a Hall of Justice complex being demolished to make space for a new library as the new Scott M. Mathesson Courthouse was under construction two blocks to the west. Fourth South Street itself was undergoing the early work required to allow it to carry a new light rail TRAX line up to the university and its Olympic venues. Detective Jill Candland found the Honorable Judge Dennis M. Fuchs, who read the Information and the Statement of Probable Cause. Jill raised her right hand, swore what was contained in the Information was true and correct to the best of the detective's knowledge and belief, signed and dated the Information. Judge Fuchs signed and dated the Information, reviewed and approved the requested bail and signed the Warrant of Arrest. In the Office of the Clerk of the Court in the basement, Jill found the chief deputy clerk Byron

"Killer" Stark, who penned the name David Earl Mead between the pre-printed line leader "State of Utah v." and the next available pre-printed case number, 971015212FS, and wrote this number on the faces of the Information and warrant. After confirming the judge's signature, Killer stamped the court's seal over both, initialed the stamps, found a pink court file, which was sent to data entry where the court's computer assigned the case to the Honorable Phillip J. Palmer. Jill went back through our office, gestured with the signed warrant and walked out to her car. She'd arranged for officers to meet her at David's current home.

I got on the phone, first to Anne Sulton in Denver, then to the Stokeses in the Springs. Mary Stokes called me later in the day seeking more detail than I'd given her folks and asked why this wasn't filed as a Cap. Although there was an explanation, I didn't make it. Tales of politics and games-manship, particularly bragging about the result, would have been inappropriate and insensitive. Mary's bringing up the date voiced the unasked question the others shared: why had this taken so long? Again, I chose not to answer.

10

Arrested

A few months back, after the civil case settled and David's share had gone to pay his legal fees, he filed for bankruptcy, Valley Ground Service went under and the Mead house was sold. Jill and other officers responded to a report of a domestic violence stabbing near the Trolley Square shopping center to find paramedics treating David Mead for assorted scratches, abrasions and a minor stab wound in the upper arm.

"Hi, David."

"Hi, Jill."

"What happened?"

"You don't want to know."

"Well, actually, I do. You know, the job and all."

Inside the house officers were dealing with David's new interest, an extremely intoxicated young woman who, finding herself in a state of partial undress, put on a somewhat short skirt over her head as a top. Jawing on, not about if she'd punctured David with a sharp object but why he deserved it, she was transported and booked. David was given a police incident number and told how the case would be processed. Before the sun came up David started repeatedly calling the jail, pleading for the lady's release, announcing that he wouldn't press charges. It was not lost that David might not want someone he'd confided in to be surrounded by so many police officers. However, when approached, the new-found flame answered with an oblique reference to pounding sand. Because of my involvement in the investigation of Pam's death, I was deliberately and correctly kept out of the loop when the stabbing was screened. It was declined, but I was provided police reports.

On the morning of August 15, 1997, Jill and her fellow officers arrived at David's home to find him standing in the open front door talking on a cordless phone. They walked up to David who said to his correspondent, "I've gotta go now. Jill's here to arrest me." He clicked off the phone, set it down just inside the door, stepped out, closed the door behind him and surrendered as requested. He was searched, handcuffed and transported to the Salt Lake County Jail in the doomed Hall of Justice complex. David Earl Mead was booked, photographed, fingerprinted, searched more thoroughly, interviewed about medical or other special needs, provided prisoner clothing, assigned a booking, or "SO," number, 0222121, to track him on this and any future occasions he might be jailed and an "OTN" or Offense Tracking Number 10098374 for criminal justice agencies to follow this case and coordinate it with the distinct numbers each agency seems driven to assign. David listed his employment as a self-employed handyman, his local ties as two of his brothers, no income or assets and his marital status as widower.

The weekend passed uneventfully and at 9:30 on the

morning of Monday the eighteenth, David appeared by means of a video hookup in the courtroom of Judge Robert K. Hilder to be arraigned. Within a two-minute span, Mead was informed of the charges against him, informed that pre-trial services was not recommending that their agency supervise him on a recognizance release, appointed a public defender from the LDA upon David's plea of poverty and assigned a date for a roll call hearing. Judge Hilder checked with his clerk who announced it would be before Judge Palmer on Tuesday August 26 at two o'clock in the afternoon and that LDA would assign Francis Palacios and David Mack to the case. I'd already told John Hill at Legal Defenders that Jack Hendrix, a past and current LDA client, was going to be an essential witness for the State. Everyone understood that Fran and Dave would only hold the fort till John designated conflicts counsel. A packet of documents that was our down payment on discovery was handed over to the defenders' representative to forward to the appropriate parties.

In the early afternoon of August 26, I went down a Hall of Justice walkway with benches, planters and pavement, whose maintenance was being ignored in light of the upcoming demolition, to Judge Palmer's courtroom in the Seventh Judicial Circuit Court. I was a few minutes early, but not the first to arrive; my party opponents, conflicts co-counsel Richard P. Mauro and Benjamin A. Hamilton, were waiting. Jail transportation hadn't yet brought Mead up through the series of tunnels, elevators and holding cells that connected the jail to the courtroom and His Honor was tied up in his chambers with a short stack of phone calls.

I asked if they'd received their discovery. Acknowledging they had, Rich asked if I was serious about going forward with this case. We postured back and forth for a few minutes before Rich noted that it was him and me, Jill and Todd Grey, just like old times. Ben gave a puzzled look; Rich would let him in on the history later.

The prisoner door opened and the jail transportation deputy announced the defendant had arrived. Rich and Ben went back into the holding cell to talk with their client, the deputy and I shot the breeze and I collected my thoughts. A few minutes passed before Gloria, Judge Palmer's longtime clerk, announced he was on his way. The deputy informed the defense and helped a handcuffed and shackled David Earl Mead make his way to a chair at the defense table where I saw him in person for the first time. David Earl Mead stood tall and lean with stylishly long dark hair and good features given to exaggerated expressions. Jill told me Mead reminded her of Ted Bundy, but I didn't immediately see the resemblance.

His Honor Palmer, one of the anchors of the courts, came in and everyone stood as he took the bench. He was in the last few months of his service, retiring before the move to the new Mathesson Courthouse. Since, simultaneous with the physical move, the circuit and district courts were being merged, with new computer and telephone systems to be mastered, His Honor demonstrated he did not lack for common sense.

We got on to the business of the day, which was to set a date for the preliminary hearing. This was clearly not a case that would be plea-bargained. With Mead adamant we couldn't prove he did it, he wasn't about to plead and we weren't about to offer a lesser offense. Since David was incarcerated, the preliminary hearing would come up quickly, but Rich Mauro had another idea: what if David were out of custody? We wouldn't need an emergency setting for a complex prelim, and isn't a quarter million bucks an unfair amount of bail? Rich started out, as any good lawyer would, by exercising the defendant's right to have an appropriate bail set and suggested $25,000, or, at worst, $50,000 even on a homicide. Rich had done his homework; Wally Bugden was waiting in the wings.

Rich asked the court to allow Wally to address the proceedings and Judge Palmer agreed. Wally related that he was David's lawyer on the civil case where the plaintiff had not prevailed despite the lower burden. He opined at some length that this was a weak case where even the civil matter barely survived a motion for summary judgment. He claimed it was driven by the Stokes family, Anne Sulton and improper motive but didn't address why David elected to settle for the 15 percent that only covered expenses already incurred. Finally, Wally hit the only two relevant issues in a bond hearing: Was David a flight risk? Was David a clear and present danger to himself, to the community or to specific people? Wally listed several reasons why he felt David was neither. Rich picked up the ball and tied together much of what Wally laid out: David had lived in Salt Lake his entire life and, by the State's own theory of the case, the person in danger was no longer at risk. I countered that now David had no real property, business, regular job, wife, nor other indicia of ties to the community. He was a flight risk and, I felt, a danger to potential witnesses.

Rich used the opportunity to suggest that the dotted line on this baby ran up and down the amount of $100,000 and Judge Palmer quickly agreed. David announced he could probably come up with that amount, so a long setting on the prelim would be okay. My first response was to ask for an additional condition of release to be a "No Contact" requirement to prevent David, but not his attorneys or investigators, from approaching witnesses in the case, which was granted without disagreement. My second response was to ask why, if David could cover a $100,000 bail, he was entitled to a publicly funded team of attorneys.

You would have thought I was burning a flag from the defense team's reaction. "How dare the State question a defendant's right to representation?"

"Well, actually, as a taxpayer, I think it's a fair topic for enquiry!"

So did Judge Palmer. I wasn't questioning if he should be represented, but whether or not the public ought to foot the bill. David poor-mouthed that friends and relatives would post a property bond in that amount, but his own resources and prospects were gone, leaving him indigent. Judge Palmer did not disturb his appointment.

We set the prelim for two days, December 17 and 18. Rich and Ben gave the court their Appearance of Counsel and Demand for Discovery, Judge Palmer told them to prepare the Order for Reduction of Bail and Dave Mack filed a Withdrawal of Counsel/Substitution of Conflicts Counsel on behalf of LDA. The judge asked us if there was anything else we needed to handle that afternoon and there wasn't. We stood, the judge left and the jailer took David back to the holding cell. Ben and I stayed and talked, hit some details on mechanics and small talk. Rich left with a bounce in his step.

Rich, an intense man of considerable talent, is a nice person, very well liked within the circles of the defense bar who gets along with our side at arm's length. Short and wiry like an amateur wrestler, he reflected changing fashions in his clothing, eyewear, hair length and dark, dense facial hair. He isn't always comfortable around prosecutors. After I won an angry case with Rich a while back that involved Jill and the ME, we'd assumed some distance.

I'd known Ben Hamilton for a number of years. He's a sole practitioner who does criminal defense work, among other chores, a good lawyer who has carried on a successful solo practice where many others have fallen by the wayside. He and I have been opponents on several cases and taken a couple to trial. A bit taller than me, a conservative dresser, with short light brown hair and a genuine smile, Ben is a very open and pleasant man who looks like a young lawyer, an even keel through the choppy waters of the profession, a good counterpoint to Rich's volatility.

The next day Ben brought the bond reduction order over to court. Judge Palmer wasn't available, but Judge Fuchs signed in his stead. David's cobbling of the property bond took longer than he hoped, but on September 23, he was released from custody.

11

Preparing for a Mini Trial

Over the next months, Rich, Ben and I went back and forth about the tons of evidence. Wally and David Mead got all the materials from the civil trial to Rich and Ben as Anne had for me. Matt Jenkins's work on David's and Valley Ground Service's finances was a new body of evidence for both sides and by mid-November there was a consensus that neither side would be ready to do their best job a month out. We each had other cases on our plates; the tyranny of the immediate afflicts lawyers, too. I phoned the Stokeses who weren't happy, but understood; we'd talked before about the probability of continuances along the line.

In Utah a preliminary hearing is a version of a mini-trial where the State is required to put sufficient evidence before a judge to show there exists probable cause to infer that the crimes charged were committed and the person charged committed them, and that there's enough of a case to get bound over. It's a good test of any "iffy" witnesses. The burden is lower than at trial, but testimony and evidence bear the same level of examination and scrutiny. It's rare that a case is thrown out at prelim, but common for some charges to be altered or dismissed at that level. Occasionally, the State is able to amend up or add charges, but it is extremely rare for the State to resurrect charges lost at prelim.

A judge is a law-trained practitioner, so it's not necessary to give an opening statement, conduct jury education, lay background for witnesses like cops or the ME or put witnesses in logical sequence. The decision of which witnesses to call is not as easy as it might seem. It's not a question of showing the hand to the defense—they've seen everything through discovery—just not revealing how the case will be presented. Sequence, emphasis and flourish can be held in reserve and close to the vest.

Phil Palmer's cases had been assigned to Her Honor Ann C. Boyden. Judge Boyden is a McConkie, the oldest, most established and respected family of lawyers in Utah. A very LDS family, eleven currently practice under the name of McConkie alone. Judge Boyden carries a calm strength borne of an upbringing that has steadied her in both her professional path and family life, which includes a wonderful child with large challenges. She is a judge who commands the courtroom through professional presence. Far from what is portrayed of courtrooms in popular media, where every voice raises louder than the last, Judge Boyden speaks softly so everyone must become quiet and listen. When she rules against a party—and she has ruled against me—there is neither ambiguity nor edge to the decision. The terms courtesy and courtly derive from the word court; anticipated rancor of our prelim would be tempered.

I sat down with my assistant Michelle to talk over strategy and mechanics: What witnesses should be subpoenaed? Which witness on which day? What contacts and witness preparation would be necessary for Winnetka Walls, Jack Hendrix or Bill Morgan? Did we have good addresses on everyone? What was Winnie's latest version of events? Would she appear or is she on board Team Mead? Did we need to talk to Dr. Grey about the changes in the autopsy findings? How should we present Matt Jenkins's analysis? Had I heard about Jill's reassignment?

My shock was palatable. "Jill's reassignment?" I said stumbling.

Michelle nodded. "Patrol Officer and Union President Jill Candland is no longer Detective Jill Candland." The Chief had demoted her. It was alleged that the detective blatantly mishandled a firearm in evidence in a homicide, but it was also loudly rumored that the Chief was not supportive of unions.

Salt Lake City Police Chief Ruben Ortega had come from the Phoenix, Arizona, Police Department in 1992. Dark hair and eyes, a wiry build and the angular features of *los indios* set out an intense and serious nature; his only smiles seemed forced. Ruben Ortega has many positive qualities and skills, but not the ability to be professionally warm, fuzzy and endearing. Ruben intended to be benevolent. He was in charge and wouldn't tolerate dissent from any quarter, certainly not from a union.

As to Jill, the story I later learned was that, in a homicide assigned to Jill, a civilian witness came across what turned out to be the murder weapon some days after a killing in a business area south of Salt Lake's downtown. The merchant let his dog out into the alley to answer nature's call only to have the tail-wagging, proud pup return carrying a handgun in its mouth. This gentleman took it from the pooch, made sure it was safe, locked it up, went home and called a detective he knew personally, who called Jill at her home. Jill recognized the tie-in to the downtown killing, called the merchant and said she'd pick it up when he opened first thing Monday morning. She did and, after taking a statement, petting the pup, properly bagging and tagging the weapon, took it to the PSB.

The obvious reaction at the working level of the PD and the DA was delighted surprise and congratulations. For those lying in wait for the union it was opportunity. Why wasn't the merchant required to return to his shop at that instant? What evidentiary value was lost by this delay? The fact that no-longer-pristine evidence had been handled by a bystander and a bowser and moved from its original position was lost on command. Jill was toast.

A development covered by the Rules of Discovery, Rich and Ben were entitled to know, because it affected a witness's credibility. The jurors were going to hear about what kind of a detective investigated this matter and the sort of work she was known to do. I ran into Rich in the courthouse a few days later and, before I could tell him, he asked if I had heard about the demotion. He does his homework, has good sources and couldn't quite contain a little rolling laugh before changing the subject and losing the smirk.

As the months passed we chose our preliminary strategy. We'd call the core witnesses: Jill; Dr. Grey; Winnie; Jack; Matt Jenkins; the first officer at the scene, Mike Jensen; Chris Ahern from the SLCPD Airport Unit and David's ex-

employee Bill Morgan. We'd use Sinie Stokes as our foundational witness for the records of the civil case instead of flying Anne Sulton over from Denver. The Stokeses would be
there; it would give the family a small measure of participation and a chance to look David straight in the eye. I wanted
to see how he reacted. We broke our two days set for prelim
into four half-day units and subpoenaed witnesses based on
our best guess of how long each would take, knowing that
everyone except Ahern and Jensen would be in for grueling
cross.

We selected two photos from the scene and an exemplar
brick as exhibits. Matt Jenkins would provide summaries and
charts of the finances and Todd Grey his reports. We'd only
use one photo from the autopsy, the one of the wound on the
back of Pam's head, no blowups, only prints for Her Honor,
no showy materials that might be hurtful to the family or sensational to the public. We had David's depositions, statements
and the like copied, bookmarked and tabbed to relevant passages and got subpoenas out just before I left for a vacation
with my family in Rome.

Michelle was in charge for the next two weeks. I'm not a
cell phone person, but I rented one with worldwide reach for
emergencies. Only Michelle and my Aunt Bunny's assisted
living center had the number, a ring I hoped not to hear.

The day I returned to the office, Jill and Michelle briefed
me on a few happenings: Jack was in prison, he'd be easy to
find; Winnie wasn't happy with us, her loyalty pendulum was
swinging David's way, but said she would testify; Matt was
doing well; I needed to meet with him and know what to ask
him; it wouldn't hurt to sit down with Dr. Grey; Jill had been
able to talk to Bill Morgan; others didn't need immediate
attention. Getting Patrol Officer Jill Candland to the hearing
was a problem. We'd need to issue her separate and individual subpoenas for each day of the prelim and each day we
needed her for preparation. She was no longer a detective and
there were no provisions for leaving her shift duties to work
with the DA. We complied. It was easier than fighting someone else's bureaucracy.

February moved into March and preparation for the Mead
preliminary hearing squeezed between other cases that

crossed my desk. I got the Mead defense's first Supplemental Request for Discovery, the anticipated demand for every record ever kept about Jack Hendrix from the nursery to the present.

On Monday, March 9, I went over the battle plan with Jill and Meesh. I asked Michelle to call the prison and make sure that they knew their transportation officers were bringing Jack on Thursday afternoon. Jill was to go over to the PD, retrieve her Homicide Book and give Ahern, Dr. Grey and Ms. Walls final calls. I felt well prepared and ready.

Winnie had changed attorneys and Kurt Frankenburg, her new counsel, wanted a call. Phoning him, I gave Kurt the assurances that we weren't looking at his client as a party or accessory to the death. He asked me to send him a fax to that effect.

Only a detective may take a detective's Homicide Book out of the detectives' offices. Since Jill was no longer an official detective, I got on the phone to Sergeant Jerry Mendez. Jerry and I go back a long, long way, including a case of a hammer murderer who feigned insanity over a period of years before we overcame his act, won the conviction and had our judge order restitution of hundreds of thousands of dollars for the services conned out of the state mental hospital. But now Jerry was under the gun.

"Jerry, just let me check it out."

"Howie, you're not a detective."

"Assign the case to someone else and let them check it out and bring it over."

"I'm not allowed to do that."

"Okay!"

Being an old timer with old friends has its advantages. I felt a lot could be accomplished by Deputy Chief Mac Connole walking across the hall to his boss's office, closing the door and advocating common sense. Mac came through and the Homicide Book was on my desk Tuesday morning.

Michelle looked nervous when she walked into my office within an hour of Jill's call. Jack wasn't at the prison: he was out in the sticks, way out in the sticks fighting forest fires.

It seems Jack was told by his girlfriend that if he didn't make some serious changes in his life, starting with the drugs, she was history. She suggested the Latter-day Saints faith, in which both were raised, might be a good place to start. Jack, to his great credit, approached the LDS ministries who served the inmates and they took Jack under their wing.

Some very good people quietly do this largely unglamorous task of preaching well beyond the choir. This work of living their faith brought Jack a long way, figuratively, which was wonderful, and literally, which looked disastrous. Jack cleaned up his act, was doing super and earned privileges and a volunteer's spot on the prison's "Flame 'n Goes" fire fighters. He was in rural southern Utah helping fight a wildfire and there was no way the prison could get him to court on Thursday.

Again, it's often who you know that counts. In this case who some people I knew, knew. The governor didn't need his plane Friday morning, his pilot is a state trooper, a helicopter fighting the fire was within range of the Moab airport and Meesh was able to coordinate the details. Jack could be in court Friday afternoon with a few extra minutes to spare. We juggled our witnesses to accommodate that. I was in hock for a whole lot of favors to a whole lot of good people.

The Stokes family got into town Wednesday. We'd talked on the phone and met briefly during the federal trial, but Garfield and Sinie Stokes, their daughter Romaine Jake, her husband George and Roger Tinsley were there. Mary Stokes and Anne Sulton were unable to attend. When they got to my office, I introduced them to my right arm, Michelle, and put them under the wing of Mitzi, one of our victim/witness counselors. The DA Counseling Unit—a crew of fine people with a tough, unappreciated job—does a lot of the emotional heavy lifting on violent or sex cases where staying in touch is important for victims, but staying at arm's length is critical for attorneys.

We talked for a while about the state of the case, evidence, anticipated presentation, expectations and hopes. I warned them about the medical examiner's testimony. We would be using few photographs, no blow-ups, but Dr. Grey and I would be carrying on a colloquy in very cold and clinical terms about their daughter and her body. I'd give fair warning when this occurred if they wanted to opt out. No, it would be rough, brutal more likely, but opting out is not the Stokes family's style. There was remaining tension from the long delay in filing, but we were getting more comfortable with each other. Garfield and I talked about how each of us came to be retired army. They saw the pictures in my office and we talked about our kids. I never miss a chance to brag about my kids.

I asked Pam's mother if she had a picture of her daughter. "Yes," she said. I explained since I was calling her to be my foundational witness, I wanted her to show a picture to the judge and put a face, literally, on David's crime. Mrs. Stokes retrieved from her purse a narrow full-length picture of Pam off to and facing one side of the picture. Sinie saw the question in my eye and unfolded the picture to show David Mead on the flip side standing behind his bride. The reason for the fold was obvious.

Romaine asked me directly if we were going to win. "I can't make any promises beyond doing the best I can with the evidence that is available." She asked why Mary wasn't subpoenaed to testify about her conversation with Pam and David's phone call with Stormy. I explained, "I can't get that into evidence because of the Hearsay Rule, but down the road we might be able to get in some of David's statements about the call." My answer didn't satisfy her, or me, or anyone else, but it was one of the cards we'd been dealt.

The pleasantries of goodbye were tinged with some anxiety and sadness because of the significance of the events of the next day. We agreed to meet at my office in the morning.

12

The First Shot

The morning arrived with more surprises when I found out that Officer Mike Jensen, the first to arrive at the Mead's home, my anticipated witness after Mrs. Stokes, had been in an automobile accident.

"How bad?"

"Not all that bad. But he's being looked at this morning."

"You got his mobile?"

"Yeah."

"Tell him to take care of himself and get well. We'll put him on tomorrow."

"Okay."

Cops are in wrecks much more frequently than most folks would think, unless they consider what cops really do for a living, every day, for us, for not nearly enough pay.

Everyone grabbed a jacket for the crisp spring day and walked to court. We congregated in Judge Boyden's courtroom in the Circuit Court Building. Rich, Ben and David were there along with several members of David's family and their private investigator Randall Carrington. A few of Pamela's old friends and Pastor Davis were there to support us. A fair segment of the press showed up along with some attorneys from both sides of the aisle whose presence wasn't immediately required in some other court. Her Honor walked in, all rose, she took the bench and, in keeping with her gentler style, announced rather than gaveled the case of *State of Utah v. David E. Mead* to order.

There are preliminary matters to any court hearing, even a preliminary hearing: the court reporter was sworn in and got lists of witnesses and spellings; I told the court about the quirks in witness scheduling; she suggested I fill in with portions of Jill's testimony.

Rich invoked the Exclusionary Rule. It looked like those old *Perry Mason* episodes where, at precisely seven minutes to the hour, as Counselor Mason bore down on a fragile witness, someone would stand up in the gallery and announce that they, not Perry's client, had done the dirty deed! But in reality that never happens. Witnesses are excluded from listening to other witnesses testify. If you look at it in a favorable light, they're excluded so they don't listen to each other and mold their memory around overheard testimony instead of personal recollection. We need their independent witness. If you look in a light less favorable, they're denied an opportunity to participate in a crafted false story or know what to expect from a rugged cross examination.

An unintended consequence of the Exclusionary Rule was a situation where a victim was further victimized by being locked out of the bulk of a hearing, but the victims' rights movement forced courts and lawmakers to address this wrong. When I announced that I intended to call Mrs. Stokes, Rich moved her exclusion and proffered that all the Stokes family were potential witnesses at trial. He saw them as my witnesses to lay a foundation for a yet unannounced expert on a new and unique theory of "staged homicides." This was new to me, something even my experienced lawyer's mind hadn't envisioned. Rich countered that he might just call them himself to address prior statements given in depositions or interrogatories. There was quite a bit of discussion, a record made of Rich's objection, but the family was not excluded.

Rich and I each designated our principal investigators as exceptions to the Exclusionary Rule. Jill joined me at counsel table and I passed her a blank legal pad so she could take notes and suggest questions to ask. I always check with my case manager before I hand over a witness. Rich designated Randy, who took a seat on the bench in front of the bar, immediately behind an already crowded defense table. All other actual or potential witnesses were admonished not to discuss this case with each other or anyone other than the attorneys and sent out of the courtroom.

"You may call your first witness, Mr. Lemcke."

"Thank you, Your Honor. The State calls Sinie Stokes to the stand."

With quiet resolve, Pam's mother walked out ahead of the bar, stood before Judge Boyden's clerk, raised her right hand and swore to tell the truth. Then she made her way to the witness stand where the bailiff helped her adjust the microphone, gave her a paper cup of water and backed away.

"Would you please state your full, true and correct name and spell your last name for the record?"

We established that she was from Denver and the mother of the decedent. I've always believed that if I'm going to use the familiar as a form of address or reference in a courtroom setting I should get permission first and asked Mrs. Stokes if it was all right if I referred to her daughter by her first name, Pamela. She said it was and told the court when her daughter was born and that she'd died at the age of twenty-nine. Sinie told us she knew the defendant, David Mead, as the man who married Pam, and identified him as the third person at the defense table. It is a small detail, but in every prelim or trial, someone has to identify the defendant.

My other need from Pam's mother was to lay foundation for the materials from the civil trial. I brought up that she and Garfield were the plaintiffs, showed her a number of documents and asked her to identify them. We talked about the lawsuit and Rich started a pattern of technical objections. Rich objected to any mention of insurance on the basis of Rule 411, which says that jurors in a civil tort are not to be told about liability insurance. Were someone to slip and fall in my home, the jury would decide if I was at fault and what I ought to pay for the injuries. A homeowner's policy wouldn't be relevant to liability or damages or evidence in a civil suit. However, were I to kill someone in order to benefit from a life insurance policy, that policy would be very relevant in a criminal prosecution. Objection overruled!

I don't mean to say, or even infer, that all Rich's objections were badly taken or unsuccessful or that mine were all well taken and received, because it wouldn't be fair, and it wouldn't be true. Rich's style is to be an aggressive, zealous and effective advocate and that works for him. I guess that

I'm just a little more laid back and that's what works for me. Rich tends to be demanding of witnesses and voice objections, while I tend to be more conversational and let some potential objections go.

After I got through my direct examination of Mrs. Stokes, Rich started his cross by asking her the outcome of the civil trial. Through the cross, subsequent re-direct, re-cross and so forth, it came out that there was a hung jury, known to be eleven to one for the Stokeses, and that the civil burden was lower and unmet, but David settled for only 15 percent of the policy's value. I forgot to ask Sinie to show Judge Boyden the picture of Pam folded away from David but I did see her showing it to several people in the courtroom. During the breaks some of the reporters did interviews and the television outfits, needing "visuals" for their stories, videotaped Sinie with the photo.

It was Todd Grey's turn.

Todd's a pro and knows his way to the witness stand. I briefly laid out his credentials and experience as foundation for getting his opinions as an expert before the court. With a judge familiar with the law and the office and duties of a medical examiner there was no need to educate the court, just make a record. Dr. Grey had testified before, including on this case during the civil trial.

We started out with the doctor's first observations upon receiving Pam for autopsy. He told the court about her clothing including the orthopedic shoes, the fact that there was dirt consistent with her wet body lying on the ground, the pins from the bunion surgery extending out of the toes, and the frothy plugs in the nostrils. I asked Dr. Grey about lividity on the back, buttocks and legs and what it meant. We talked about the temperature of the body as twice measured, along with the temperatures of the air and the water, indicating a very approximate time of death. We discussed the injuries to her body and mentioned the scrapes to her abdomen and her right elbow. We talked about the concept of pre-, peri- and post-mortem wounds occurring before, close to or after the time of death. The damage to her elbow and stomach was peri-mortem and we talked at length about the peri-mortem wound to the right side of the back of Pamela's head. The rest of her body was free of injuries, which was inconsistent with Pamela falling on or across the jumbled rocks and bricks that made up the collar of the fishpond.

Our discussion included the observations of the head wound examined after Pam's hair was cut away, observations about the hair itself and what the doctor saw of the damage beneath her skull. Pam's hair was curly and thick, not just in its constitution but its cut as well, sufficient to have cushioned a lesser blow. The wound itself cut deeply: "It penetrated through to the underlying tissues, did not cause fracturing of the skull, did not have any associated injuries within the brain." A fairly straight-line laceration a little over an inch long with the "superior undermining" tissue damage, there was tissue damage outside of the intact skull, but none underneath. Whatever caused the wound had a relatively straight edge and was moving up relative to the back of her head, a blow sufficient to have caused disorientation, concussion and possibly brief unconsciousness, any of which could easily contribute to the inability of someone to rescue him- or herself from drowning.

One of the Meads' neighbors had dismantled a patio and given David the leftover bricks that became the inner ring of the fishpond's collar. Although David's family buried those as they filled in the pond, the neighbor had some left over and had provided one to Jill during the investigation. I marked that brick as a "demonstrative exhibit" and handed it to Dr. Grey who confirmed such a brick was capable of causing the wound. We addressed the idea of how the blow would have been struck: straight up, but only if Pam were standing erect; were she bent over at the waist or lying on the couch, the mechanics of the attack would be different.

We discussed two issues that arose from David's version of events: he found Pam floating face down in the water and pulled her out himself. He was, by all accounts, the only one who ever saw her in the water. First of all, would she have been floating? Then, could we determine how long she'd been in the water and place the time of death with any certainty? Todd knew that folks don't go in the water, drown and immediately bob up to the surface. Her clothing wasn't blousy and floating is a function of density, body fat content, water temperature and time in the water. Pamela Mead wasn't a fat person by any measure and, even if she were, floating was caused by gasses from tissue decomposition and wouldn't take place for days, even if the water were warm. This water was 67 degrees and ". . . the body would most likely be submerged."

There are generally agreed-upon formulae for body cooling in either air or water and the doctor could apply these to David's statements that he last saw her alive at 8:30 and first saw her in the water at 11:10. He concluded Pamela probably went into the water closer to 8:30 than 11.

I asked Todd about Pam's surgery and if walking would be uncomfortable. Mercifully, I felt we did not have to discuss the autopsy's internal findings or talk about the methods of those examinations.

We got to the history of the changes in Dr. Grey's conclusions as to manner of death. Rich was anxious to get into what he felt was the meat of one of his avenues of defense, but I merely touched on the area. We talked about the dates of the initial finding of accident, the change to pending, the change to homicide and the inputs Todd received to make those changes. I asked what pressure was placed on Todd to make those changes during that month and ten days. There was none; this was his independent decision on how to certify the death. We both knew what he was looking at on cross, and we each knew how we were to react.

"Thank you, Doctor. No further questions."

"Mr. Mauro."

Rich did not disappoint. In a small and rather tight community, like that of those who practice criminal law in Salt Lake, trends are easy to spot. Every lawyer in Utah is required to acquire twenty-four "CLEs" or hours of continuing legal education every two years, usually at seminars the defense bar or the prosecutors' organization sponsors. For months after a particularly effective speaker spins their magic, the other side will see a new tack or technique tossed their way on almost every case we try. I don't know who they brought in that year, but their thing was cross-examination by definition accomplished by staccato questioning of the witness.

"Dr. Grey, you testified you are a forensic pathologist. Is that correct?"

"Yes."

"And that's a different job than what Ms. Candland does. Is that correct?"

"Yes."

"She is a police officer?"

"Yes."

"And you have an office on Medical Drive. Is that correct?"

"That is correct."

"And you have a place where you perform autopsies?"

"That is correct."

"And you don't go out and interview witnesses? Do you?"

For some time we went on about what Todd was and what he wasn't. The effect of the questioning was almost a sneer set to elicit only an answer of yes or no. That's known as controlling the witness, a good technique in any cross. Rich's goal was to try to show that Dr. Grey's opinion on manner of death was the result of inputs beyond the autopsy, outside his zone of expertise and therefore invalid. He was trying to show that the medical examiner was either trying to be a cop or was pressured out of his role by the cops. Todd is a pro and I'm not bad either; we might not have enjoyed this but we could handle it.

The questioning continued about what constitutes an autopsy: an outside examination, open up the chest, examination inside the body cavity, inside the head, but not witness interviews. Aside from the insensitivity toward the family, the line of questions was designed to irritate the witness and the prosecutor and was succeeding.

Rich handed the witness Defense Exhibit #1, a copy of the original death certificate that certified the manner of death as accidental. Todd identified the document, it was moved for admission, I waived objection without examining it further and it was received. Rich, as he should have, used this as a launching pad for his line of attack but hardly went into the details of the autopsy and never mentioned Dr. Sperry. If the Medical Examiner viewed the death as an accident after the autopsy then he should maintain that same finding. Other evidence was beyond the ME's expertise and shouldn't even be considered.

Cross-examination in a preliminary hearing can be a very calculated step in preparation for trial. The defense might be very tough or abrasive with a witness, hoping to cause them to arrive with a nervous or angry affect in front of the jury. They may be very gentle or forgo an entire line of questioning to relax and later ambush a witness. Sometimes an attorney will elicit otherwise meaningless details to create minute conflicts in the trial testimony and make the witness appear less credible. "Today you say that person was 5'7" and 150 pounds. Didn't you testify, at the prelim, under oath, before a judge, that he was about 5'6" and 155 pounds?" The prosecutor and the witness do well to observe the prelim's cross to anticipate trial tactics, but a good defense attorney—and Mauro and Hamilton fill that bill—will often try to stay a chess move ahead or drag a red herring across the cross. Rich also made sure the expert witness and the other lawyer knew he was well prepared, referring Dr. Grey back to his deposition, civil trial testimony and reports with questions about technical minutiae.

The major thrust of the questioning concerned the fact that Dr. Grey's two amendments followed information provided by Jill. Since a great deal of this information consisted of the statements of Winnetka Walls and James Hendrix, wasn't it incumbent on Todd to go beyond the detective and judge the credibility of those actual witnesses? Rich knew Todd neither met nor personally interviewed either witness and both witnesses had things that bore on their credibility. Mauro continually referred to Ms. Walls as Winnie, as a person he and Todd were personally familiar with, as though they were ridiculing her over a beer. I've always thought a courtroom proceeding deserved a courtly dissertation and don't believe it was lost on Judge Boyden that an adult woman's name was treated so cavalierly in her courtroom.

Finally I broke in and objected that the defense was trying to impeach Walls and Hendrix through Dr. Grey. I said that each would take the stand and their credibility could be examined firsthand. The judge agreed and we moved on.

Todd was questioned about how much his finding

depended upon the investigation conducted by Jill, the cops and ME's investigator Ken Farnsworth, what they'd done, what they hadn't done and the fact they'd abandoned that scene under the impression of an accident.

We moved on to the meeting on the sixth floor of the PSB with Jill, Greg Skordas and some of the police brass and got back to patronizing.

"You went to the police station?"

"Uh huh."

"You went to the Salt Lake City Police Station?"

"Yes, on Third."

"For a meeting?"

"Yes."

"And there were four police officers there?"

"Yes."

"Ms. Candland?"

"Yes."

"Sergeant Roberts?"

"Correct."

The idea here was to hint that the Chief Medical Examiner for the State of Utah was bullied, pressured or cajoled into changing his opinion to placate or please cops and prosecutors.

The questioning finally got to the observations of the autopsy itself. Rich went into the surgery involving Pam's feet and how difficult it made walking on a wet surface in special shoes. The orthopedic shoes she was wearing had smooth soles that would have been slippery when wet and open toes that allowed the steel pins to protrude and made them subject to being bumped, causing excruciating pain. Yes, Todd felt that, along with the underlying condition of her feet, would have made balance difficult. Although the defense wanted to infer that Pam could have easily fallen and struck her head as she fell into the pond, it also begged the question, why would she be walking around in the dark on a collection of loose rocks in the first place?

Rich questioned Dr. Grey about the abrasions on Pamela's body, those on the elbow and the abdomen as well as the absence of other trauma. There was no tissue under the fingernails, which remained smooth and intact; her clothing was intact and had no distortion, ripping or tearing, nor were there any "defensive wounds" that would indicate a struggle. The abrasions on the elbow and midsection were patterned and could have been caused by falling over rocks on her way into the pond. Could these have been caused by the forepaws of a dog like Baron jumping up on the victim and knocking her backwards? Certainly.

Wasn't the wound to the back of her head as consistent with falling on a brick as being struck by one? Well, yes and no. Quickly, Rich took the brick, stood in front of the doctor, demonstrated a swing straight up in the air and asked the ME if this were a way to effectively strike with power. Todd didn't think it would be.

The cross-examination ended by a line of questioning that emphasized that the original finding of accident as manner of death was based on all of the scientific evidence that Dr. Todd Grey, Chief Medical Examiner for the State of Utah, had ever had before him in this case and changed based entirely on evidence passed along by others, external to the autopsy.

"Nothing further, Your Honor."

"Mr. Lemcke, any redirect?"

I posed a few questions to emphasize that the autopsy is one component of the medical examiner's investigation, a very important component certainly, but not the whole of the input the office normally and routinely gathers. I went back over the obvious—that the pond was destroyed and Pam's remains interred by David and his surrogates, making further physical examination almost impossible. Briefly we reviewed the evidence that Todd received as he changed his conclusions. It's not only defense attorneys who use red herrings during prelims; a staunch defense by the prosecution of the importance of the ME's conclusion masked my belief that ultimately the only meaningful determination of manner of death would be by the jury who heard this case.

Then I asked Jill to come over from the prosecution table into the well, picked up the brick and asked my detective to bend forward at the waist. Standing on her left side I swung the brick in slow motion over her back coming forward, stopping just above her head and asked if this appeared to be a better way to put some power into the blow. Todd agreed and

I asked if this would cause the superior undermining of the wound he observed. Again, he agreed before I had him reaffirm that the nature of the blow was relative to the posture of the victim. I let Jill stand up and got a look complaining about the length of my theatrics.

I asked the doc, if Pamela had been struck when she was bent over looking into the pool, could she have struck an elbow and/or scraped her stomach on the rocks while falling into the water? He agreed. And was the blow sufficient to impair her to where she might have been easily held in the water by the clothing or hair or where she might even drown on her own? Again, the ME answered affirmatively.

After this I invited Todd Grey into the well. Theater begets theater. Posturing earns posturing. I stood him looking face to face, or more accurately face to top of head, at the now upright detective.

"Are you intimidated by Detective Candland?"

"Only when she has her gun pointed at me."

"Has she done that lately?"

"Never done that."

"Has she done that in this case?"

"Never!"

"Do you work with these people on a routine basis?"

"Yes, I do."

"Are you intimidated by them?"

"No!"

"Have you ever told them that you disagree with them?"

"Yes."

"You get along?"

"Yes."

"Have you ever told me you disagree with me?"

"Yes."

"We still get along?"

"Yes."

"Part of the job, isn't it?"

"Yes!"

"No further questions."

Rich popped out of his chair and asked Todd if he had his autopsy report in front of him.

"Have any injuries to the top of the head?"

"Top, no."

"Any injuries to the top of the forehead?"

"No."

We went on to the nose, mouth and shoulders and noted it looked like there were bricks and rocks outside of the pond, that were never measured and were probably pretty hard. There was no indication, other than the wound to the back of the head, that Pam fell face first onto the rocks. Again it begged a question, best asked well down the road, why there were no injuries indicating the victim ever fell onto a pile of rocks.

Dr. Todd Grey's morning on the stand was over, Rich and I were out of questions and it was almost noon. After a brief discussion about scheduling and the problems in bringing in Jack Hendrix, we agreed to reconvene at 1:30 and adjourned. As Jill and I sorted what we needed to prepare for her testimony, Garfield and Sinie were out in the hall talking to the reporters, giving them the opportunity to videotape the folded photo of Pam and David.

13

More Courtroom Haggling

We gathered in my office a little after one. Michelle, who was doing yeoman's service making sure everything and everyone was in order for the afternoon's session, showed me messages, said she'd take care of them and explain why I wouldn't be able to return most calls for another day or so. The troop formed and we headed back out.

It was the custom of the DA's staff to jay-walk to court directly across 400 South, often to the amusement of the SLCPD who used great flourish issuing citations routinely dismissed after appropriate groveling. But it is one of the busier streets at the edge of Salt Lake's downtown and

Garfield and Sinie aren't the sort of folks I wanted out dodging traffic, so we walked to the crosswalk at the corner. It was a pretty day and Jill and I were walking behind the Stokeses when I noticed Pam's mother was carrying what first appeared to be a small purse on a long strap. It looked to be leather with gilt on narrow sides and a tiny ribbon coming out through that gilt. Then I recognized what it was. We got to the corner. While we waited for the traffic light to turn green, I leaned over to Sinie. "What passage do you have marked?"

"What do you mean?" She smiled.

"Your Bible."

"You recognize it?"

"Yeah. Just like my mom's. What passage?"

"John 3:20. Evil things done in the darkness will be brought forth into the light."

I thought about that. "I guess that's what we're working towards."

"Keep up the good work."

We crossed the street and got up to court without more small talk. I was in awe of Mrs. Sinie Stokes and her faith. Not faith in Howie Lemcke, Jill Candland or our agencies, although she clearly had to put her reliance in us for secular justice. This was Faith with a capital F, in ultimate Justice with the capital J that sustains people through unimaginable wrongs. A drop of water was reminded how wonderful was the wine and a case that had always been important grew more so.

I started the direct exam by asking Jill to describe what she observed when she was called out to the scene at the Mead house just past midnight the morning of August 16. I handed her the photographs we selected and Jill affirmed they were "fair and accurate representations" and used them to describe the layout and conditions she found. She explained how the area was cordoned off with police tape and portable light banks set up to illuminate the otherwise darkened yard. The questioning went over the cops and civilians she found there and Pam. She described the Meads' backyard with its lack of landscaping, the pond, the collars of bricks and rocks, the plastic liner, the nearby pile of dirt leftover from excavating the pond, Baron, his doghouse and chain. She held the photographs where the judge could see, explained the contents of each picture and some rough dimensions. I handed the witness the exemplar brick that she confirmed was not from the pond but had been provided by the neighbor. The photos and the brick were moved into evidence without objection.

Then I asked my detective about the defendant and how she was directed to David, then released from the restraint of handcuffs, sitting in the front seat of Mike Jensen's police car, wet and wrapped in a blanket. He still appeared to be hysterical and attempts to talk to him made it evident that no interview was possible at that time. She noticed no marks nor tears on his face and told the court that she could hear him wail from the time she arrived until David left with his relatives.

After that we moved the questioning to Jill's examination of the scene itself. She told Judge Boyden how Ken Farnsworth from the ME's office arrived, the two made a preliminary examination of Pamela's body, noticed the injury to the head and the blood. While Ken examined the body further she obtained a high-powered flashlight, painstakingly examined each rock and brick that hadn't been pulled into the pond for traces of blood or hair but found none.

Jill was briefed on the observations of other officers, the interviews they'd conducted and findings and measurements that Ken Farnsworth gathered. The court learned about the search of the home, the absence of negative evidence and the continuing inability to interview David Mead. When asked what the officers knew at that point about the Meads, the detective responded, "That they were a loving couple and happily married couple. That they were married approximately three years and there were no problems anyone was aware of."

She told us that by three or four in the morning she'd finished her work at the Mead house and caught a short night's rest before arriving at the Office of the Medical Examiner to witness the 8:30 autopsy. The witness continued that by the time she left that office for the PSB, she'd concluded the death of Pamela Camille Stokes Mead was an unfortunate accident. Pending the outcome of toxicology results, Dr. Grey's final ruling and an interview with David for a few clarifying details, there was no further investigation anticipated or intended on the detective's part. It was a shame that David's brothers felt they had to shelter the widower, so the file remained open on her desk.

Of course, this was sarcasm to torment the defense. When Angela called a couple of days later and brought Winnetka Walls in, the file could have been easily retrieved. I questioned Jill about the visit from Winnie, what was said and Jill's impressions. She related how Ms. Walls was visibly shaking during the interview and how what was said made the detective want to look further into what she'd learned. Rich objected on the basis of hearsay and I responded that this was "not being admitted for the truth of the matter asserted," rather as a device to show how and why the detective proceeded. Besides, Ms. Walls would be called to the stand herself to place her own, non-hearsay statements on the record later into the prelim.

We talked about how Jill sought out Gayle Fairfield who, in turn, referred the officer to Jane Dryer at Pennington's Denver regional office. Ms. Dreyer said the policy had indeed been issued on December 14, 1993, and she'd been contacted on August 17 by someone identifying himself as David Mead's brother who wanted the paperwork on the claim sent as quickly as possible. That person seemed very concerned and asked her to act quickly and not reveal to anyone else the amount of the policy.

Jill testified about further efforts to interview David, receiving the flowers at her office and the eventual interview. She told the judge about the problem with the tape recorder, the detail of that interview and questions aimed at creating a reaction as much as an answer, about who might have done this or would be above suspicion. Detective Candland spoke of David's lack of surprise or other emotion and how he pinched his nose or put tissues up to his face as if he were crying.

"Were there any tears?"

"Not that I observed. No."

I questioned my witness about how Wade Wayment informed her of a person in the Davis County Jail who wanted to talk about the fishpond case. The courtroom got to hear how the detective interviewed Hendrix and what he had to say. Rich entered the same hearsay objection he had about Winnie, I gave the same response and we continued. This started with Jack's long and tortured account of his dealings with David from the time Jack got out of the Utah State Prison till he wound up in the Davis County Jail. Had he tried to sell his story to Jill for a plea bargain on the robbery of David and Winnie? Had he sought any particular reward for coming forward? What was his motive?

He didn't want to wind up dead, without anyone knowing how or why.

I asked where the investigation went and Jill related how she kept her command and Dr. Grey advised of the developments, first met with Pam's family, conducted more interviews of Ms. Walls and Mr. Hendrix and attempted to interview one of David's brothers, who requested an attorney. The brother wasn't a suspect or charged; although he had nothing to say we got his reticence into evidence.

Jill talked about the meeting with Todd Grey, Greg Skordas and the SLCPD Detective Division command. After briefly talking about Greg, his position before the election and the handover to me, I had her make a record of the role of the prosecutors' office and the typical dealings of the PD and the DA before a case is even screened. We laid out our decision to hold off on the criminal case while we sat back to see what might arise out of the civil proceedings. When asked what in fact had developed, she mentioned Bill Morgan and a jewelry salesman who helped David select a customized bauble for Winnie. There was also the test of how witnesses like Ms. Walls and Mr. Hendrix held up on the stand, how well plaintiff's and defendant's experts came across and David Earl Mead. What would he have to say when he was examined? How would David look on the stand or at counsel table? How would David react if he didn't get the money? Would he be disciplined enough in the long term not to brag to someone else? What documentation could Anne Sulton ferret out?

What might fall out of the trees that Roger Tinsley shook so briskly and so well?

We got into the Capital Hill/Salt Lake City Airport drive time experiments that followed our meeting Bill Morgan and our re-examination of the layout of the Salt Lake City Airport.

Finally, I wanted to give the defense a taste of how I intended to use David's statements and referred my detective to the collection identified by Mrs. Stokes. These had been collectively marked as a single exhibit and I had Jill retrieve David's sworn statement to Pennington's investigator John James, a statement of my party opponent, therefore not hearsay. Rich objected on the basis of foundation, claiming we hadn't properly shown the statement was the actual statement of David Mead. I countered that Mrs. Stokes was a party to that lawsuit and these are her documents. Judge Boyden agreed that there was sufficient foundation to admit David's own words in this prelim.

"What specifically is the statement of Mr. Mead?"

" 'As soon as I saw her in the pond, I jumped in and I started screaming. I struggled, I don't know how long. There was a lot of blood. I remember trying to push her out of the pond. It was so slippery I was struggling and I finally got her out of the pond.' "

"Does that comport with your observations of the scene?"

"No!"

"I have no other questions of this witness at this time."

Rich took my place at the lectern. "Ms. Candland, you are on patrol now?"

"Yes."

"You are not a detective anymore?"

"No."

Rich was also giving a taste of the future, went no further down this path but wanted us to know that he was a meticulous attorney who did his homework. The cross-examination quickly turned to the night of Pam's death, again in staccato cadence. We sat quietly and heard again a description of how Detective Jill Candland drove to the location, parked the car against the curb, got out of the car, walked toward the house, saw police officers, who were SLCPD officers, and some crime scene tape, that was yellow tape, that comes on a roll and a lot of other things. Eventually we returned to substance.

Rich crossed Jill about the number and disposition of the cops at the scene before asking where Pamela's body was found, how it was situated, Pam's height, weight and build. Next, the examination turned to the neighbors Jill and other officers encountered—who they were, where they lived, what they heard and did before, during and after all the screaming, including Barry Baxter and his efforts at CPR—then back to officers, hierarchy and assignments.

After this, the court heard about Jill's physical examination of the scene with emphasis on what she didn't do—count and measure each brick or stone—or didn't see—marks indicating a struggle or a body being dragged. The cross emphasized what the police didn't do—go into the pond themselves and retrieve those rocks and bricks David pulled in. The rocks and Pamela's clothing, article by article, were not examined in the laboratory for blood, nor was the length of Baron's dog chain measured, even though Jill had testified it easily reached the fishpond.

Mr. Mauro then directed Officer Candland to her encounters with Winnetka Walls and Jack Hendrix. She described the procedure when someone comes to the SLCPD headquarters and signs in at the front desk. There's a big glass cage, a police officer on the other side of the glass, a log book to sign and a little visitors' badge, about this big, that pins on your jacket.

I objected. "Your Honor, this is interesting, but why is it probative?"

"It is completely probative, Judge! It is the circumstances!"

"You may answer," Her Honor instructed the witness with a tone in her voice noting the court was growing weary of the tack. At least my objection broke the rhythm.

The cross about Winnie was fairly brief; it dealt with which officers were present, the fact Don Bell asked most of the questions and never went into Ms. Walls's varied versions. Hendrix was a different story, as Rich used his questioning of Jill to go over Jack's history one more time, starting with

the details of Jack's home invasion robbery of David and
Winnie on Center Street. We moved into his prior convictions and bad acts including Jack's admission to the detective about consuming massive quantities of cocaine around
the time of Pam's death. Jill was aware of those in quantity
and quality, that Jack's case was plea-bargained down and
Jack treated less harshly in return for his guilty plea.

We visited Detective Candland's dealings with then Chief
Deputy County Attorney Greg Skordas around the time of
Pam's death. Rich asked whether Greg was aware of each
unit element of evidence Jill accumulated. But he didn't file
charges, did he? In August? Jill responded that she hadn't
asked him to do that. In September? Same response. All that
year?

"Your Honor . . ." I whined.

Judge Boyden got right to the point, asking why this was
relevant. Mauro responded that Mr. Lemcke had asked questions about Jill's dealings with Greg Skordas and Her Honor
allowed he could continue down that line of questioning, but
only so far. Rich wanted to hint that Greg turned the case
down for want of substance, but Jill was savvy enough to
keep reminding everyone she never screened the fishpond
case with Greg or asked him to file it. The cross-examination
ended and I moved into re-direct.

Briefly I had Jill emphasize the only person who saw, or
claimed to see, Pamela in the fishpond was the defendant. We
went over a few times from the police dispatch logs: the first
9-1-1 call was at 11:13 PM and the last crime lab tech left at
3:25 AM.

I asked Jill if she remembered Rich's questions about
Jack's cocaine binge.

"So, who did Mr. Hendrix say he got that cocaine from?"

"Objection. Hearsay."

We argued back and forth for a while in another opportunity to air the idea that the coke was Mead's down payment
on murder. Rich said his questions only went to Jack's credibility as a junkie, but I countered that Jack wasn't on the
stand and the immediate issue was the detective's perception
of Jack as someone whose version she might rely on.

"In the same vein, where had Hendrix told you he had gotten the cocaine from?"

"From David Mead."

I asked about details of the first dope gift and later payment Hendrix reported and if Jack Hendrix presented himself to this experienced police officer as a person who would have other means to obtain nine hundred dollars and sixty-six grams of coke. Jill observed that he did not.

I returned to what was presented to Skordas and had Jill tell the court how much she learned in 1994 about the financial condition of David Mead and Valley Ground Service. She said that although some of this did come to light early on from Pamela's family, the detail was developed during the civil lawsuit. I referred her to David's statement that there was a lot of blood and then asked about the clothing Pam was wearing, which showed no sign of blood, including the white socks and tee shirt.

The first re-direct examination concluded by asking what would have become of the PD's investigation had Jack and Winnie not independently come forward. In all probability it would have been closed out as an accident, Dr. Grey would never have been approached for further consultation and no others avenues pursued.

Rich returned, asking if there was any scientific analysis of the water or the clothing for blood. There had not been.

"Did you promise Jack Hendrix he wouldn't go to prison?"

"No."

Rich handed the witness back to me.

"What did you ever offer Jack Hendrix?"

"Mr. Hendrix didn't ever ask me for anything. What I offered him . . . I wrote a letter to the Board of Pardons, after he was already in prison, expressing that he had been a cooperative witness in a case. And whatever impact that had on the Board of Pardons, I don't know."

"What did you promise him?"

"Nothing."

I asked Jill if she ever took part in, or was aware of, any other offers to Jack. She said no. Then I asked if, in her lengthy experience, she was aware of Vernice Ah Ching,

Jack's LDA, getting good deals for her clients. Rich objected and Her Honor sustained when Rich made a valid point: isn't it Howie Lemcke's office that makes any decision to reduce those charges? So I asked if this seasoned detective had ever encountered my office reducing a charge contrary to the wishes of the cops. She replied that we had. Rich asked if he could have a copy of the letter to the board, we agreed and Jill was off the hot seat.

Jill never located Mike Jensen. We explained the situation to Judge Boyden who took recess for the day and agreed to return at nine in the morning. It was just past three thirty and there was some afternoon left, so we gathered a box full of papers to take to the office. Tomorrow would be a full day with Ms. Walls, Jack Hendrix, Matt Jenkins, Bill Morgan, Chris Ahern and, hopefully, Mike Jensen. The Stokeses were in the hallway talking to the press and Jill and I waited to walk back to the office with the family. After we exchanged impressions of the day, the Stokeses said they wanted to walk back to their car at their own pace; they'd meet us in court in the morning. I suspect, though I've never asked, that a life-long smoker like Garfield needed to stop and work on that first good ciggi-butt after the session and that last one before.

Back at the office we briefed Michelle and a few of my comrades who saw us came by and offered impressions. Jill and I went over what the morning might bring and went to our respective offices to catch up on phone calls. We'd meet here about eight thirty. I didn't get home for the early news, but the kids told me what they saw. I caught the ten o'clock coverage to see Sinie holding the folded picture of Pam, dealing with reporters' questions in quiet dignity and sadness. Each of the stations displayed a close-up of the photo, first only Pam, then unfolded to show the couple. No reporters opined on who was winning. I flipped off the TV. Sleep didn't come quickly as I replayed the day in my mind over and over again.

14

The Surprise Phone Call

Although I got to work a little early the next morning—my kids knew to hustle on Dad's-going-to-court mornings—the phone was ringing incessantly, this and that needed review or signature and I was going to be late for court. Jill was across the fourth floor common area comparing notes with an attorney on another case and Meesh had ducked out somewhere. I put on my blazer and reading glasses, picked up the cardboard box, stepped out of the office and the phone rang. Pick it up? Let it roll over to message? *Oh, hell, I'm going to be late anyway.* I stepped back in and put the box on a chair.

"This is Howie."

"Is this Mr. Lem . . . ? I need to talk to the person prosecuting David Mead," said the voice of an adult woman who was having a problem with calm. All I needed at that moment was a David fan or someone who didn't see a crime in harming people of color.

"This is Howard Lemcke. I'm the prosecutor on *Mead.* How can I help you?"

"Mr. Lemcke, I think that I have some information you ought to know."

"Okay. Sure! What would that be? Who . . . ? Who is this, please? Could you tell me who I'm talking to?"

"No! I don't want to tell you my name!" Oh, good, an anonymous caller.

"Okay, then why don't you tell me what it is you feel I oughta know?"

"David . . . Well, David Mead was dating women who weren't his wife and . . . Well, you know, when he was married and he was talking to them . . . he was talking about, you know, killing his wife."

"This is Stormy? Isn't it?"

"I told you that I didn't want to tell you my name!" Her voice was almost loud enough to hurt.

"Okay. Okay, let's be cool. Don't hang up. Person who isn't Stormy, just talk to me. Okay?"

"Okay. I didn't want to tell you who I was."

"That's okay. I still have no idea what your last name is."

"I bet you have caller ID."

"No. I work for the county and they'd never spring for anything that expensive. Besides, you probably came in through the front desk and got transferred up here."

"Yeah. Can I just talk to you without you asking my name?"

"Sure." Of all the things I've done in my life that involved juggling more than one affect at a time, this was the toughest. I had to keep a cool demeanor on the phone with Stormy while I had to get someone else's, anyone else's, attention. Michelle had returned to her desk but was talking to someone and Jill was all the way across the fourth floor. I'd stretched the phone cords until the console was dangling between the two cords connecting my desk, the console and me. *God, please don't let the connections pop*. I was halfway out of my doorway gesturing with my free hand and a foot to anyone who might see it, but nobody looked. "So tell me why you called today." At least my voice pretended calm. I went on. "If somehow I happen to lose this connection, will you please call back? I don't have caller ID."

"Okay. Umm? This is going to sound silly, Mr. Lemcke. Did you say Howie?"

"Yeah. I'm a junior, so it's Howie. And nothing's silly."

Greg, my supervisor stepped out of his office to see his charge gesturing like an idiot, cocked his head down against one side of his chest and looked over with a bemused, unspoken question. I gritted my teeth in a display of desperation and pumped my free hand pointing at Michelle as I listened to the reply.

"I wasn't ever going to call. But I watched the news last night. Did you see that?" There was pain in that voice.

Greg shrugged his shoulders, walked over and tapped Meesh on the shoulder. She turned around, saw me gesturing wildly in a gathering motion towards her, giggled, covered her mouth with her hands and walked over as a small crowd that didn't yet include Jill noticed the deranged attorney and gathered.

"Yeah, I saw parts of it. What was it you saw? What . . . what was it caught your eye?" Michelle recognized a big part of my dilemma and helped me get my phone console back safely onto my desk.

"It was when I saw Pam's mother, Sinie. Sinie?"

I helped with the pronunciation, "Sinie." I grabbed a legal pad, flipped it over and wrote across the entire cardboard back, "IT'S STORMY!!!" Jaws dropped as I swung my pointing finger sideways from the elbow towards where Jill was talking and two or three people sprinted across the office.

"I watched her . . . You know, I don't usually watch the news. I could see her pain. Mr. Lemcke . . . Howie . . . Howie?"

"I'm fine. Please do." Jill came over dragged by others, looking bewildered, Michelle held the legal pad out with both hands and Jill shoved through the new-formed crowd asking questions with her eyes.

"I saw her. I saw a mother's pain. I just can't imagine the pain of losing a child. You know I'm a mother myself . . . No, you wouldn't know that . . . Now I'm telling you who I am, aren't I?"

"No. You're still safe. Talk to me. Please."

"When I saw her hold that picture of Pam . . . I . . . I . . . I knew I couldn't . . . I knew that I couldn't . . . I had to call. I changed my mind, but then I watched the news again, at ten, and . . ." The pain in the voice was real. I could see tears on a face I couldn't yet envision.

"Okay, person who may or may not be Stormy, what are you doing for lunch?"

"It is Stormy and I guess I'm meeting you."

I scrunched my eyes shut and pumped my fist next to my shoulder to silent raised arms, dances and high fives outside my office door. Stormy and I talked for about five more minutes and figured out a time and place to meet for lunch. I told her I'd be with Detective Jill Candland and described how we were dressed. I didn't ask for her last name or anything more specific than the part of town where she worked in order to pick a restaurant. I'd pick up the check. As the conversation ended I did my best to be as calming as possible and not provide reason or excuse to flinch and not show up. I hung up with pleasantries, turned to my colleagues waiting in happy tension who exploded into cheers.

I was going to be late for court! We jaywalked. Briskly.

I took Rich and Ben aside and told them that I had gotten a telephone call from a potential witness but didn't know if the person would show up for a proposed lunch meeting or what they might have to offer. I refused specifics because I'd heard fear in Stormy's voice and had no idea if David knew how to locate her or if she were ready to come forward.

Winnetka Walls has a tiny voice to start with; being nervous reduced it even more. At the start and several times down the road I had to ask her to speak up. Kurt Frankenburg was there and I made record of his representation of Winnie before I had her identify for the record David Mead.

I asked when the two had met, the circumstances of their dating and when and how she learned David was a married man. Uncomfortably, she told Judge Boyden how the relationship evolved, testifying that David helped Winnetka move out of her parents' home into an apartment where David paid the rent. When I started to ask about the trips the two took together Ben Hamilton began a series of objections largely based on relevancy. I explained a two-fold relevancy: the money David spent would tie in down the road with our financial analysis; the nature and depth of the relationship would be very important when ultimatums and answers arose closer to Pam's death. The questioning continued as we talked about gifts. Objection. We continued through the gifts.

After Ms. Walls told the court that for a time she moved into the home on Center, I asked about sexual relationships—Objection!—that were recorded—Objection!!!—that were the subject of Ms. Walls's threats and ultimatums to David Mead in the weeks before the drowning. We continued: the lovemaking had been recorded on videotape and there was a threat that tapes would be sent to Pam if David didn't leave his wife. When we got to when these threats took place, the examination and the witness's memory bogged down.

This wasn't unexpected: we'd speculated about, and prepared for, the swings of an emotional pendulum. I stepped from the podium to the State's table where Jill, without a word or prompt, handed me the first of Winnie's prior statements. There's requisite technique for using prior statements to either impeach a witness or refresh their memory: ask the underlying question; get either the inconsistent answer or declaration the witness can't remember; present the witness with his or her "prior recollection recorded"; have the witness review the document; ask if the witness's recollection is refreshed; quote the document into the record.

I handed my witness the transcript of her original interview with the cops. She confirmed the transcript was, to the best of her knowledge, accurate and those were her words. The first interview was a little messy because some of Winnie's statements came through Angela, but we found the first ultimatum about the videotapes and placed it within a month of the death.

As I started into David's response, Ben interrupted. Winnetka's mother had come to court to support her child on a difficult day in a very public forum, something we encourage for fragile witnesses. Ben noted the presence of Winnie's mom, declared that mom might be a potential witness in the case and should be removed from the courtroom under the Exclusionary Rule. Legally sound, factually iffy because mom would at best be an extremely tangential witness, but a well-struck blow. It broke the rhythm, yanked the witness's security blanket from her arms and unnerved her. Ms. Wall's mother left the courtroom and direct became even more labored. One lawyer to another, I can begrudgingly admire a good lick when it's laid on me. You never know; some day I may find an opening to use it.

Back to David's response. "What did he say?"

"He said everything was going to be okay. We were going to be together."

"All right, and did he tell you how that was going to happen?"

"Yeah."

"What did he say was going to happen?"

"Said there would be a nasty spill, that he would have an alibi . . . Basically."

"That there would be a nasty spill and that he would have an alibi?" A question is a wonderful device to repeat important testimony.

"Yes."

"Did he say when this was going to take place?"

"No."

"If you would read on to page twenty? Go ahead and read page twenty. Tell us now what he said about the details of the nasty spill or what would happen to Pam."

"Said that . . ."

"I will object to what the document says!"

On it went, as slowly, painfully we crawled forward learning that the alibi may include David at the airport, at work, and the nasty spill may look like a robbery. We heard what Walls learned from Mead about the insurance policies, what David and Winnie could do with that sort of money and the consequences to David's ownership of Valley Ground Service in the event of divorce.

We stepped head-on into Ms. Wall's history of inconsistent statements. When a lawyer calls a witness who has some weaknesses, he or she always wants to put those weaknesses on the table. If the party opponent brings out on cross prior convictions, bias or prior inconsistent statements, it makes it seem the presenter was hiding the flaw. It's always best to present a witness as internally consistent with who and what the witness is. Winnetka Walls was, in my opinion, one of David's other victims, one who had been and was still being used as a pawn to play or sacrifice as the needs of the game dictated. She made statements all over the map, but these had to be put in the context of what she was still going through. I felt that, seen in its whole cloth, what she said rang true.

Yes, she recanted her original statements to the cops, wrote a handwritten letter from California at David's request, after he moved her there, had it notarized and sent it to him. Winnetka Walls told Judge Boyden how she loved David, wanted to help him and just make everything better. I showed her a copy of that letter, identified it and offered to move its admission on behalf of the defense. Ben said that he wasn't ready.

We talked about the Stokeses' lawsuit, starting with the attempt to depose Ms. Walls when she declined to answer under the protections of the Fifth Amendment, Anne Sulton's reaction that taking the Fifth implied guilt and Winnie being named as a defendant in the civil suit. My witness recounted how she ended up recanting the recanting, being deposed, being dropped from the lawsuit and testifying in the federal trial.

I asked the witness which statement was true. She told me there were things in each that were true and things that were not. Starting with the statements to the cops, Winnetka disclaimed several of Angela's statements to the officers where exaggeration and amplification distorted what Winnie told Angela, but she thought "everything else may be pretty much true." I had the statement to the cops marked and moved as an exhibit, "of course subject to cross-examination."

Ben objected as hearsay, although it was clearly within one of the rule's exceptions. The court had barely overruled the objection when Rich Mauro rose in a loud and angry voice, "Can you state the basis for the record?"

Judge Boyden met this challenge more calmly than many jurists, stated that hearsay requires a declarant who isn't present and subject to cross, but Rich continued in the same tone.

I broke in. "Your Honor, might we have one of the two making the objections?" With more than one attorney per side, custom and courtesy puts one lawyer per witness; breaking in is a faux pas almost on the scale of bad attitude or challenging a judge.

"And that will be the process that we follow, Mr. Mauro."

"I was just trying to preserve the record. That's all. And . . . I will sit down."

"That is my ruling."

Ben picked up the challenge but, sensing the atmosphere, did so with great reserve. We went back and forth a few more times before I got back to my witness, who felt the tension and became even quieter. With encouragement from the court, I coaxed back her voice and got Winnie to say three more times, in increasing volume, what she told Jill was what she believed to be true.

I didn't confront her on the detailed content of the hand-written and notarized California letter; Ben was ready to go there. My best strategy would be response, so I told the judge direct was over. Her Honor asked Winnie how she was holding up and if she was ready for cross-examination.

Ben went right to the handwritten letter by trying to elevate its dignity and status as a sworn statement, reminding all that the interview with the cops wasn't under oath and obviously was much less reliable than a statement sworn before a notary. I guess that Ben went to that same seminar, because he went into the staccato, incremental technique and touched each point in a separate question and answer. We learned that Ms. Walls's letter was telling the truth, the whole truth, nothing but the truth, that she signed the statement, before a notary public, was placed under oath by the notary public and swore to tell the truth. I'll leave you to imagine the rest, which was worse than you're imagining.

Finally, questions found substance in the relationship that developed between David and his newfound romantic interest. Ben briefly ran a line of questions to say David really hadn't spent all that much on Winnie's rent and got in that Ms. Walls had given Mr. Mead many ultimatums. She was given a first taste of hard and personal cross-examination, an appetizer in anticipation of the banquet of trial as Ben publicly explored her heart. We listened to the witness's answers about dating, becoming emotionally involved, physically involved, caring for him and knowing it was wrong before her voice tailed off to the point she was admonished to speak up. The room turned to the woman who couldn't leave David Mead, was very much in love, found it hard to deal with, heard only excuses, had her feelings hurt and didn't want to share her first love with anyone else. Her deep and genuine emotions were laid raw to the world as her voice fell off sadly, again and again.

The defense took her to the time close to Pam's death and her feelings about days without contact from David. At the point she went with Angela to the PSB she was driven by anger. It wasn't even David who called to break the news and told her to keep distant and quiet. After the salt that David loved his wife was rubbed into Winnetka's wounds a few more times, the examination turned to implications that her statement to the police was but lies born of revenge. She responded sadly but affirmatively to questions describing her as screwed up, upset, depressed, angry, deeply hurt, feeling used, a mere sex toy, wanting to hurt her tormenter, before Ben forgot the old lawyer's saying: if you're looking to taint with implication, leave it as implication.

"The statement you made to the police was a lie, isn't that right?"

"Not all of it. No."

"There was some truth in it?"

"Yes!"

"But . . . there's some truth in every lie, isn't there?"

"Objection! Your Honor, that's argumentative. Maybe philosophical, but argumentative."

"It is." The court laughed and tensions momentarily drained.

Ben drew Winnie to the federal lawsuit and aimed at her heart, how her name appeared in the press, named as "a mistress," her embarrassed family calling and people who walked by staring at this young woman. Why, she was asked, did she hire a lawyer and work her way out of the lawsuit? He pounded, she was "enticed" to do "almost anything" to get out of the lawsuit, avoid paying for a lawyer; she had little money, not even a decent car, to get out from under the pressure of family, friends and her community.

At one point Ben asked about what she asked her lawyer to do and Kurt Frankenburg interjected that Ben was wandering close to Winnie's lawyer/client privilege. Ben objected to Kurt's interjection, those two went at it, the judge and I rested on the sidelines and Ms. Walls squirmed uncomfortably on the stand. Winnetka Walls's heartfelt love of David Mead was not about to be returned by his representatives.

Jill and I often discussed how much witness preparation to give Winnie but feared, given her mercurial swings of loyalty and underlying fear of the process, we'd do more harm than good. We knew she was fragile, were never sure if on any given day she'd appear and didn't want her to feel pressured by both camps, so we took a chance to do very little in the way of courtroom prep and rehearsal. This was brutal, but she was holding together and getting a good dose of the concept that David's loyalty was, cruelly, only to David, and David's attorneys' loyalties were, correctly, only to David. How she'd do in trial would be the payoff.

After another round reaffirming the regal dignity of the handwritten, notarized California letter, Benjamin Hamilton went after my witness as if she were my pawn. "And you've been coached before coming in to testify today by Mr. Lemcke? Isn't that right?"

Very softly "No."

"You had an interview with him . . ." Ben started as I cut in referring to the last question and answer.

"Can she please answer that out loud?" I raised my voice. "I want that on the record?"

"You may answer the question," Judge Boyden advised the witness who found herself suddenly in the center of a storm.

"I think it was on the record," was Ben's retort.

"I did not hear it." The judge was firm. "I would like the answer."

I cut to the chase, interjecting loudly out of turn. "Question was, did I coach you?"

"No. You did not."

"Thank you."

Angrily, my party opponent stated to the witness in barely the inflection of a question, "He brought you in and talked to you beforehand and prepared your testimony!?"

"I spoke with him, but . . ."

"Thank you!" She was cut off abruptly as Ben turned on his heel and sat down.

No one had yet moved to admit either Winnetka's handwritten, notarized California letter or the transcript of the first interview, so I got up and moved the latter. Ben got up and moved the former and argued against my exhibit. The judge listened, admitted the transcript and asked if I objected to the letter. I didn't. Her Honor took note that Ms. Walls had been on the stand for quite a while and called a short recess.

After the break, Judge Boyden took the bench and told us that she would limit admission of the transcript to those portions brought out in court, which was fine. Back on stage, I asked the witness if she recalled the long list of questions on cross-examination about her motives to testify in the federal trial and the oath taking on the handwritten letter. Was she under oath during the federal testimony? Yes, and there, under oath, she testified that what she told the cops was true, but her voice disappeared again and the judge nudged the witness into volume.

I showed her the affidavit that she gave the Stokeses in anticipation of the federal trial. Resisting the temptation to frame a long series of incremental questions, I asked if this was also a sworn statement and reached the logical conclusion of my "rehabilitating" an impeached witness. "Okay. Are you telling us . . . today, that you are telling us the truth, today?"

"To the questions you are asking, yes!"

"No further questions."

Ben was finished as well, but Rich Mauro wasn't.

"I guess that the only thing we would ask is the State notify us of someplace to get a hold of Ms. Walls in case we want to interview her." That was the last message Team Mead sent to the witness, at least that day.

"Mr. Frankenburg is in the directory." I was irritated and it showed.

As soon as Ms. Walls saw the assembled cameras, microphones and reporters she grabbed her waiting and anxious mother, covered her own face and dashed for the elevator.

15

Fun, Games and More Serious Considerations

Salt Lake City Police Department Sergeant Christopher Ahern explained that in August, he was assigned to the police detail at the Salt Lake City International Airport and confirmed Jill's testimony that she called him to see if there was any way to verify if David had been at the airport. Chris explained the system of badges, personal identification numbers and control points that recorded the time, place and person assigned the badge and PIN for each passage.

"What does that record show?" I asked.

Rich objected on hearsay and the court overruled, recognizing the business record exception. Rich renewed his objection, asked for and received permission to *voir dire* the witness. In this context *voir dire* is a procedure that allows a lawyer to ask a few questions out of turn to clarify or short cut testimony or build foundation for an objection. Rich's questions led to Chris conceding that he was not the keeper of those records. Once again Rich objected, but it still was overruled.

Sgt. Ahern viewed a record that showed on August 15, at 20:51 hours, 8:51 in the evening, David's card gained its holder entrance to the airport through Gate 13. Chris explained Gate 13 was a vehicle access gate about 250 yards south of Terminal #1 and I had him draw a rough sketch of the airport showing the terminals, concourses, Gate 13 and Valley Ground Service.

Rich Mauro asked Chris Ahern where the physical record was and whether a copy was handed over to Detective Candland and the prosecution. The sergeant responded that he didn't have such a record, he didn't know if one existed and he's never handed over such a document. He did talk to an officer he remembers to be Jill Candland on August 16, 1994, and obtained a printout from the security access system that told him about the entry through Gate 13.

After Rich asked Ahern a number of questions about the mechanics of going through a control point with a badge and PIN and the number of vehicle gates and doorway control points, Sgt. Ahern's testimony was concluded; he was excused and made way for Matt Jenkins.

Joseph Mathew Jenkins, CPA was an expert witness, a subset of witnesses who are allowed to offer opinions, expert opinions. It's necessary to set out their credentials as foundation for the opinion. Dr. Grey was an expert, but the physician's art is so readily recognized that credentialing an MD, especially in a prelim, is normally short and *pro-forma*.

Matt required a little more introduction, so we ran through his academic history, status as Director of Licensing for the State of Utah, Department of Commerce, Division of Securities and Acting Division CPA, and duties of his offices. Matt and I have worked together on securities fraud cases and, with Utah the reputed "Scam Capital" of the country, he spends a lot of his time auditing broker/dealers and investment advisors. I asked, with tongue firmly in smiling cheek, "Do you have some problems with them, now and again?"

"At times," he returned with a knowing smile.

We moved into the sad financial affairs of David Earl Mead and/or Valley Ground Service. I asked him what documents he'd reviewed in preparation for prelim and he described subcategories within the approximately one-foot-thick stack of paper. To steer him to the financial conditions of VGS, I handed Matt a chart summarizing his finding that he prepared from the records of what United, Continental and Northwest airlines paid VGS. It was a "summary of voluminous business records," another hearsay exception. Matt pointed out the contents, I moved the chart, Ben objected on foundation and asked to *voir dire*.

Ben focused on the fact that Matt used incomplete records to create the exhibit. Matt responded this was the best he could come up with given what was available and that it correlated closely with VGS's bank documents; the holes in the data were not the creation of the prosecution. When Ben tried to box Matt into certain corners things got a bit chippy.

"Just try to answer the question I asked you!"

"Time out!"

"Try to answer my question!" Chippy begot chippy. Standing at the podium Ben held up a set of papers. "Are you familiar with this document, this memo you wrote up for Howie Lemcke?"

"I can't read that from here."

I had several opportunities to object, but this was just too much fun. The judge cast me a glance that asked "Why?" I just smiled, put my hands behind my head and leaned back. When Ben put out a question involving detailed minutiae from the records, Matt replied he couldn't remember the detail but could get it from his laptop. I picked the computer up, walked forward, holding it like a waiter's tray and asked a syrupy "Oh, may I?" The judge cut off the banter, admitted the chart and made me resume direct.

I handed Matt another chart that showed outflow from VGS to persons named Mead, David and his blood family, which was marked, moved, objected, noted and admitted. "Based on your examination of these records and your preparing of State's 10 and State's 11, were you able to form an opinion about the . . . not the condition, but the trend of Valley Ground Service going into the summer before Pam Mead's death?"

"Yes, I was."

"What is that, sir?"

Ben Hamilton interposed that the incomplete nature of the records did not provide a foundation for an expert opinion. I countered it went to the weight the court ought to give the opinion, not admissibility; the court agreed, overruled the objection and said weight ought to be argued at summation.

After the question was re-asked, Jenkins said it was his opinion that the trend for VGS was financial difficulties based on drastically falling revenues. Interspersed between arguments surrounding objections, the opinion continued that per-quarter revenues had fallen from around $70,000 to $35,000 two years later. Some were as low as $11,000 and the departure of Continental Airlines was one of several complicating factors. Further, David Mead was taking cash out of the business as soon as it came available, building no reserves and withdrawing as much money as was possible. It was all going quite well till the lawyer conducting direct tripped all over his own tongue.

"That would lead you to believe what . . . other than . . . in terms of . . . well . . . I'm sorry . . ."

"Objection! That's calling for speculation. I don't think that this is the basis of an expert opinion. This is speculation as to what he believes might be based on information. His opinion was that David was not building up a business but instead maintaining a business."

I had to chuckle, "Your Honor, it's kind of interesting that he's objecting to a question I haven't been able to form."

"A question has not been asked!" With amusement in her voice, Her Honor confirmed my observation.

With my brain and mouth in the same gear, it was time to ask the witness, based on what he'd learned, what effect factoring in the money David Mead was spending on Winnetka Walls would have on his opinion. We crawled through objections. After going over VGS's outflow, I asked Matt about his knowledge and experience in the field of life insurance.

Jenkins replied that for several years while he was a securities broker he was licensed and gained some familiarity with insurance. Matt was aware of the theories and norms in the industry about appropriate amounts of coverage for people in certain circumstances. Again a forest of objections sprang up, including another interjection from Rich followed by admonishment from the court. J. Mathew Jenkins opined that, with the added factor that they had no dependent children, $250,000 with double-indemnity for people in the Meads' financial circumstances was excessive by industry norms.

Ben went to the insurance issues with questions designed to show that Matt didn't know enough about the Meads and VGS to give a good opinion about their needs. Ben focused on the incomplete nature of the records before he brought Matt back to Mead payees on VGS checks and asked if any of those checks were written to Pam. There were none; she didn't appear to be an employee. How about Winnetka Walls? Ben was trying to show David hadn't been supporting her by writing company checks. Matt keyed up the proper file on the laptop to the accompaniment of strange electronic music, realized where the mystery tune was coming from, shut off the laptop's speaker and answered that no such checks were written to Ms. Walls.

Ben asked if David Mead wasn't very good at keeping records, so poor that he might not have a handle on VGS's finances. Matt agreed. For emphasis Ben started questioning David's late tax filings, some of which weren't filed till after Anne Sulton was on the case.

On re-direct, I brought out another point. "You were asked about the status of Pamela Mead as an employee. You have gone over the purchase agreement?"

"Yes."

"Who was, according to the purchase agreement, sole owner of Valley Ground Service?"

"Pamela C. Mead."

"Thank you. No further questions."

It was about eleven thirty. We had a brief discussion of the status and location of several exhibits and agreed it was a good time to take a recess. Judge Boyden asked how many more witnesses I had.

"We anticipate three, potentially four. I got a phone call this morning, Your Honor. I need to leave to interview someone who may be a potential witness. She kind of phoned me out of the blue this morning." With that, the judge instructed us to return at 1:30. Apprehensive, I headed out with Jill to see if the mysterious Stormy would appear.

16

The Surprise Witness

As our car pulled into traffic, I called my assistant Michelle on the mobile phone to see if Stormy had called again. She hadn't, so I headed with Jill for a Mexican restaurant about five miles south of downtown. We role-played at some length about how to handle various situations and who would do what in several events and got there about ten to noon. The hostess led us to a booth against a divider wall that wasn't ideal, but would do. We were going to sit on opposite sides; when we made contact with Stormy, I would get out, Jill would move to the wall and I would by gesture allow Stormy to choose to sit separately on her own side of the booth or on the outside next to the female detective. We didn't want to give the impression of trapping her. We told the waitress we were expecting a third person and would order lunch when she arrived.

Noon came and went, as did the waitress on several occasions. There were no unaccompanied female diners and Jill made a trip to the restroom to see if Stormy got there ahead of us. Could she be there with someone else? Could she have flinched and decided not to come at all? We were into some very strange people-watching and speculation. Aren't exotic dancers generally very tall? Don't they normally have other unique physical features? Some of our fellow patrons wondered what was up with this strange couple who had no eyes for each other.

Five after, ten after, quarter after, nothing! We might as well just enjoy a good lunch and get back to court. The waitress returned and we were in the process of ordering when a petite, pretty young woman, her face framed by medium-length brown hair, walked into the restaurant alone, looking around for someone and obviously uncomfortable.

"Stormy?" I inquired.

"Howie? I'm sorry, Mr. Lem . . ."

"Howie's okay. Please have a seat.

"Stormy, this is Jill Candland. She's a detective with the Salt Lake City Police Department."

Stormy got into the booth next to Jill. The waitress, with every right to be irritated, remained polite and said she'd come back in a few minutes.

Stormy wasn't ready to let us know her last name. That wasn't really okay, but we said it was. She was here. It was clear she was scared but not of us. We placed an order to break the tension and keep the waitress happy and after very little small talk I asked Stormy why this morning, why the call this particular morning? She had a brief choke of emotion, paused to take a sip of water and elaborated on what she'd said in the morning's phone call. Jill gently drew out Stormy's story, wisely not bringing out her notepad.

In a soft, trembling voice, Stormy started with the televised news the night before when she was doing mommy chores around dinnertime, heard the name David Mead and stopped to watch. David wasn't on, but Mrs. Stokes was being interviewed by the reporters. Stormy, the single mother of small children, heard the pain in another mother's voice and watched the photograph unfold. Her eyes glistened from reflections dancing on newly formed tears, her voice wavered ever so slightly and she told us that she wanted to just ignore it, let it go away, but got her kids into bed and watched the late news to reaffirm it was the man she knew folded behind the photo. After a bad night tossing and turning, unable to sleep, she made the call.

Our curiosity turned to the content of the call Pam overheard, but Stormy took us through some background. She met David in a club in late 1991 when suddenly single, out on the town with some girlfriends. David Earl Mead invited her onto the floor. They danced, conversed and saw each other for a couple of weeks. After that Stormy didn't see David until April of 1993 when she and a girlfriend ran into him. The two dated for a couple of months, until one day at lunch the charming suitor made an announcement: he was a married man.

She was shocked and dismayed, angry and hurt and made him drive her back to her work without further ado. She wanted no part of this. Part of the reason she was now a single mom was that she had been cheated on. Having been through it, Stormy couldn't do that to another woman. She had no idea that David was married.

He continued to call, but she resisted his efforts to date her. Was David separated? No, but his wife was an airline stewardess and often out of town, which gave him the ability and opportunity to forecast his availability. David really wanted Stormy to know how unhappy he was in his marriage. She asked why he didn't just confront the situation and ask for a divorce. Mead told her that such a move would cost him his business. According to Stormy, she told him she wouldn't see him while he was a married man.

But Mead was persistent. One day he called Stormy at her work and elaborated on the situation of his company, a family-owned business with financial problems. His wife's family gave him some financial backing that made the business part Pam's and were he to get a divorce the business would go to Pam. He did suggest a better solution: it would be easier to kill Pam and collect the insurance money. Stormy told us that before she could react and say anything beyond a few words David was off the line. The line was still open but he wasn't on the other end until he came back and said, "She's on the line. Pam's on the line," and left for several minutes more. Mead finally came back and explained that Pam picked up the extension and overheard David saying all these things to Stormy. Pam was "distraught," out on the front porch throwing things. David's lighthearted tone of voice made Stormy feel David thought it was funny.

David called back and made other efforts to take Stormy out, but she wouldn't date him. A few weeks after the overheard conversation, he called and said that Pam left him for her parents' home. He called a couple of times after that and asked her out to concerts: Janet Jackson and Def Leppard. She wouldn't go and he didn't call back. She did, somewhere in the course of time, stop by his house unannounced. David was home and asked her in and she noticed there were pictures on the wall of David and Pamela that weren't on those walls before. She asked and David told her that he and his brother had it down to a science how to put up or take down pictures and other personal objects when Pam was out of town.

My prosecutor's mind sorted through all this and I could see Jill's detective juices were flowing. Certain things were important here. How would Stormy learn about the business except from David? Their overheard conversation was before David and Pam took out insurance policies. Was this the genesis of David's plan, when he started the year of the perfect husband? Those two concerts would be one-time events. We could fix the dates: Salt Lake doesn't get big name concerts several times. If the pictures were on the wall, Pam would have been home. Did this happen after she returned from her folks' home in the Springs?

Jill and I both did our best not to become threatening, come on too strong and frighten away our newfound, yet-unidentified witness. Terribly tense, we worked at being relaxed. We each had the duties of our offices but liked Stormy as a person from the moment we met her and it was easy to see we found an emotional moment.

Then she told us that she probably never would have come forward had it not been for how she learned Pam was dead. A typically busy single mother of small children, she didn't pay much attention to the news, missed the drowning and hadn't noticed the press coverage when the lawsuit was filed. The first Stormy heard about the death was when David showed up and instructed Stormy not to come forward.

I sat up straight, startled. "Say what!?"

Then Stormy told us about an extraordinary and frightening day somewhere in mid-1995. She'd last seen David the year before and had since taken a new job working for a commercial video distributor in Salt Lake when, out of the blue, David Mead walked into her office. She asked if he had bought a video store and become one of her customers. He said no, he'd come to talk to her about something important. His demeanor was tense and serious and she rode a wave of fear that he might have come to admit he had AIDS; the two had once been intimate. David took a chair, but got up, paced, put his hands on the front of her desk, leaned over facing her and said, "I don't know if you know or not, but my wife Pam died in a mysterious, freak accident last August."

David, not in response to any questioning, as Stormy was too stunned to question or comment, continued to volunteer his tale. Pam and David were living near the capital at a point in their marriage where they were talking about having children. Pam had some sort of an operation on her feet. He went to work one day and when he returned home he, or someone else, found her drowning in a three-foot pond in the backyard. He continued to give the stunned Stormy details and waved his right hand into the air as he related how she had a wound to the back of her head that went up. "Don't you think if she was assaulted or attacked that the hit would have been down?" he asked as he swung the hand back down.

Even as Stormy remained unable to form questions, David told her that the Stokeses sued him, felt he was somehow responsible for Pam's death and wanted to deny him the insurance money. He repeatedly mentioned that it was a civil suit, not a criminal matter, and only about money. He leaned over her desk and stated grimly that the Stokeses' investigators were out there, following David, looking for her.

Finally, Stormy was able to interject "Would they have followed you here today?"

"Well . . . you know . . . if they find you . . . you will be followed." He responded to her next obvious question, continued to lean forward over her desk and didn't want her to come forward or talk to them, particularly about two things: the overheard telephone call and that the two had been intimate.

I could see revulsion matching my own welling in Jill's eyes and asked how David had brought these up. Stormy paused while she pursed her lips in a mix of sorrow and anger and said he had asked if she remembered the phone call. She said that she did, he told her that he didn't remember it. Then he asked if she remembered when they made love. She said yes. He replied that he didn't remember that either. By then this fine, fine human being was less than an arm's length from her face.

Sitting in this restaurant I could see this young woman's face mirror the firming resolve she must have summoned that day in her office as she told us how she got up, put her arm around David, told him that she had more information than she needed, turned him to the door, wished him luck and gently ushered him out. It was evident she still carried the fear she must have felt returning to her desk. There were people looking for her. The one who found her felt that killing a woman for insurance dollars was an option, that woman was dead and insurance dollars were involved.

Stormy asked how good our case was. Did we have a chance of winning? What other evidence did we have? Jill told her we thought that we had a shot, a tough shot, a real tough shot. I told her we were foreclosed for the time being from sharing our other evidence or witnesses and gave a brief explanation of the Exclusionary Rule that was less than satisfying. Finally, we told Stormy it would be a much better case with her, especially in the light of what we'd learned over lunch. She didn't react immediately but was obviously churning in decision. We tried to move the conversation to the lunch, a lot of good Mexican food was getting cold. The waitress, a pro in her own right, recognized the tension in the booth and avoided the normal ceremonies.

The lunch hour grew long and it was time to address the pivotal question. Would she testify? Although my rapport with Stormy was good, I felt as another woman and obviously sympathetic, Jill would have a better chance. It was clear this job needed to fall to Jill. With genuine sincerity, she looked at Stormy and asked if she were willing to help. In small tears Stormy said she was.

I took care of the check, treating our waitress generously for her wise discretion, while Jill gathered requisite information. After phone calls to let Stormy's employer know that she would be needed in court for a few hours, assurances that we would cover that with a subpoena and agreement on transportation to court and back, I had one more question. After all her name was Stormy. "Stormy? Pardon me for asking, but . . . are you now or have you ever been an exotic dancer?"

She looked at me quizzically. Jill started to explain the situation when Stormy looked down at her body, looked up at me and laughed. Jill apologized for the stupid lawyer and briefly set forth the story. Stormy smiled.

But her face changed and she looked at me with worry and a request. Her two children were grade schoolers and she wanted a chance to prepare them for the flood of publicity headed their way. She wanted to tell them herself before classmates teased them about what they saw on the news. I told her I had no control over the press and it was a valid fear. "I don't know what I can do, but I'll do what I can." We headed to court.

Back at the office we walked in with our prize. My office mates, who had no idea of how big this find was, greeted us with broad smiles. I briefed them very quickly and said we'd bring Stormy in through the hallways serving the judicial chambers to avoid a confrontation in the public corridors. The Stokeses were out ahead of us—I suspect Garfield needed a last smoke—and one of my crew said they'd catch up with the family and let them know.

We went in through the side door, up the elevator to five, down the corridor to Judge Boyden's courtroom. Jill waited with Stormy in the jury room and I entered the courtroom, walked up and told Ben and Rich we'd found Stormy. Rich was in the process of demanding more explanation when the clerk stood, announced Her Honor and called the courtroom to order. Judge Boyden took the bench and asked who was

the next witness the State intended to call. I said Bill Morgan
was present but not our first witness, Judge Boyden admonished Morgan on the Exclusionary Rule, told him to wait outside the courtroom and asked who that first witness might be.
I said I had a witness that had not been listed, explained that
I'd known her last name for less than an hour. "Have you
given the name to defense council?"

"About thirty seconds ago!"

"Mr. Mauro?"

"We obviously want to put an objection on the record. We
haven't had notice. We haven't had a name, address. Haven't
had a telephone number. Haven't had the criminal history.
We haven't had the statement. We don't know where the
statement is. We should be entitled to have any statements
she's given to law enforcement available for us to cross-
examine the witness. We don't have any of those. We object
on that basis!"

"Thank you. Mr. Lemcke, do you wish to respond?"

"Yes, Your Honor. We got a phone call this morning from
this witness. We met her at lunch. We did not know her last
name until an hour ago. The data that counsel asks for,
including statements to the police . . . to this point . . . there
have not yet . . . been any." I walked to the corridor door and
pushed it open. The State was about to call Stormy to the
stand.

Jill led Stormy into the courtroom. The judge said I could
put Stormy on, but Rich was entitled to continue till another
day to allow him to prepare his cross-examination. Jill was
watching what else went on in court, including David Mead,
and later asked me through a smoker's-cough-laced laugh,
"Have you ever seen anyone who looks like he just swal-
lowed glass?"

I put Stormy's name on the record and asked her about our
dealings that day, the anonymous call and the lunch and if
she knew the defendant in this case. She pointed him out and
made record of what he was wearing and where he was sitting. We went to when, where and how she met Mead, then
when, where and how she came to learn she'd been dating a
married man.

Rich was interposing objections at almost every question.

He said that each of my questions were intended only to bring in facts that would besmirch David's good name.

We crawled through objections that turned accusatory. "I don't know if this woman called the prosecutor's office for the first time or not. But it's a quarter to two and they come up with a witness. The case is four years old and, suddenly, at 1:45 on March 12 they march in a woman named Stormy. I think it is unfair for the prosecution to bring this witness, rattle off things we don't know about for the first time four years later when everything has been fleshed out in this case."

I responded that this case hasn't been fleshed out, because the defendant hasn't been honest about the existence of this witness. In fact, the defendant made affirmative effort to prevent the witness from coming forward or testifying.

"We don't have any of that!" was the angry cutoff at mid-sentence.

Judge Ann C. Boyden may have a gentle nature, but she has the tools to take control of a charged situation, speaking where hers is the only voice not raised, consequently the only voice anyone still listens to. Things calmed down and Rich, twice, put on the record that he wasn't suggesting any bad faith or improper conduct on my part. I made a point of not saying that the real surprise wasn't Stormy's existence but that we'd found her after their client's steps to prevent it. Even if his lawyers were unaware, David Earl Mead well knew who and where she was. The judge decided the best course was to continue Stormy's testimony till a later day, after Stormy could submit to a recorded police interview to be provided to the defense. This was logical and we'd expected it. Rich asked for the opportunity to interview Stormy and Judge Boyden said that would be entirely up to the witness. Jill took Stormy out the front door through the newly energized press corps.

Later, I asked the Fourth Estate a favor, something I had absolutely no right to demand of a free press: Could they show a moment's mercy to Stormy? This went down today, Stormy was a single mom who hadn't been able to prepare her kids for the publicity. Could they, please, not use her last name or her face for one day, only one day, to give her a chance to prepare her family? There was a brief silence, a look of soft humanity in professional eyes and no answers. This would be a decision of anchors and editors, made only if reporters would sell the concept. Reporters are good people and have needs, too. I told them that after Stormy testified in May, I'd do my damndest to have her cooperate with them.

17

Interesting Witnesses

I called the injured Mike Jensen ahead of Bill Morgan, and we moved quickly through his testimony. The officer summoned on the report of screaming arrived to find a female, cold to the touch, without a carotid pulse lying on the ground next to a backyard pond and a male standing in that pond with water up to his chest. When asked to point out that male person in the courtroom he chose Ben Hamilton. "Hey. They look similar. It's been a long time." I didn't sweat that one. It was no problem; identification wasn't an issue in this case.

Mike described David Mead as hysterical, screaming, making little sense and refusing the officer's requests and orders to get out of the pond. Eventually he was able to get Mead out of the pond but, with David in hysterics and one person already dead, the officer elected to handcuff Mead for everyone's safety and put the wet widower in the front seat of his police car, wrapped in a blanket. Mead calmed down, plenty of other officers arrived and Jensen felt comfortable removing the cuffs.

The officer went through a description of the pond, particularly the collar of loose rocks and bricks he described as approximately three feet, or one large step, wide. We used photos of the scene to point out for the judge, who leaned toward the witness, what each showed. The witness said that when he arrived Pam was out of the pond, on her back in the dirt. Mike described the Meads' dog Baron as about the size of a small German shepherd and noted Baron was off his chain when the officer arrived.

As his testimony continued, Mike Jensen told how he'd stayed with David Mead for the duration but was never able to converse beyond bits and pieces, sobs and screams and little that made sense. Mead seemed angry with himself. He had just finished the fishpond, blamed himself for the death and felt that his wife must have slipped and fallen: she just had surgery and her balance was poor. If he hadn't built the pond she might still be alive.

"What did you notice of him, in terms of tears?"

"I didn't notice any tears."

"No further questions."

Rich Mauro took this witness and went to the reasons for handcuffing the defendant when Mead wasn't under arrest. Rich had Mike reaffirm he was the first cop at the scene, asked which neighbors or civilian witnesses were already present, if he had interviewed any of the civilians; he hadn't. Mike looked over the report and, his memory refreshed, admitted he talked to some of the neighbors but didn't interview them in the official sense. Rich had him tell the court that, according to those neighbors, the Meads seemed to get along just fine. After Mauro made Officer Jensen admit he hadn't measured the depth or width of the pond or length of the dog chain, he handed back the witness.

There's an old axiom in the law that an attorney ought never ask a question where he doesn't know the answer. I forgot that and asked Mike Jensen if the scene were being treated as an accident or a crime scene, fully expecting him to say that the cops were treating this as an accident, but he came back and responded that every scene is treated as a crime scene until there's a determination of what happened. I quickly changed the subject, asking a few questions about David disassembling the fishpond from within and how Mike stopped that from happening.

Rich asked Mike Jensen if he counted the rocks or the bricks at the scene, he hadn't and his turn on the stand was over. Bill Morgan was up.

I hadn't dealt much with Mr. Morgan since he'd announced his existence walking into the courthouse during the federal trial, so I was introducing him to myself as well as to the court. Bill testified he knew David because he worked for Mead and Valley Ground Service in 1993 and 1994. He explained how VGS cleaned interiors, refilled water tanks and emptied lavatories for Northwest, Continental and the other airlines.

According to Mr. Morgan he'd worked the evening of the fifteenth, came in about seven or eight o'clock and cleaned two planes. He took his son with him that evening to help out, didn't see David Mead at the airport and learned of Pam's death from a baggage handler the next evening.

It was their responsibility that night to totally clean the Continental from end to end, including the galley, vacuuming, going through the seats, emptying trash from the containers and seat-back pockets, picking up any loose items and straightening out the magazines, pillows and blankets. That would normally be a couple of man-hours of work but strangely, when he got on the aircraft, Morgan noticed someone had already done a "quick clean," what VGS did on flights that arrived late, had a short turnaround or only enough time for a cosmetic slicking up. Bill had done this work long enough to recognize a plane that had been visited by such a procedure. How long would a quick clean take? Fifteen minutes, maybe thirty, fifteen if you were pushing and, since the plane just arrived in Salt Lake, "Someone had jumped on the plane and done this job."

I asked again if Morgan saw David that night. He hadn't. The last time Bill Morgan saw Mead at the airport, David was coming in through the air cargo service; he couldn't recall ever seeing David come in any other way.

Mauro was brief on his cross-examination, having Morgan admit that his estimates of time were approximate and that he had no idea whether or not David Mead might have been there at some other time.

My next witness produced stares and gasps from the spectators. Jack Hendrix was called to the stand and came out of the courtroom's holding cell in his official white Utah State Prison jumpsuit with large hand-stenciled labels, leg shackles and front-facing handcuffs laced through a belly chain padlocked in the small of his back as an un-sugar-coated prison inmate. I learned he got off the fire line with just enough time to shower up and get into clean duds before hopping aboard His Excellency the Governor's official wings.

Jack shuffled past between the prosecution table and the clerk's bench the best he could, stopped, turned to the clerk, raised his right hand as much as his chains allowed and was sworn. With help from the bailiff, he got up the one step and sat down. The bailiff adjusted the microphone and brought the witness a paper cup of water from the cooler. Jack shrugged a demonstration that the kind gesture was futile because the cuffs prevented him from lifting the cup to his mouth. The cup remained on the stand for want of a better, less embarrassing option.

After Jack put his name on the record, I asked about his attire. He told the courtroom he was an inmate at the Utah State Prison, almost three years on this last stint, a multiply convicted felon in and out of prison for eight years. He was doing time for robbery with convictions for burglaries, thefts, car thefts and a gun charge. Jack Hendrix and David Mead were cousins, their mothers were sisters and Jack was currently in prison for robbing his cousin David Mead.

Hendrix told the court that, although their families had briefly lived together when the two men were children, Jack and David weren't particularly close. Jack met Pam a few times briefly and once went to their home on Capital Hill. Jack said he was surprised when his mom told him David contacted her. Just out from another stretch in the joint, he got the phone number and called. Interestingly, Jack Hendrix's courtroom voice and demeanor were almost soft. I had to remind him regularly to speak up.

The next day he and David got together and rode around in his cousin's car, got a hamburger, sat and talked some. David asked how Jack was doing on the outside and if Jack knew someone who would kill David's wife.

I zeroed in on that remark while rumbles could be heard in the courtroom. "He asked you if you would kill his wife? How does one start up a conversation 'will you kill my wife?' What was the first thing he asked you, in that regard?"

"He asked me if I would kill my girlfriend."

"Who was your girlfriend?"

"An ex-girlfriend."

"Did he say . . . why you would kill your ex-girlfriend?"

". . . said I would kill her for . . . would come into the value of two hundred thousand dollars . . ."

"So . . . it was how much money it would take to kill your ex-girlfriend?"

"Yeah, I said, yeah, I would."

"Then what did he say?"

"Then he asked me about . . . if I would kill his wife . . . or if I knew somebody who would."

"Did he tell you how much he was going to pay you to kill his wife?"

". . . said around thirty thousand dollars." It was a grim version of the old joke that ends, "Now that we've established what you are, we're just haggling price."

The witness said David wanted it to look like a break-in and gave his newly freed cousin a little present; it was in the ashtray. Jack looked and found eight grams of cocaine wrapped in a hundred dollar bill. Some professions call that earnest money; mine calls it a retainer. Jack also told us David made inquiries about Jack dealing a little dope for David as well. Rich objected and was overruled.

Then Jack told us about the next day, when cousin David picked him up and the two drove around for some time before David asked about the proposed killing. Jack lied that a proper hit man had been identified but not yet contacted and Mead presented Hendrix with fifty-eight additional grams of coke, eight hundred dollars in cash and a set of scales. They talked about Hendrix selling the dope and splitting the profits or recycling those profits into more dope. Jack spoke to his cousin in earnest tones about contacting that hit man but Jack Hendrix, junkie, had other plans.

"What did you plan to do with that cocaine and that money?"

"Shoot it!"

"You were going to consume it?"

"Yes!"

"And what, in fact, did you do with that cocaine?"

"Used it."

"Did you use . . . What did you do with the thousand dollars in cash?"

"Used it."

"For what?"

"Coke."

My witness on the stand readily admitted he was an addict, a junkie, at that moment a recovering addict, but he'd always be an addict who could only hope and pray to remain a recovering addict. At the time he was meeting with David, Jack was an addict without modifying adjectives, who saw dope and cash, a doper's dream, and was more than willing to tell David anything he wanted to hear and get his junkie hands on that beautiful stash. Would he kill his ex-girlfriend? Hell, yes! Would he kill Pam? Hell, yes! Would he kill anyone David named? Whatever you want to hear, Cuz, just give me the haul.

So for two weeks, he can't be real sure but that was his best guess, Jack had one bodacious binge. His girlfriend, who'd stuck by Jack through more than a few bad times, reached her limit and kicked him out. He took up with another woman until the dope and the money ran out, then stole a few things, which he traded for more drugs. At some point he called his mother, found her crying and learned David's wife died, had slipped in a pond and drowned.

Jack asked where his *bereaved* cousin was. When his mother told Jack David was staying at Tommy's, Jack and his new woman went over to the Mead house, broke in and stole things, which were quickly fenced for more drugs, went back a second time and stole more. But his new friend's probation officer showed up, saw the goods and arrested her before the party pals got to their fence. Fortunately for Jack, the PO didn't recognize Hendrix, realize his status and arrest him, too. Among his other misdeeds during the two-week toot, Mr. Hendrix ignored the reporting requirements of his contract of parole and became a fugitive. Jack went to the Meads' one more time but only stole a few things out of the shed.

As Jack's mind came out of the fog, he realized that he'd better confront David. After all, David gave him nine hundred dollars and sixty-six grams of blow and Jack had neither kept up his end to market the drugs nor kill the spouse, although the latter chore was now moot. Jack got to David's house, found his cousin and offered his condolences. The boys walked to a nearby store, got some beers, went to a couple of strip clubs and talked. David said that he was suspected in his wife's death and "they" wanted him to take a polygraph. Mead boasted that, anticipating this, he went to libraries, studied polygraphs till he knew more about polys than the polygrapher he paid to administer the exam and passed with flying colors.

Hendrix never directly asked Mead if he killed Pam, but he did ask how David was doing now that he had all that insurance and begged David's forgiveness for not keeping his word. The widower, who seemed sad at home, but much less so at the strip clubs, admitted he thought Jack would go ahead and use those drugs, just being out of prison and all, and held no grudge.

There was a way that Jack could work off the debt. David wanted to enlarge his garage to be able to store a boat and Jack could dig the footings for an hourly wage. Jack agreed and started digging the hole in Mead's backyard. When he noticed David putting a For Sale By Owner sign in the front yard, Jack's brain went into gear. Putting the house up for sale and enlarging the garage for a new boat were not logical companion scenarios and someone had just died in a recent excavation in that very backyard. Were cement footings poured over this parole violator's body lying in the bottom of a hole he had just dug, he'd never be missed, never be found and never be able to tell what he knew. In a fit of common sense, Jack Hendrix ran.

Rich interposed a series of objections based on relevance, speculation and 403/404(b). The judge decided I was pushing the envelope on relevancy and becoming quite speculative so we moved to the robbery of David and Winnie. Jack admitted he went to David's house to rob his cousin three weeks or a month after Pam's death, with a newfound drug friend and a gun. He didn't remember his co-defendant's name.

When they arrived, David and a girl, whose name he got from reading the charges against him, were there. Twenty minutes after the robbery Hendrix and cohort were on their way to the Davis County Jail, their escape up the interstate cut short by the electronic miracles of 9-1-1, police radio and the sharp eyes of the Utah Highway Patrol. "Now I am in a mess."

According to Jack he called his sister the next morning and laid out the whole story, tried to "justify" everything to her, but she had known her brother too well for too long and wasn't about to buy into "justifications." She called him back with the name of a detective to whom Jack ought to talk. Was that Jill Candland? He didn't think so, didn't remember so well, hadn't slept well, still coming down off the drugs but remembered she was the one who came and talked to him in the Davis clink where he told her his story.

I finished my direct exam of Jack Hendrix by asking when, before Jack met with David for burgers and dope, he last saw or talked with his cousin. It had been a long time, maybe Thanksgiving the year before.

It had been a busy and eventful afternoon, so Her Honor called a break.

After about twenty minutes we got going again and it was obvious Richard R. Mauro, Esq. had prepared for this cross-examination long and well. He started out by placing an easel with a full-sized white sketchpad sitting in the well in front of the witness.

"Mr. Hendrix, I want to ask you some questions about your criminal record. Do you understand?"

"Uh huh."

Rich's combative enthusiasm flowed "Is that yes?"

"Yes." The judge asked Hendrix to speak up as Rich handed a computer printout of Jack's "rap sheet" to the witness. Rich crafted questions to include the obvious thickness of the document and the fact it went back to 1982. I slipped in a saccharine offer to post no objection to the rap sheet being admitted as an exhibit. Rich knew that once admitted a document "speaks for itself" and a witness can no longer be questioned on the writing's contents, but in a bravado demonstration of how prepared he was in this case, he moved the exhibit and moved on. Jack was asked, in turn, about every one of the several aliases he'd used in the past. No, that was not his name. Yes, he's used that; that was dishonest; he gave that name to police; that was a lie to a police agency; he did that in an attempt to get out of trouble. Name after name after name, each in turn, was written on the sketchpad.

Then Rich moved to the robbery of Mead and Walls in staccato detail. You were in a car? With your co-defendant? There were guns? Some were loaded? You were charged? Each charge was written on the sketchpad. These are the potential punishments? Each maximum sentence was listed. You did three burglaries at David's before the robbery? Each would be this charge? Each would carry this penalty? The impressive list grew and grew and by now Jack was only nodding in response. Everyone had given up asking him to raise the volume. Rich asked the witness if he went to the police about Mead's proposed contract to kill Pam after he learned of her death. He had not. Before the first burglary? Before the second? The third? The robbery? Not till he was in jail and looking at returning to prison? He didn't tell his PO? He didn't tell the PO that picked up his binge-mate? Not till he was in custody?

Next the questioning went into talks with Detectives Wade Wayment and Jill Candland. How many times did each talk to him? Several. Ever searching for the prosecutorial misconduct that every true-believer defense attorney knows deep down in his soul is always there, Rich asked "Mr. Lemcke did come by and talk to you? Right?"

"No!"

Rebuffed, Rich responded with sarcasm "It was . . . Jill?"

"Yes." There was a change in the witness, whose posture grew from hangdog to erect as the familiar form "Jill" was used repeatedly without last name or title and pronounced as if it contained twice its actual letters. Chained to a chair, his voice grew strong and attitude evolved from deferential to combative. In my old engineering days, I learned of processes where something most people would view as pretty hard, like "mild" steel, would be beaten and subjected to extremes of heat and become harder and tougher and stronger. As I watched, State's witness Jack Hendrix, a person most people would view as pretty hard, was worked by heat and pounding and becoming harder and tougher and stronger before my eyes.

The questioning turned to Jack's history of getting arrested and released. He'd violated more than one probation, parole and pre-trial supervised release in his day.

Rich announced he was going to ask a series of questions and I asked the court if he'd just ask the questions and skip the announcements. Jack broke in that Mauro knew as well as anyone how the system of arrest and release works; Rich agreed and Judge Boyden intervened: "Let Mr. Mauro ask the questions. Mr. Mauro, ask the questions and allow the witness to answer."

Rich got into incidents where Jack was arrested and never charged. The sketchpad groaned under the magic marker. Uncharged conduct isn't a proper subject for impeachment, but I held my objection until Mauro started to ask if all these were somehow the arresting officer's fault. I put in an objection, which was overruled, to let the witness know I believed that this was argumentative, abusive and unnecessary. Alliance building never hurts.

Mauro then moved into questions about whether there were deals and promises that Jack got in return for his testimony in the case at hand. The truth was the only promise he ever got was Jill's letter to the Board after Jack went to prison. What incentive did Jack have to honor his part of the bargain after he was committed? Jack got a plea bargain, a "package" or "global" deal to clear up the several cases on his plate, a good deal, not a great deal. Nonetheless, referring generously to the sketchpad, Rich went back and forth with Hendrix, comparing potential sentences on crimes charged and uncharged to sentences actually imposed, to the layman the deal of the century.

Rich, in a very studied line of questions, got Jack to admit that when each of the events took place only Jack and David were present with no corroborating witnesses. After impeaching Hendrix with some differences in his testimony that day and the transcripts from the civil case, Mauro walked up to the witness with a group of new documents and explained they were releases he wanted Jack to sign to allow Rich access to all sorts of Jack's personal records.

I stood up and objected. Jack's LDA Vernice Ah Ching knew Jack was testifying today and wanted Mauro to contact her before making any demands of her client outside the courtroom. "He knows that Mr. Hendrix is a represented person and . . ."

I was cut off. "No! He is not! I am going to tell you because I was a Legal Defender. Legal Defender's contract for representing Mr. Hendrix has ended. I know the contract because I worked there for seven years."

My turn to cut in, looking at the judge, and gesturing toward Rich "He was not working there at the time Mr. Hendrix was represented on these charges?"

Jack picked up the theme, cut in on me and addressed Rich directly "You know what? I would sign those, but you have an attitude."

It was the court's turn, and when the judge takes her turn, it's the last turn. "Don't answer that. This is not an appropriate question for cross-examination. It is outside the scope. And, if there's any question Mr. Hendrix is represented, he will not be able to sign those until he's had an opportunity to discuss it with his attorney. If he is not represented, then we will deal with that then. Do you have other cross-examination?"

The questioning traveled to Jack Hendrix's 1994 sentencing. Back and forth between the witness and the sketchpad, magic marker in hand, the defense attorney flowed through a series of questions designed, once again, to demonstrate that when Jack got a chance to complete a drug program, it was a deal beyond belief. That might have played well before a lay jury, but everyone in our courtroom knew that it was a tough program few are strong enough to complete, but those few are numbered in the program's history of success in shepherding addicts. Jack didn't succeed, but he learned something there, because he was succeeding in prison. Inadvertently, Rich's last group of questions made that point.

"Even though you went to prison, Jill still wrote a letter on your behalf? Right?"

"Yes."

"A letter to the Board of Pardons?"

"Yes."

"Asking that they give you special consideration?"

"Yes."

"You are a firefighter now?"

"Yes. Squad leader," he told us with pride.

"Squad leader . . . or firefighter . . . that's a privilege in prison? Isn't it?"

"No. You have to earn it."

On redirect, I walked to the sketchpad, contrasting magic marker in hand and smartly popped off the cap. Hoping my party opponent would flinch while wondering what I would do to his exhibit, I waved the marker about the page and asked incoherently "Is that second one five to life . . . ? Or five . . . ? No . . . That's life . . . Okay. Sorry."

Then I walked back to the podium and, my point having been made, snapped the cap back on the pen and looked at the witness as directly as I could. "This chart aside, did you tell us the truth today?"

"Yes, I am telling the truth!"

"No further questions."

Rich was done and wanted to talk to Hendrix about the releases, but Jack Hendrix looked at Rich. "If you had good intentions, I would sign it. But you don't have good intentions, so I won't sign it." When Judge Boyden told the shackled witness his testimony had concluded, Jack got up and, with the strong arm of the law to assist his balance, hobbled down from the stand and walked away despite Rich still asking, "So your answer is no?"

It was four o'clock and we gathered up our goodies to head back to the office. I spoke briefly with the Stokeses about the day's events and the continuance, but I had one more important piece of business waiting outside the chambers.

It had been a day of interesting witnesses. Winnie, Matt, Bill Morgan, Jack and Stormy, but the press was interested in Stormy.

That night I got home fairly deep into the dinnertime news cycle and was met at the door by an excited family asking who was this Stormy, the one with the blue dot on her face? With TV remote firmly in hand, I anxiously watched the tail end summaries and the teasers for the ten o'clock cycle. To my great satisfaction in the underlying decency of all people, no station, nor paper, nor service used Stormy's face or last name. The coverage was extensive and led the news, but to a humane journalistic person they gave her that day. Some just used "a surprise witness"; some wouldn't use her name or face till May. Delighted, I could only imagine how Stormy felt. I did not imagine, however, how Winnetka Walls felt. I should have.

In the two months or so mid-prelim, Stormy came in to give us a videotaped interview in one of the conference rooms in my office. Three of us and an investigator as cameraman spent a couple of hours in a relatively relaxed setting, at least compared to the courtroom. Stormy, who was grateful for the soft touch the press laid on her, said she'd given a lot of thought to what we'd talked about over lunch and recalled more detail. We asked her to continue to mull over those details as the process wore on. She asked us to tell her about other witnesses and evidence. We couldn't but promised to get together after all this, when all questions could be answered.

We were not only aware David Mead once tried with some success to intimidate this witness, but we were trying to prove he'd already killed to get his way.

18

Stormy

As we gathered in Judge Ann C. Boyden's courtroom in the brand new Scott M. Mathesson Courthouse, we learned by and through his attorney of record, Richard P. Mauro, that the defendant, David Earl Mead, had a beef. When the press picked up on the legend of Stormy the exotic dancer and the dutiful search of police for that elusive specter, Mauro read the articles and was shocked at the implication his client misled the world as to Stormy's identity. Mr. Mauro announced he'd reviewed all of David's prior statements and admissions and found no such false statements. Her Honor asked if I had any response. I told her this was between the defense and the press. I didn't say it, but I knew the court and the press would learn that very morning about David Mead's less humorous attempts to prevent the world from discovering Stormy. I also realized that Rich was falling afoul of an old Texas axiom: you can't win a pissin' contest with a newspaper, 'cause they drink ink by the barrel.

Stormy was formally introduced to audiences well primed to hear what she had to say, her fear of David tempered by the support around her, and started her testimony by telling the courtroom of the two dance club meetings with David and how the second led to dating. She spoke of the dates, the fact that she had been to his home, how she learned her suitor was spoken for and the telephone call Pam overheard.

"What did he tell you about his marriage?"

Mauro objected. This conversation occurred one year before this action. "I don't think it is relevant. If it is relevant, it is subject to 403. It is misleading . . . prejudicial. The prejudice outweighs any probative value."

I used the opportunity to restate good evidence and argue the case: "The time frames here are relevant. I would ask the court to, in fact, to wait on the ruling of the relevance of the time frame until my witness's testimony about things that happened between her and David Mead, where David Mead told her, in the context of the civil federal proceedings, to deny the fact that certain conversations, where he said that he was going to kill his wife for the insurance policy, took place."

"I will allow you to continue at this time."

Like other lawyers I have an ego and occasionally, with help of adult beverage, view myself as grandly eloquent. It is humbling to go over my transcribed words that fail to form full or coherent sentences, or to realize that when I try to "pound the facts" that I, in fact, develop a speech tic.

David Mead elected to talk to others in some detail about his marriage, his business and his options: important detail that Stormy, like Jack and Winnie, could have only gotten from David. The only contact any of these three ever had was when Jack robbed Winnie. None had met Matt Jenkins; this wasn't a crew in conspiracy. David said his family owned it first, but the Stokeses gave him financial backing, so VGS was part Pam's. David feared VGS would go to Pamela in a divorce.

"What did he suggest might be a better solution?"

"He suggested that killing Pam would solve his problems."

"Did he say how he was going to do that?"

"He said it would be easier to have her killed and then collect the insurance money."

"Did he mention an amount of insurance?"

"I am not sure . . . at this time . . . at this conversation or the following conversation in '95, which time the insurance came in eventually. . . ."

"What was the number he got?"

"Five hundred thousand."

Soon we got to the point where Mead announced that his wife picked up the extension. When asked about David's tone, Stormy gave a voice example first of a serious David as she quoted "easier to have her killed" and a nonchalant, almost humorous caller "she's throwing stuff all over."

When Stormy asked if she could speak with Pam directly, David asked why and was told she wanted to assure Mrs. Mead there was nothing going on between the two: Stormy would not help a married man cheat on his wife. David refused.

A couple of weeks later, Mead called, announced his wife had left him and asked Stormy out. She refused and didn't date him after that, although she testified about the concert offers, the visit to David's home and the rotating collection of photographs.

"When was the first time you found out that Pam Mead had died?"

"It was in 1995, after May and prior to November."

"How was it you came to find out Pam Mead had died?"

"David Mead came to my place of business."

Stormy testified about the location of her job and that she'd changed employers since she last talked to Mead. Rich Mauro interposed a lengthy objection on relevance and 403.

Her Honor sounded worn. "I know. And you have a continuing objection. I will allow the testimony."

"What was his demeanor at the time?"

"The situation was tense. His demeanor at the time was . . . kind of like . . . He said, 'I was going to send you flowers first' and 'I was going to send you flowers.' He used to send me a lot of flowers." I gave Jill a teasing wink to rub it in that the detective wasn't alone on Mead's FTD route. She scowled.

The testimony moved through the encounter, the posture, descriptions of the "mysterious freak accident" and the head injury, what Mead said about the civil lawsuit, investigators, the advisability of not coming forward and suggested selective memory.

We got to Stormy's state of mind as David left her office, the advice of her acquaintances and precautions for her safety. Rich continued to object on relevancy; I said it was relevant and "bolstered" my witness, a tactic usually objectionable but probative here for this witness's state of mind.

I finished direct with the circumstances and timing of how Stormy, Jill and I came to meet. Judge Boyden invited cross and ruled on Rich's ongoing objection, "I found that the testimony was relevant, as well as the probativeness was not outweighed by the prejudicial nature of it."

Richard P. Mauro went right for the throat, no finesse; he was direct on cross. "Stormy, you said you don't know much about this business, but you do know about the truth? Don't you?"

"That's a fact. Yes!" Her back was up from her first answer.

Rich Mauro went directly to Stormy's dealings with me and Jill Candland, hinting that he didn't believe the account of how she appeared mid-prelim. He alluded she'd been spoon-fed information by "the State" and was testifying to that, not her own witness. She was clearly irritated by the tenure of the examination and parried Mauro's thrusts to discredit her integrity.

After a series of questions designed to show that semantic differences in her videotaped account and direct exam were sustentative, Rich took on Roger "Action Jackson" Tinsley through this surrogate. "Did he tell you the investigator was following people?"

"He said it was, particularly, him."

"Did he tell you that the investigator was lying to people . . . about him?"

"I don't think so."

"Did he tell you that his lawyer filed a protective order to prevent the investigator for the plaintiffs from lying about David?"

"I don't believe so."

"Did he tell you that he had a court hearing with affidavits of witnesses that said the investigator had been lying?"

"I don't recall that. No."

I was getting the *Why don't you object?* glance from the bench, lead detective and wise co-workers in the gallery, but this was going my way. I probably owed Roger an apology for not standing up to defend him, but I was sure he understood. Had David Mead told Stormy any of this, it might have been a legitimate basis for her staying out of the way, but he didn't; Mead just scared her off. David lost that hearing, too.

Rich went looking for Stormy the exotic dancer. What was she told? That David said she was an exotic dancer. Who told her that? She read it in the papers the next day. What did Lemcke tell you? That the cops went out to the clubs looking for a dancer named Stormy. Did he tell you why they were doing that? No.

Then the questioning became darker. "If Mr. Mead were to say that you had two children, that would have been the truth?"

"Uh huh."

"If he were to say that you had two boys, that would have been the truth?"

"That is correct." Her eyes sparked anger.

"If he would have said your children . . . your oldest child, was between the ages of five to seven, that would have been true?"

"Yes."

"Your youngest child . . . three to five, that would have been the truth?"

Pamela Camille Stokes Mead
at her job as a flight attendant.
Courtesy of Mr. & Mrs. Garfield Stokes

The photo
of Pamela and
David Mead that
Pam's mother kept
in her wallet, folded
to hide David.
*Courtesy of Mr. & Mrs.
Garfield Stokes*

Booking photo of David Earl Mead
after his initial arrest three years
to the day after Pam's death.
Courtesy of Salt Lake City Police Department

TOP: Police photo of the brick and stone collar surrounding the fishpond where Pam died; CENTER: Police photo of the Meads' backyard on the night of Pam's death; BOTTOM: Curious neighbors gather in front of the Meads' house the night of Pam's drowning. *Courtesy of Salt Lake City Police Department*

Jill Candland as a rookie officer. She became the homicide detective assigned to Pam's death.
Courtesy of Salt Lake City Police Department

The Honorable Ann C. Boyden, the judge who presided at David Mead's preliminary hearing.
Courtesy of the State of Utah Third Judicial District Court

Anne Sulton, the Stokeses' attorney, in their wrongful death suit against David.
Courtesy of Anne Sulton & The Jackson Advocate

Pam's sister Mary Stokes, private investigator Roger "Action Jackson" Tinsley, and Pam's mother, Sinie Stokes, outside the courtroom during David Mead's trial. *Courtesy of Kristan Jacobsen, Deseret Morning News*

U.S. Magistrate Judge Ronald N. Boyce, the jurist assigned to consider a motion that, if granted, would dismiss the wrongful death case against David Mead. *Courtesy of the SJ Quinney College of Law, the University of Utah*

Detective Jill Candland and Howard Lemcke outside the court-room during the trial of David Mead. *Courtesy of Kristan Jacobsen, Deseret Morning News*

Pastor France Davis, who provided spiritual guidance to Pam during her life and constant firm, but wise and kind counsel for Howie and the people of Salt Lake City. *Courtesy of Pastor France Davis & Calvary Baptist Church*

ABOVE: Howard Lemcke argues the case for the prosecution. *Courtesy of the District Attorney for Salt Lake County* LEFT: Michelle Watson, aka Meesh, Howie's assistant. *Courtesy of Michelle Watson & Love Communications Advertising Agency*

District Attorney David Yocom, whose victory or defeat in the election determined who would prosecute David Mead. *Courtesy of the District Attorney for Salt Lake County*

The Honorable J. Dennis Frederick, presiding judge
at David Mead's criminal trial.
Courtesy of Chuck Wing, Deseret Morning News

Dr. Kris Sperry, Medical Examiner
for the State of Georgia.
Courtesy Dr. Sperry

Expert witness
Matthew Jenkins, CPA,
on the stand.
*Courtesy of Mr. & Mrs.
Matthew Jenkins*

David Mead's prison mug shot.
Courtesy of State of Utah Department of Corrections

After the verdict, Detective Jill Candland hugs Pam's mother, Sinie Stokes, as Pam's sister Mary Stokes looks on.
Courtesy of Kristan Jacobsen, Deseret Morning News

It was time to break in, although I was wondering if Rich might don a monocle, tap a riding crop on his palm and announce "Vee know vere your children are." "Your Honor, I will object. I think Mr. Mauro may have some interest in the battle with the press. This isn't particularly the forum for it. This is beyond the scope of cross-examination."

The court allowed it. Stormy was in fighting shape: don't ever threaten a mother's cubs.

Rich wandered down that path for a few more questions, touched on the fact Stormy was once cited for simple assault and moved back to dealings with David Mead. He had the witness go into some detail of the dating and her conversations with the client. Had she taken notes of these? He asked about her economic circumstances during that time with a hint she might have been preying on an available man and then, bitter learning the prize was taken, made this up.

Mauro started to make some inroads. Stormy said that she was shocked, shaken and disturbed that David was a married man, "You were married at that time, too? Weren't you?"

"Only by name," sadly. "Only by name. We had been separated for years."

She hadn't told Candland or me or even Mead. By the time of her dealings with David Mead, the divorce was in process.

When she heard David felt it might be preferable to kill Pam for the money, did she call the police? Did she call Pam to warn her? After she learned of Pam's death, did she call the police? Did she ever contact the Stokeses? "You seem to strike me as a person that would want to protect someone, if they were in danger, and help them?"

"Yes," weakly.

"You have a pretty good sense of when someone might be in danger? Is that a fair statement?"

"In a general way, I guess."

"If you felt someone was in danger, you would get on the phone and call the police?"

"Yes." There were a few more questions to hint that Stormy saw no real danger and deepen the witness's sense of guilt for not calling the cops before or after Pam died.

A few more questions confirmed that, other than what

David told her, Stormy knew no details of the insurance or the death. Rich had no other questions, Stormy was excused and, after confirming with the clerk that all offered exhibits were admitted, the State rested. Jill walked Stormy out to the corridor and our part of the bargain with the Fourth Estate.

Judge Boyden asked if the defense intended to call any witnesses. As is typical in a prelim they didn't. Rich advised the client of his right to testify but advised David not to. David agreed with his attorney, the defense rested and we moved to argument.

As the "moving party" in this motion to bind over the charges for trial, I got to go first and also last "in rebuttal." I started out restating the charges, misstating the Solicitation of Homicide as Attempted Homicide, being corrected by Her Honor and getting back on track. I re-started with that solicitation charge and its requirement for a "substantial step" being taken toward that end and feelings that a two-stage down payment of $900 and sixty-six grams of cocaine was substantial. The evidence before the court on Count II was uncontroverted; the defense had mercilessly crossed Jack Hendrix on his persona and motives but never asked him a single question to refute his version of events, the only version before the court.

Then I moved to the evidentiary foundation for Pam's death as a homicide. That was circumstantial, entirely circumstantial, but they were strong circumstances. While Pam was having her autopsy, the defendant's family was disassembling the instrument of her death. There were three witnesses with whom the defendant discussed the killing of Pam Mead before it took place who heard how and why it should be done. Matt Jenkins testified about the finances of David Earl Mead and Valley Ground Service, confirming what Mead told other witnesses about the ownership status of VGS and why a divorce would put the Mead family business into Stokes family hands. Jenkins also showed that the projected disappearing income from disappearing airline contracts combined with David's looting of VGS left an infusion of insurance funds as Mead's only shot to maintain VGS and his lifestyle.

Pamela Camille Stokes Mead died from drowning, but

was it an accident or murder? What did the findings show? There was a wound to the back of the head, small abrasions to the elbow and the torso. There was an absence of other injuries to the back of her head, neck, shoulders, back, buttocks and legs. Had she fallen on the pile of rocks and bricks she certainly would have sustained more injuries and she would have had to fall uphill after she hit her head to get into the water. Coincidentally, the only person who ever saw her in the water was the defendant, David Earl Mead.

The ME's findings were changed, twice, but must be viewed from the vantage point of what circumstances were visible to the cops and ME at those times. I reminded the court that on the night of the death, everyone saw a perfect loving couple and a widower who a police agency confirmed had been at the airport. They didn't know about Bill Morgan, the concepts of quick clean and airport access, Winnie, Jack, Stormy or insurance proceeds. They hadn't consulted Matt Jenkins to hear of the inordinate nature of a half million-dollar insurance policy for a childless spouse who had just left a nineteen-thousand-dollar-a-year job. Each of the ME's three successive findings had to be viewed in the light of evolving circumstances.

Given Pam's feet with pins extending from her toes, even beyond the open-toed orthopedic slippers, walking in and of itself would be painful. Imagine walking uphill across the unlit moonscape of that backyard, past the dog, over a three-foot collar of rocks and bricks to feed fish. She landed on those rocks and only sustained a single wound that showed an upward blow to the back of her head. The only fall consistent with these circumstances was the nasty slip and fall David predicted to Winnetka Walls.

I returned briefly to Count II, repeated that it was uncontroverted, noted Jack Hendrix may not be the sort of person folks run into at church, but asked, "Is church on the weekend where you'd go to find someone to kill your wife?" I felt the State met the legal standard for bindover at a preliminary hearing.

Before I sat down, I took the opportunity to raise the temperature a mite. In Utah, a prosecutor can move to amend charges during or at the end of a prelim. So, without ever forming it as a motion, I went on, "The question . . . I think . . . right now is whether or not we have met the standard that would . . . in fact, because this was so clearly done for gain, bind this over as a capital offense?"

I found the right button. Rich rose loud and angry. "Judge, I will object to that. This is not a capital hearing. I mean . . . "

Ben, who was slotted to do the closing argument, got to his feet and sat Rich down. The judge never addressed my non-motion, but my stunt was universally recognized with the stares and glares I got from the several corners of the courtroom. Ben would, quite justifiably, chew on me in a private moment down the road.

Ben Hamilton also started with Count II and challenged my characterization of the evidence, particularly the cash and dope as a down payment, taking the position that these were seed money for a little family drug trafficking. He argued that there was never a contractual meeting of the minds between David and Jack of sufficient clarity to say a substantial step was taken or actual offer or solicitation from the defendant. Ben maintained what happened was a collection of *What if*s too nebulous to support bindover. I turned to ask Jill to find Jack's testimony in the March 12 transcript; she was on that job before I asked.

The defense addressed the homicide and went to the ME's findings, noting Dr. Grey's testimony that of the several choices available to him after the autopsy, including "unknown," Todd made a professional, reasoned decision to choose accidental. Since Dr. Grey believed Pam died closer to eight thirty than eleven thirty that evening, she may have walked out to the fishpond in the daylight. Jill passed a note saying that she'd check the time of sunset. Hamilton noted Dr. Grey admitted there were scenarios involving accidents consistent with his findings.

Referring to the physical injuries, Hamilton discounted my opinion that if Pam fell on the rock collar she would necessarily receive more injuries. He proffered that Baron was loose, a big, boisterous dog known to jump up on people, and might have struck Pam with sufficient force to propel his owner across the collar and width of the pool. She might have struck her head on the way down on the far side of the pond.

Jill and I simultaneously startled, looked at each other and took notes.

Ben turned to the witnesses' observations of David Mead after his wife's death. He came home, the lights were off and his wife wasn't home. He called around, looked for her, found her facedown in the pond and freaked out, certainly a normal reaction. How would any of us react to the discovery of the death of a loved one? There was testimony the Meads had a loving relationship! Jill squirmed enough to jiggle the table.

Ben noted Officer Jensen's testimony about the blame David Mead heaped upon himself in hysterics for having created the fishpond, the instrument of his wife's death. Would a guilty person draw suspicion to himself? Wouldn't that person be defensive? Wouldn't a schemer forge a coherent story instead of wailing uncontrollably?

There were inconsistent details in Jack's version: this didn't appear to be a robbery gone bad; Pam wasn't shot. There was also the fact that Winnetka Walls had given David Mead many ultimatums. Why was this one different? We'd never watched the Walls/Mead action videos but exchanged small grins.

Ben took some time to sort through the reams of material the defense discovered about Jack Hendrix's past, why he simply shouldn't be believed, and reemphasized the valid point that the death of Pamela Mead had not gone down per David's plan. Why would a killer set up two completely inconsistent plans? Didn't Hendrix have a motive of revenge for David calling the police after the robbery?

He dealt with Stormy, called her testimony confused and her memory selective. Why couldn't she remember specific dates when she claims to remember conversations? Isn't she, perhaps, an angry, spurned lover or a woman angered by David's lack of candor about his marital status? "Obviously there's something going on there."

Ben Hamilton's last point was that, if this were a staged-accident homicide, his client David Earl Mead had to be ever so precise. David, a man with no medical training, would have to strike Pam in the head just enough to incapacitate her, get her to and into the fishpond without leaving signs of a struggle or alerting his neighbors. Although Pam had those pins in her toes, she wasn't medicated, not a small woman and probably able to "do some damage to David" had she fought him. "It just doesn't make sense. We would ask the court to not bind either of these counts over for trial."

Although Ben finished strongly, I was feeling my oats and got up to rebut. As to Ben's contention that I mischaracterized the evidence about Jack striking a deal with David, I read from the transcript: question, answer, question, answer, back through "if I would kill his wife," seven separate references to killing Pam and five mentions of killing the ex-girlfriend.

I rebutted Ben's contention of Pam fighting back with the evidence that she was struck from behind. I thought Ben was wrong about the sequence of Jack and Winnie's meetings with David during Pam's lifetime, Jack's fall into the arms of Morphius and the completion of the fishpond. I reminded the room that, the night of the death and the day of the autopsy, all the investigators were of one voice: this was an accident.

But I couldn't let go of Baron, figuratively. "And let me briefly address, at the risk of dignifying the theory of 'Bruce Lee, the dog.' " With my best, or if you prefer worst, faux karate postures, gestures and accents I continued, "Somehow this dog would rise up, would knock Pamela . . . incidentally the dog would not leave any scratches from its claws or bruises from its paws . . . presumably over the ring of rocks, over the width of the pool . . . so that she would have been spinning through the air . . . and strike only her head on the far side, slip into the water and perish."

I finished up admitting that this was a circumstantial case but one of strong circumstances, emphasizing that Pam died in a manner and time frame her husband suggested to one witness, assured another witness and solicited a third witness that she ought to die and told Her Honor that the State had met its burden as defined by Utah law.

Judge Boyden noted that given the nature of this case she gave both sides all the time we wanted to fully develop our arguments. She spoke of the legal standard in a preliminary hearing to view evidence in a light most favorable to the State, then after a brief review of the evidence and a comment on whether the money and cocaine were for killing or future sales, she found the State met its burden and the case would be bound over for trial. The judge's clerk typed a few entries into her computer, wrote a few words on a slip of paper and handed it to Judge Boyden.

"So Mr. Mead will be bound over on both counts, as charged. The assigned judge in this case would be Judge Frederick. The initial appearance before Judge Frederick on this matter for further scheduling will be May 15, 1998."

Richard P. Mauro quietly asked, "I will be out of town May 15. Can we do it the week after that?"

The clerk, then the judge, offered the twenty-ninth. We all agreed and the clerk entered that date along with David Earl Mead's first formally entered pleas: not guilty. We each withdrew our exhibits, thanked Judge Boyden and the court personnel. The prelim was over at 11:01 and David, his lawyers and a few supporters walked out to the corridor and the press, who were pushing to meet noon deadlines. Jill and I stayed in the courtroom to give the defense its space and talk to the Stokes family.

We had drawn His Honor J. Dennis Frederick, the most no-nonsense judge the Third Judicial District Court had to offer, a man who had no trouble making a decision. Was that good or bad for us? Neither, and both. If we proved our case, he would send David Mead to prison in a heartbeat. If we didn't, he would dismiss it just as quickly. There wouldn't be any of the morning's karate theatrics. No one would be so foolish as to attempt to talk him out of a ruling; this would be a straightforward trial without surprises. With His Honor Frederick, you know what you're going to get and better be prepared to go get it.

I explained to the family that the May 29 hearing would only be held to set dates for motions and other matters of substance I knew would soon flow my way. When were we looking to go to trial? Probably the fall. One other quality of this judge, he doesn't put things off. We exchanged hugs and went to greet reporters. I asked Detective Jill if she was ready to face the summer of the motions and she asked if I was.

19

Minor Motions, Serious Concerns

Fourth Floor, North Corridor, first courtroom on the left, room N41 of the Scott M. Matheson Courthouse is an enormous space, windowless, largely undecorated and slightly wider than it is long. As you walk in, the jury box is on your left and the holding cell door to your right. The bench, with the witness stand toward the jury box and the clerk's station to the right, takes up half of the back wall. The jury door is in the left corner, the judge's entrance all the way to the right. Entering, Judge J. Dennis Frederick needs about four steps before he walks behind the clerk and takes the bench. A tall, lean man, His Honor strides from door to bench with robes flowing behind a determined gait, takes the bench and gets underway without undue ceremony or small talk.

Just past nine o'clock the morning of May 29, everyone was in place. Immediately before the bar, left of the center aisle, the prosecutors' table had a Deputy DA "covering the calendar" with files for most of the thirty or forty or so calendared cases. Some were, like *State v. Mead*, District Court Arraignments and others scheduling conferences, changes of plea, sentencings, orders to show cause, bench warrants or motions not requiring a great amount of time to present or argue. The State's table was the base for prosecutors covering non-routine matters that required personal attention.

The defense table on the right to accommodate incarcerated clients is normally abuzz with attorneys ducking in and out between the court and the holding cell, completing court calendars or awaiting their turn before His Honor. There are only three or four chairs and a narrow bench whose back is the bar, so defense attorneys mill around in hope of being first to capture the podium.

David Earl Mead and a small group of his supporters sat in the gallery on the defense side. Rich was there; Ben had a conflict but gave Rich notes on trials and events already calendared. About four or five items into the proceedings, Rich and I made the standard eye contact to acknowledge we were ready and per custom Rich as the defense attorney moved to the podium. "Your Honor, could the court please call the *Mead* matter?" Judge Frederick gave his clerk Cindy a facial expression of acknowledgment and was handed the file.

"State of Utah versus David E. Mead, 971015212, appearances please."

"Howard Lemcke for the State, Your Honor." I walked up alongside Rich.

"Richard Mauro for the defendant, Your Honor, who is present. Mr. Mead . . ." Rich gestured and Mead came up to the podium as well, "will also be represented by Benjamin Hamilton. Mr. Hamilton has a conflict, but he's given me his calendar."

"Are you retained?"

"No. We're on the conflicts contract from LDA."

"Well, all right. What are we going to do? Do you want a trial date?"

"Yes. We were thinking of early '99."

Judge Frederick peered through the space between his glasses and eyebrows and announced that the trial would come much sooner than that. Rich informed the court that this was a complex case on entirely circumstantial facts and he'd file many motions. I chuckled to myself on the last point and, when Judge Frederick asked, agreed about the complexity. The judge asked how long Mead would take to try. I said probably two weeks, but Rich thought much longer. His Honor consulted with Cindy and his calendar and scheduled the case for ten days commencing September 8, 1998, at 10:00 AM. Jury instructions were due September 8; he would hear all motions on August 28 at 9:00; motions and responses were to be timely made.

I braced myself for motions that didn't come. There were only a few days left in May and those passed without the expected onslaught. June, July and the first week of August passed in eerie quiet on the motion front.

Before June was over, Neal Gunnarson, the elected District Attorney, was a lame duck beaten badly in the Republican primary with over a half a year remaining in his term. Dave Yocom was unopposed as a Democrat and the November race matched two candidates not currently working in the office. Even though the future was undefined, we wouldn't have to face the ongoing tension of daily encounters with in-house candidates whose every expression begged the question of that moment's loyalty. Neal took the statesman's route and ran the shop without employing his last months as a vehicle for revenge. He'd still support the work, make the big decisions, resist settling old grudges and largely stay out of the way.

The defense wouldn't be the only side filing motions. I had a few. I gave notice of experts I might call accompanied by *curriculum vitae,* or CV, the new age term for resumé, and copies of any experts' reports. I also gave notice I intended to offer hearsay, the videotaped deposition of Kevin Harris from the federal civil case.

I intended to call several experts: Dr. Grey; Matt Jenkins; Pennington's investigator John James and Dr. Grey's cohort at the ME's office, Dr. Maureen Frikke. Maureen, a good friend of Jill's, was in on a lot of the discussions and could address Mead's claim of finding his wife floating face down in that dirty old water. This stereotype of old cinema, a convention that allowed an audience to see the character dead without showing his face, gave the actor the opportunity to breathe through a tube and a tank but just isn't realistic. I gathered Todd's and Maureen's CVs from our file and stapled those along with another copy of the autopsy report for submission. I screwed up.

I received somewhat miffed calls from both doctors to the effect that this was Dr. Grey's case and it was proper for me to call only Todd, who was well able to field questions about drowning and floating and did so in the prelim. I stepped on protocol and sensitivity within the profession and had little left to do but apologize.

I listed John James as a potential expert not because of his witness to David Mead's statements but because he was aware of the norms for insurance coverage.

It became clear the defense would file their motions at the last moment, compressing the time I had to respond. Since gamesmanship was in the air, I gave Supervising Special Agent Mary Ellen O'.Toole of the FBI a call. If Dr. Sperry took the stand and were asked about the red flags of staged homicide and denied or challenged those, Supervising Special Agent Mary Ellen O'Toole became a potential rebuttal witness I just had to list. Would she fax me her CV? With all sorts of admonitions about authorizations and higher headquarters, Dr. O'Toole, Ph.D. transmitted a stunningly impressive CV that would seize the attention of any attorney.

David's attorneys filed their first three motions on August 6. I filed mine the next day. The salvo included Notice of Intent to Call Expert Witnesses, Motion to Allow a Pretrial Juror Questionnaire, and Motion for Individual In-Chambers Voir Dire of Jurors.

The defense announced two experts, Dr. Kris Sperry and Dr. Paul France. Dr. Sperry was expected but Dr. France was a surprise. He was noticed up in the federal case as a counter-expert to Dr. Smith of Michigan, who claimed expertise on hypothermia and still-water drowning. Smith was to testify about the unlikelihood of Pam's body floating after only a few hours and the mechanics of accidental and non-accidental falls that could put Pam into the water with her particular wounds. He had sent Anne Sulton a videotape showing his wife falling off of a diving board, again and again, into the family swimming pool. However, a series of difficulties with Smith's credentials were placed before the court and he never testified.

On August 15, the fourth anniversary of Pamela's death passed with quiet notice.

The defense's other motions asked for variation in the norms of jury selection. The custom in Salt Lake is for the judge to ask *voir dire* questions of potential jurors, who are called *venire*. There are stock questions each judge asks and the sides submit proposals for the court's consideration. Follow-up questions can be asked of individuals, under certain circumstances privately in the judge's chambers. Rich and Ben wanted to send a questionnaire to the potential jurors. The *venire* would then fill out the queries and the parties would obtain copies, pore over and analyze the answers. Looking like any good exam, the proposed four-page questionnaire was a combination of true/false, multiple guess, fill-in-the-blank and short essay.

I'm not a big fan of questionnaires; they're a lot of extra work for everyone, including the court personnel. With a panel of fifty *venire*, that's two-hundred pages of handwritten answers to sort and I hadn't forgotten there were two of them, plus some in-office and volunteer helpers, to the one of me. Questionnaires put a lot of personal information about otherwise uninvolved people into some circulation, so there's a tendency for *venire* to muse on questions and what they ought to answer, not just respond. Most were questions the judge would ask anyway and I wanted the collateral information that comes with a vocal response. Some people are more relaxed, more confident, more assertive and/or more intelligent than others and that shows in eye-to-eye examination. The *venire* will, by dress, carriage, attitude and occasionally aroma, further demonstrate how seriously they view this duty of citizenship.

The defense wanted to have the attorneys rather than Judge Frederick conduct *voir dire* one juror at a time in chambers. The judge, clerk, bailiff, court reporter, defendant and all the lawyers isolate each individual juror in a small room and question them. There's salesmanship, attempts at endearment or subtle intimidation; questions are crafted as pre-opening arguments. Questions known to be objectionable can serve to put a thought or issue in the juror's mind. And in-chambers individual *voir dire* takes a long, long time. I sat down to draft my responses to these motions and got hit with round two.

Defendant's Motion to Dismiss, Defendant's Motion in Limine, Defendant's Objection to State's Notice of Intent to Call Expert Witnesses, Defendant's Second Supplemental Request for Discovery, Defendant's Memorandum in Support of Motion in Limine, Defendant's Motion in Limine to Exclude Expert Testimony of Todd Gray, Memorandum in Support of Defendant's Motion to Exclude Expert Testimony of Todd Gray and, finally for now, Motion to Compel

Discovery or Alternatively Motion to Prevent Witness from Testifying came in rapid succession.

At one point the defense put forth the proposition that this was a high profile case that "received extensive press coverage," but I reminded the court the death of Pamela Camille Stokes Mead had been little but a curiosity four years ago. The defense did not reference any specific coverage and therefore any coverage that was inaccurate or unfair. I felt pretty good about the first batch of motions, but the second wave was worrisome.

The Motion to Dismiss complained that David Mead had been charged with both criminal homicide, murder and solicitation to commit criminal homicide. In Utah a prosecutor can't charge both an underlying crime and the inchoate form of that crime. Attempt, conspiracy and solicitation are "inchoate" offenses, one degree less serious than a completed crime. Normally, a prosecutor must elect to charge either the underlying or the inchoate offense, but this was not a normal case. David Earl Mead was charged with first trying to hire Jack Hendrix to kill Pam and then, after Jack screwed up Plan A, forging Plan B and killing his wife by other means. A and B were significantly separated in time, place, method and instrument and it was the State's contention that David tried, failed, waited, changed weapons, went forward and succeeded.

The Motion in Limine, the big one that many jurisdictions call a Motion to Suppress, is heard before trial to limit what may be presented as evidence. *In limine* means at the threshold or limit. Rich wanted to keep it all out—that's his job—and started with a narrative "Background" of his version of the relevant facts, including Wally Bugden's motion to place a protective order against Roger Tinsley, with no mention that Judge Benson denied the motion.

Stormy's statements, James Hendrix's statements, David Mead's alleged bad acts, David Mead's financial situation, statements made by Pam Mead and David Mead's post-death conduct were major headings of evidence in the State's hands whose introduction would offend the judicial conscience. The four-page motion accompanying a fifteen-page memorandum in support, plus attached exhibits, was a strange and atypical memo. A number of mistakes of fact and law weren't self-serving, just mistakes: it was Stormy who overheard the phone call or Mary Stokes on TV holding the photo of Pam and David. My opponents were feeling the time constraints generated by the August 28 hearing, now less than two weeks away, the time I had to answer these.

After setting out the relevant portions of the Utah Rules of Evidence, including old friends 403 and 404(b), the defense went into a contention that David's statements to Stormy, before and after Pam's death, and to Jack were irrelevant. David's statements to Stormy before Pam's death were too remote in time to the actual killing and didn't reflect his state of mind on August 15, 1994. The statements David made to Jack were also "at least a month or more before" the drowning. Connecting with the Motion to Dismiss, "Hendrix's statements are also irrelevant because the State is barred by statute with charging both Murder and the inchoate offense of Solicitation." David's statements to Stormy in her office after the death did not go to his state of mind at the time of the accident; their very nature would tend to hold David Earl Mead up to scorn, hate and ridicule with no evidentiary value on the issues of this case.

Obviously, the State disagreed.

Finally, the Motion in Limine addressed "David's Post-Death Conduct." Not David Mead, not Mr. Mead, just the familiar and hopefully comfortable David. The memo argued that the jurors should not be allowed to hear of David's demeanor after Pam's death, the destruction of the fishpond or any observations, opinions and conclusions about Mead's demeanor, sincerity or lack thereof. These were irrelevant to David's intent on August 15 and the prejudicial effect would clearly outweigh any probative value.

Again, the State disagreed.

Next came Richard Mauro's Initial Request for Discovery, which was a standard "boilerplate" motion submitted with his initial appearance the previous August, and we responded, per custom, with copies of all reports in our possession.

Far and away the most problematic move was the defense Motion in Limine to Exclude Expert Testimony of Todd

Grey, a clever and original tactic. Dr. Grey's second and third opinions on manner of death were not based upon the science of autopsy but on the unscientific and untested words of Winnetka Walls and Jack Hendrix. Without a proper foundation in science, the opinion of a scientist as expert was inadmissible. Were Todd to testify his amendments were based even in part on Winnie and Jack it would improperly "bolster" their testimony. Jurors would feel that if an MD relied on their statements, those two must be telling the truth, an invasion of the jury's duty to judge the credibility of witnesses. This wouldn't keep Dr. Todd Grey off the stand, but it would require him to give his expert opinion that the manner of death was accidental and seemingly agree with the defense.

Nevertheless, I felt in pretty good shape to meet the Mead motions in law and logic.

When Judge Frederick asked the date we'd like our trial, I said as soon as practical. Team Mead suggested spring or summer 1999. David would waive his right to a speedy trial. His Honor suggested October 20; he could clear his calendar for two weeks. I quickly agreed while Rich and Ben objected to not having enough time to thoroughly prepare. J. Dennis Frederick perused the docketing statement, noted that the pair had been on board for more than a year and conducted a bulky preliminary hearing. This was an important case with witnesses and family victims whose needs also deserved consideration. Cindy was keying those days into the judicial computer before the last echo of protest left the air.

Michelle had already sent out subpoenas, but we'd been in phone contact with almost all the witnesses, made them aware continuances were common and something they'd need to prepare for. I called the Stokeses myself; I owed them that. They weren't happy, but understanding and glad Judge Frederick didn't favor long or repeated continuances, but their travel arrangements were locked in as reservations. Our office has the ability to pick up travel for subpoenaed witnesses but no funding for victim families. We cobbled together a few connections including Pam's airline crew and Pastor Davis's continuing good offices. Providers universally found sympathy for the Stokeses' plight and accommodated them.

Jill, Meesh and I sat down to redo the subpoena list to place witnesses into two sessions a day for those two weeks, a guesswork process: we needed to notify each witness to be prepared to move backward or forward as the flow of the trial dictated. We had to phone each of them again, but that had some benefits. Michelle would be the pivotal contact anyone could get hold of and held the numbers for each participant. Mary from DA Administration would handle travel arrangements for out-of-towners. Neal's budget people reminded us repeatedly how expensive last minute changes were.

Jill needed twenty subpoenas, one for each morning or afternoon and I wanted another ten to help out the week before. After the expected reaction from Chief Ortega and cooler heads acting as intermediaries, I got half of those.

Within the week we returned to N41 and argued about juror questionnaires and formats for conducting *voir dire*. The oral arguments followed the logic set forth in the written briefs. Rich bore the defense arguments and was brief, reasoning that questionnaires would serve to identify prejudices and save everyone a lot of courtroom time, though he admitted he could cite no case requiring questionnaires.

I emphasized the added work questionnaires would mean for the court clerks. It wouldn't appear in the transcript but would be noticed by a seasoned jurist. I told His Honor that nothing was brought forward by the defense to demonstrate such extraordinary publicity to merit a make-work project of questionnaires.

Before Rich could insert an answer, Judge Frederick, in his typical fashion, forehead thrust forward, right fingers extended and waving, with phrases separated by short pauses, dismissed the lawyers and gave his ruling. "All right, Mr. Lemcke, thank you. I have, on past occasions, used questionnaires, but in capital cases only. Certainly, there may be, and probably is, merit to the use of questionnaires, in certain circumstances, but I am not persuaded, in this case, it is required." Nor was the judge persuaded that the individual *voir dire* was appropriate. The need might arise and, if so, would be met. The judge would entertain our questions, but he would ask them. The motions were denied and the State would prepare the order. The downside to winning a motion is that the winner needs to draft an order memorializing the court's findings, run the order back and forth between the parties and get it signed. The first oral arguments now concluded, I went back to the word processor.

In a memo entitled State's Response to Defendant's First and Second Motions for Supplemental Discovery and Motion to Compel Discovery or Alternatively to Prevent Witness from Testifying, a title easier typed than spoken, I sought to counter the entire collection. I'm a responder and tend to give back what I perceive people give me and the tenor of the defense's motion brought out sarcasm and a mean streak in my response. Under the defense theory, if I didn't provide what I didn't have, or what I wasn't even entitled to have, like Jack's co-defendant's PSR, I should be punished by having my witness excluded. I said that was just unfair and chided the defense for trying to cobble their lack of success in finding evidence into my discovery violation and sarcastically quoted portions of their motion, "The non-specifics of what 'may be contained in Mr. Hendrix's prison file' is a pond selected for a fishing expedition in hopes that it is stocked with material known not to be in possession of the District Attorney."

The Motion in Limine provided an opportunity to let the court know that there's plenty of damning stuff I knew wasn't admissible and not trying to admit, as counter to the 403/404(b) attack on my evidence being nothing but a brush with which to paint David Mead as someone so horrible he must be guilty. I wanted to be seen as the reasonable party, culling down the evidence to what was relevant while my party opponents just tried to exclude everything.

"The defendant attempts to argue that none of his conduct after his wife's death is admissible because it doesn't go to his intent at the moment of that death. Were David Mead to acknowledge that he in fact killed his wife, there might be some merit to his claim that his state of mind at the moment of the killing is the only relevant issue. The State invites the defendant to do just that."

Team Mead's objection to the State's notice to call expert witnesses was full of anger, umbrage and irony, complaining that the names, CVs and proposed testimony of our experts were turned in at the last possible minute. They were doing the same thing but griped about the "bad faith" of the prosecutor not bringing these forward long before the deadline. After all, "Mr. Lemcke has been familiar with the facts of this case for years." Interestingly, booting the trial into October laid moot these objections.

I elected not to prepare a written response to the objection on experts and just deal with it during oral argument. The tenor of the objection meant that one of my goals was met: we got under their skin. Agent O'Toole would only be available for very narrow rebuttal, Dr. Frikke's portion was going to be covered by Todd Grey, they knew about John James's interview with David and the substance of our attack on the size of the policies. It'd be better to handle it in person and come off as the calmer, more reasonable party to this lawsuit.

The attack on Dr. Grey's testimony was clever, but it seemed an odd notion that the defense would want to keep the three opinions out, when the normal tack would be to sell their expert as a man of national reputation who held firm, while ours couldn't make up his mind.

My response, even in its heading, took every opportunity to emphasize that the defense motion consistently misspelled Todd's name and started by going over the evidence Todd reviewed beyond Jack and Winnie's statements, noting both Winnie and Jack would testify and the jury would make their own assessment of credibility. I concluded, "The anger in the defendant's motion is no substitute for on-point case law. Nor are his claims of inadmissibility substitutes for cross-examination." The nastiness creeping into my submissions did not go unnoticed. In a response to my response, Todd's name was spelled correctly; mine wasn't. I let it go.

Jill and I were working out witnesses, exhibits and strategies. Even with Judge Frederick denying the defense motions on the questionnaires and individual *voir dire*, it would take at least a full day to pick our jury, maybe more. We'd need to start bringing in our witnesses the morning of the second day. Meesh wondered if we wanted to call them in that first day, so we could introduce them to the jury, a point well taken. During jury selection the lawyers introduce themselves, their client and their witnesses to the *venire*. If any of the potential jurors are familiar with them, they can announce it and allow the lawyers to challenge "for cause" or choose preemptory challenges more wisely. It also makes jury selection the "last minute" to announce witnesses. Putting on a surprise witness is wonderful drama on TV, but in a courtroom it sometimes backfires: the opponent objects and the judge excludes the witness. We generated first day subpoenas for all our witnesses except out-of-staters and experts.

Our next chore was to put together the exhibits. We had a few pictures taken the night of Pam's death and the autopsy photos, and chose a few to blow up to poster size. For the ME's testimony we had no need to show more than the head wound and the abrasions and could work from a diagram. Going beyond that wouldn't shed more light for the jury but would be painful to the family and give credence to Rich's contention that the only case I had was to inflame the jury.

We had the exemplar brick as our only piece of physical evidence. We thought about a model of the fishpond scaled for Ken and Barbie dolls; it might be useful for showing how bizarre some of Dr. France's scenarios and Ben's contention that Pam may have fallen victim to the martial arts mutt were. After some reflection, we put that idea aside, as it would be a difficult exhibit to handle.

There was a question of whether we should prepare written transcripts of the redacted Kevin Harris deposition so jurors could follow along, but we came to the conclusion that it was pretty clear, Kevin's personality was very compelling and we didn't want to distract jurors from watching.

Then the Bureau called: the profilers reached some theories and had some suggestions for how to handle Mr. Mead. David Earl Mead thought of, and dealt with, women as a consumer product, believing they were there for his convenience and to serve him, not a sexist notion as much as an egotistical one. Women weren't there to serve men, just to serve David Earl Mead.

Were David to take the stand, and I couldn't imagine he wouldn't, we needed to create a show where David saw young, pretty women—some of the women he believed ought to be at his beck and call—serving me, fetching things, handing me things, being courteous and deferential, serving me, not David. I would play the lawyer, taking complete control of the courtroom, allowing David none. I have a healthy ego, so I was in: Jill at the table, Mary Stokes in the courtroom and Meesh would be available. Stormy and Winnie could only be present during their testimony. I thought I could bring Stormy in on this, not Winnie, but there was His Honor, J. Dennis Frederick who owned N41. Any such theatrics would have to be limited to what this savvy, nononsense jurist would tolerate. I had absolutely no doubt that he'd spot gamesmanship in a heartbeat with no hesitation to call me on it. I might get some latitude, but not much.

20

Legal Haggling

The day originally set for trial found the parties gathered to argue the last bevy of motions. Rich started with his Motion to Dismiss by quoting directly from the statute, "No person shall be convicted of an inchoate and principal offense, or of both an attempt to commit and a conspiracy to commit the same offense." He made the point that to sustain a conspiracy charge the evidence must show that the solicitation "was made under circumstances strongly corroborative of the actor's intent that the offense be committed" and selected excerpts from Jack Hendrix's testimony hinting that the cash and the cocaine were an investment in dope-dealing, not a down payment on death.

I countered with an analogy that if David had tried and failed in July to kill Pam with a deer rifle but succeeded in killing her in August with a handgun, he wouldn't be entitled to a free pass for an earlier failed attempt unique in time, place and method. I read excerpts from the prelim where David led Jack to the act and the eight grams wrapped in the C-note.

Rich responded that if it were two separate crimes Mead was entitled to two separate trials, severing the counts. It had to be fish or fowl, one criminal episode, entitling dismissal of a count, or two, requiring severance. With a wave of his fingers, His Honor moved the proceedings along without hint of a finding. "All right. Now let's deal with your next motion, Mr. Mauro."

We moved to the opinions in the manner of death given by the Chief Medical Examiner for the State of Utah, Dr. Todd Grey. Rich walked through an edited history of the case. His argument abandoned any attack on the scientific underpinnings and moved entirely into complaints about bolstering witnesses.

I referred the court to all the input the ME actually received during the time he deliberated and noted the two experts the defense announced would base their opinions on input beyond the autopsy. Dr. Grey's opinions needed to be examined for weight, not admissibility.

This time waving the whole hand, "All right. Thank you. Your next motion, Mr. Mauro."

"Judge, I think the next motion would have to do with the Motion in Limine and the supporting memorandum."

"Incident to the testimony of Hendrix and Stormy?"

"Hendrix, Stormy—"

"And the bad acts?"

"Bad acts, other kinds of things."

"Let's deal with the Motion in Limine incident to the claim for exclusion of the testimony of Hendrix and Stormy, unless we've already touched upon that."

Stormy scared them. Rich found sarcasm as he spoke about how seeing Mrs. Stokes on TV "prompted" Stormy to come forward. "The argument can be made that maybe Stormy's following the news. She may be talking to people. She may be getting advice." The man whose client worked so hard to hide Stormy had a hard time believing I hadn't. Rich argued that Stormy's dealings with David before Pam's death were too remote in time, too inexact in date and much too inflammatory to be admissible.

Any dealings between Stormy and David after Pam's death should be excluded as evidence as too remote in time, not demonstrative of Mead's state of mind at the moment of Pam's death, an obvious reaction to the Stokeses' and "Action Jackson's" conduct and comportment during the civil case, when Wally Bugden filed for a restraining order. Rich characterized the confrontation in Stormy's office as David telling Stormy he just didn't remember their overheard phone conversation "happening where I threatened to kill my wife." He only sought out Stormy to protect the fair maiden from the onslaught of an evil PI. Even if David told Stormy he didn't want her to testify, it was highly prejudicial and shouldn't come in.

His Honor broke in, showing some irritation at the length of the arguments. Asking if the balance of remaining argument was about bad acts, but not waiting for an answer, he asked me, "Is it your intent, Mr. Lemcke, to concede on any of these points? Or are you proposing to offer evidence on each of them? Those that you are wishing, or intending, to concede, let's hear from them now so we can, maybe, get back to the issues."

I told the judge that my response memo contained a list of David's bad acts that I had no intention to introduce, then mentioned a few, conceding their inadmissibility. Judge Frederick turned to Rich, waved the signature finger and asked him to address only the points he felt were contested.

Mauro briefly touched on Jack Hendrix then moved to Matt Jenkins. "The State has experts from some state agency somewhere who've reviewed, as near as I can tell, evidence or documents from the airlines." Rich emphasized that the records Matt examined were incomplete and poorly kept, said Matt hadn't reviewed Mead's tax filings but didn't mention that were no tax filings until some police officer notified the taxman. How could anyone draw any conclusions, except highly prejudicial conclusions, from such a wanting database?

Richard Mauro did not want David's conduct following

Pam's death in evidence, that pond was filled in by family
and friends to protect neighborhood children. The Stokes
family isn't qualified to draw valid conclusions from the widower's alternating hysterics and calm and absence of non-
induced tears. "I'm presuming that they want to do that with
this FBI expert that we don't know anything about." He'd
seen SSA O'Toole's CV and it had the desired effect. Given
that it included participation in investigating many high-
profile crimes, and at least one of the seminars Dr. O'Toole
taught was at Harvard, that's understandable.

After touching on Rules 403 and 404(b) and whether
404(b) was effectively amended by a recent court opinion,
Rich submitted the matters to Judge Frederick. As I started to
speak, the judge cut in and asked me to address the legal
issue of the amendment of 404(b). I felt that it was more a
clarification than a sustentative change to the rule. When His
Honor asked me, "So your position is that it adds nothing
new to the previously existing balance of tests that was
engaged for admissibility of 404(b) evidence?" Rich
answered, "It clarifies how it ought to come in." His nervous
response made my point.

I blended the expected testimonies of Jack and Stormy
and how they interlocked, the details of the insurance policy
and the condition of Valley Ground Service as His Honor
stared without changing expression.

As I moved into Matt Jenkins's analysis, Judge Frederick
cut in, "What is the conclusion that you are proposing that
your expert might testify to?"

I said we were going to put on evidence of VGS's and
Mead's deteriorating financial straits that combined with
David's lifestyle and the ownership of VGS could form
motive for murder. The judge asked if we were going to
allege money laundering, collusion or theft and wanted to
know where the State "was coming from."

I told His Honor we wouldn't attempt to put on evidence
that David might have an interest in other "substances" easily taken on and off airliners and weren't going to delve into
his blood family's gambling problems beyond what they
might contribute to his overall financial condition. We would
say David talked about killing Pam in a strip club and paid

with cocaine, because those were the facts. We weren't out to smear him with collateral evidence, respected 403 and 404(b), but resisted an absolute prohibition in case the defense tried to put David's good character at issue knowing we couldn't rebut.

The judge signaled that he'd heard enough. He would take all motions "under advisement" until he found and read my responses. Then he'd let us know what he decided when he decided.

Rich came back in, "Three quick points," and an irritated hand waved resigned agreement. Rich had "heard rumors" that I was generating evidence about Pam's life insurance coverage while still employed by Continental. I hadn't very actively, but now reminded, I would.

Rich tried to reopen the discussion. His Honor turned him down, so he returned to discovery. Still unsuccessful in obtaining Jill's letter to the board and Jack's co-defendant's PSR from the Department of Corrections, Mauro used this as one more occasion to rip on Jack Hendrix, terrible human being.

"You're not suggesting that Mr. Lemcke has control of the records there?"

"No!"

His Honor's voice rose throughout the next question, "You are suggesting to me that the compulsion that's available in terms of ordering discovery in this case will prompt Mr. Lemcke to acquire the documentation?"

"No!" Mauro wanted a court order, needed an Order to Compel sent my way for procedural reasons. Judge Frederick asked if Rich consulted the records people at Corrections. "Other than a couple of telephone conversations" he hadn't, but they always take the position they won't release inmate information without a court order. Rich admitted those weren't available to me, so His Honor suggested, "In that regard, then, it may well be more productive, from your perspective, to set about subpoenaing those records from the Department of Corrections." Rich could have an expedited hearing if they fought it.

His next, and last, request fell on less barren soil. Rich still didn't have written reports from several of my expert witnesses, Maureen Frikke, Mary Ellen O'Toole, John James and Matt Jenkins. The judge asked me why.

I started with Matt, who'd testified at prelim and wasn't mentioned in their Motion of Objection. His conclusions were all, and there was a huge amount of "all," contained on the computer disc we'd already provided. I conceded neither Maureen nor John would be testifying, SSA O'Toole wouldn't prepare a report because she'd only testify, if called, about "red flags" and wouldn't draw a conclusion if this case were a staged homicide.

His Honor saw through my act in a heartbeat and let me know in no uncertain terms that a written report from a proposed expert witness was a reasonable request. Sorry, Matt! If Rich had any more issues, he was to set up a telephone conference.

The next morning Michelle brought in faxes from the next round of motions. The Third Supplemental Motion for Discovery headed this sequence, a reasonable request for detail on some of our evidence, and wouldn't be a problem. Two days later we got a Minute Entry from Judge Frederick announcing that he would continue to hold all the matters under advisement and rule on them as they arose during the trial, a routine methodology that allows a judge to hear and consider evidence in the context of the case, see the whole cloth and rule on specifics. I was fine with that, even though I got to prepare the orders the "best I could given the state of the minute entry." The defense wasn't fine with that.

My weekend passed with quiet but intense trial preparation and drafting orders. The morning of Wednesday, September 30, two weeks and six days before trial, started with a bang as a string of motions were filed with both Judge Frederick and the Utah State Supreme Court. In the law there is a procedure known as an interlocutory appeal that occurs when an attorney, dissatisfied with a trial court's decision on an issue of law prior to or during trial, petitions an appellate court to review and rule before the trial ends. If an appellate court takes an "interloc," it shuts down the trial in the court "below." When a trial is shut down in this manner it's a safe bet the party opponent, the witnesses, the jurors and the judge are not happy people. This among other good reasons is why interlocs are seldom requested and rarely granted.

His Honor Frederick received a Motion to Stay Trial Pending the Filing of a Petition for an Interlocutory Appeal while the Supremes caught Petition for Interlocutory Appeal, Petition for Extraordinary Relief Pursuant to Utah Rule of Civil Procedure 65B (d) and Motion to Stay Trial Pending Determination of Petition for Interlocutory Appeal and Petition for Extraordinary Relief accompanied by the required Statements of the Facts and Arguments. Not surprisingly the "facts" were progressively more edited: Winnie's notarized letter recanting her first statement was brought up, not the fact it followed Dr. Grey's amended findings by some months; Roger Tinsley evolved from the target of an unsuccessful petition to the "subject of a protective order in the federal civil suit." The defense memoranda in support of each motion were included; my memoranda in response weren't. Although I'd sent the defense each of my proposed findings and orders for "approval as to form," none were ever returned to me or the judge or provided to the Supremes.

I called Jill and Anne who each growled at the tactic. I dreaded passing along the news to Colorado Springs; when I caught Mrs. Stokes at home she was justifiably upset. I did my best to let her know that this ploy was very unlikely to succeed, particularly with this judge. The Supreme Court probably wouldn't buy in either, but were a wild card with the ability to order the case halted. I'd let her know how this was progressing and get them what help I could if this came to pass.

I typed up a terse, sarcastic and nasty reply. Fortunately, I got a call from Tom Brunker, an Assistant Utah Attorney General in the Appeals Division, before it was finished. The AG handles all matters before the appellate courts in a very specialized practice, which, because appellate court decisions affect future cases in the entire state, appropriately belongs in their statewide office. Tom was going to handle the interloc and wanted to see anything I had before it went up the hill, a good thing because Tom had a much calmer vantage point than I.

I finished up my "Answer" as Tom counseled appellate responses are styled, toned it down and faxed it to him. After it went back and forth a few times, I printed out and signed a clean copy for the AG's runner to hand carry along with the AG's submissions to the Supreme Court and made sure my responses to the defense motions and the still unapproved-as-to-form findings and orders were included. Tom would put together his brief and ask for expedited hearings.

Judge Frederick knows expedited; if the defense didn't want to phone conference on details we would be standing on his carpet in short order. Friday, October 2, 1998, two weeks, three weekends and one day before trial, Rich and I stood before an irritated jurist who wondered why the defendant wasn't there. Rich replied the hearing came up so fast he didn't have the opportunity to get hold of David.

"You're sure Mr. Mead . . . Mr. Mead certainly wouldn't think we were trying to do something to his detriment, if he's not here. Would he?"

Rich assured the court he was certain his client would waive the right to be present and was allowed to make his argument for bumping the trial. Rich felt that the rulings weren't adequate to guide his pre-trial preparation: he should have won all of those contests outright and knew the Supremes would agree.

"All right, Mr. Mauro. Mr. Lemcke, do you wish to respond?"

"Your Honor, the State would adamantly oppose a stay in this trial. We don't believe that the motions, when first brought, were sound. We don't believe they're sound now. We don't believe that the motions are proper for interlocutory appeal. We just—"

Cutting me off, "I . . . I'm going to deny the motion to stay, counsel. The Supreme Court may, of course, decide to reverse me and that's fine . . . and, Mr. Mauro, obviously if the Supremes disagree with me, you can be sure and let us all know." The sarcasm wasn't disguised.

"I will." Rich asked to raise a few more issues, including SSA O'Toole's not yet submitted report and was told these weren't calendared and wouldn't be considered.

Seeing an opening, I told His Honor that I hadn't timely

provided that within the thirty-day requirement, so I wouldn't be able to call this witness, unless of course Rich was successful in bumping the trial and giving me fresh time to get the report. I got the hoped-for wince from Rich and a sly smile from the bench.

Rich mentioned his continuing troubles getting compliance from the Department of Corrections. I repeated, "I'm not standing between the defense and the evidence." Interrupting, the judge reminded us of his offer of a conference call. We walked out of a tense hearing that took a total of twelve minutes. My call to Sinie took longer.

Tom got our paperwork to the Utah Supreme Court on the ninth with eleven days to go, including the Columbus Day holiday and my wife's and my twenty-fourth anniversary.

The office recognized the escalating situation. My supervisors and colleagues did all they could to get day-to-day assignments and routine matters off my plate. The Salt Lake City Police Department conceded the series of subpoenas for now Patrol Officer Candland to help during the last week of trial prep. Michelle declared, "I'm going to protect my Howie." She did and did so well. The victim/witness counselors and travel coordinators stepped into high gear. So did Ben Hamilton.

Ben and I agreed some time back to cooperate on redacting the videotape of Kevin Harris's deposition and each had copies of the tape and a court reporter's transcript made from the depo. The transcript was very helpful, because every word is on a numbered page and line allowing us to communicate with precision and quickly locate words in question. Starting in August, Ben would send me listings of portions of the tape he believed to be objectionable. I'd respond either agreeing, disagreeing or asking why. We'd been back and forth with a pretty even flow. I anticipated tying it up, with a redacted video in Ben's and my hands in short order. Ben sent a letter to ask if I would be willing to draft a memorandum about the content of the Harris deposition and the context of how I hoped to employ it in the State's case. I replied, "With only two business days until we meet our jurors, I would not be willing to do that." My reply accompanied the videotape redacted to the agreed-upon content.

A high point of the last week was the graphics and color of Matt Jenkins's "Light and Magic Show." Jill and I went over to the State Division of Securities, sat in a conference room with a bunch from Matt's shop and previewed his PowerPoint presentation of the sad financial states of David Earl Mead and Valley Ground Service the summer of Pam's death. Matt had his laptop computer hooked up to a projector and a printer, so whatever was on his screen was projected, could be printed as hardcopy, marked and moved. He has a good sense of graphics and color and could find and display almost any variation on the data. What was the outflow in February? Click, click, that's it. The inflow from only the airlines in December '93? Got it! Anything else, counselor? A bodacious way to present the story of David's financial spiral.

I told Matt, "I'll need you on the third or fourth day of trial." I left happy, almost confident.

21

Plan of Revenge

I called Stormy and we talked for a bit. It was likely the defense would try to trip her up on minutiae or detail from her earlier testimony. She asked if I had transcripts and told me where she was working and living; I agreed to bring them by.

When I asked Michelle about Jack Hendrix, Jill told us that Jack had been granted parole; he and his girlfriend were married and available for trial. But Michelle had been unable to get hold of Winnie and was told by her mom that Winnie had left town and wanted nothing to do with the case. There had been tension and, although Michelle had done well as our go-between, it was on my shoulders now. Without Winnie, we'd be in trouble.

I got hold of Mrs. Walls, asked to talk and mentioned the

fact that her daughter was one of David Mead's victims, too. Mrs. Walls knew David Earl Mead, who was arrogant enough to come to her home with her daughter for Sunday dinner and told the Wallses that he would "solve the problem." He actually said he would "murder" Pam, laughed as if it were a joke and toyed with Winnie's parents as one more device to control Winnie. When Mr. Walls told David he'd seen Pam on crutches with bandaged feet, David announced he ran over Pam's feet with his car, just to teach her a lesson. Even though David employed all his fabled charm, Mrs. Walls's maternal instincts left her very ill at ease. But, who more than our own children reacts with such disdain to our loving concern for their well-being when we're just trying to interfere in their happiness? Two parents commiserated at length.

I was able to assure Mrs. Walls that I hoped I wasn't simply one more person who only saw her daughter as someone to be used and discarded for my own ends. I wanted to convict David for what he did to another pretty young woman who trusted his intentions. He should pay for that and be stopped from further victimizing Winnetka or anyone else. She gave me a phone number in a neighboring state.

I got an answering machine that confirmed what Mrs. Walls told me about her daughter's new work schedule. That night after dinner I called from home. Winnetka Walls picked up on the second ring and almost hung up when she learned who it was. Taking a cue from her mother's insights, I chose not to push but to apologize, not to threaten but to listen, not to plead but to understand. Winnie needed to vent, deserved to vent, had a lot to vent about and she did. Ms. Walls recognized, as did her mother, that a whole string of people lost track of the humanity of Winnetka Walls. That string, which ran from David Mead to Howard Lemcke, saw Winnetka Walls, human being, child of God and our sister, as nothing more than an object to be used for our own needs. Those needs met, each moved on.

"Do you remember the prelim? Did you see the coverage? I was the 'kept woman'; Stormy was the hero. She got a blue dot on her face. She was protected. They showed my face. They showed my mother's face! Do you know what it's like to have your neighbors walk by your house and stare?" She was absolutely correct. There was nothing I could argue. Even given the circumstances surrounding Stormy's dramatic discovery and the history of Ms. Walls's continual battle with the parties, there was nothing I wanted to argue. It was a fair question.

She'd been sued, accused, threatened, lied to and ignored. The man who said he loved her set lawyers upon her to call her every name in the book and say she wasn't worthy of belief. And he showed up in court with another woman! And it hurt; God, it hurt. All I could do was listen. If I were sitting across from her, I could nod or offer the support of a gentle hand, but I couldn't even do that little over the wires.

She asked me if the conditions of David's pretrial release allowed him to travel out of the State of Utah. I didn't believe they did but wasn't completely certain. Why do you ask? Because David came to visit Winnie last week. You don't say? He came to ask her to marry him, a fine device to make his bride unavailable as a witness under spousal privilege. Wasn't that what she'd been dreaming about for years? How did she respond?

When Winnetka told me she turned him down cold, I had to ask why. First of all, he didn't bring a ring. Oh, he bent down on one knee all right, but he didn't bring a ring. He also didn't care one bit that she was with child, and not David's. That made no difference at all; they should get married right away, as soon as possible. Why not? Aren't we young and in love? But even David's best efforts were transparent.

Out of curiosity I asked if David had anything to say about the case. Oh, he knows the prosecution doesn't stand a chance; he'll have those jurors eating out of his hand. There'll be women jurors and he'll own them. Then he'll sue everyone, kill some of you, and we can live happily ever after, move to Mexico or Hawaii and open a dive shop. David told Ms. Walls he was buying a condo in Palm Springs in her name so it would be more difficult for the Stokes family to find. VGS was gone, so why not?

Kill some of us? Allegedly David had a list of people and methods and intended to get away with those, too.

The steam out of her for the moment, we fell into conversation. We'd been on the line for about two hours and I'd never popped my question because we had matters of import to discuss, like childbirth, child raising and the immense support needed for both. In the end it was Winnetka Walls who brought the subject up. She'd come to Salt Lake the weekend before the trial and be at her folks' house; I could reach her there. She didn't know if she'd come to court, wouldn't know till that day, till that moment. I offered to try to get her airline tickets, but she turned me down. If she came, it wouldn't be because we bought her testimony: it would entirely be Winnetka Walls, capable and independent human being. I said that flying her in wasn't buying her testimony and promised to call. We said good night and hung up. I lay there, spent from sharing real pain, thinking less of myself for failing to recognize someone else's humanity. I found tears for each of us. If Winnetka Walls took the stand, I wouldn't try to hurt her, but I would do my job, even if it did.

At least one other witness was a problem, David's brother. It wasn't kind but I needed him for certain detail within the case. When he resisted the subpoena, I turned to "personal service." A subpoena is an order, not a request, from a court, with serious consequences for not showing up. I got hold of a DA investigator, explained the situation and set him on task. After a pointed telephone call, David's brother saw the advantage of not being served in his workplace by uniformed cadres and agreed to accept his subpoena, if we would please slip it under his door at home.

I got a call from Ben Hamilton asking me what I wanted of David's brother, hinting that he was part of Team Mead and asked Ben to intervene. David's brother was on my list of potential witnesses and I'd deal with him directly. Ben recognized this and the conversation ended amicably. I'd wait till he was on the stand to deal directly with the brother.

The motion practice wasn't quite over. On Friday the ninth, Rich filed a Motion to Sever—hold a separate trial for each count—that Judge Frederick set for argument on Friday the sixteenth. Telegraphed during the Motion to Dismiss, it was expected, but we were getting real close to trial. On Wednesday the fourteenth, everyone got a letter from the Supreme Court saying they'd received the interlocutory appeal and assigned it.

• • •

David Mead made it to this hearing. Rich argued that the court, by not dismissing either the murder or the solicitation, was required to sever them, to say it was either one crime or two. He argued this case met the standard and went into a series of accusations about what the State was trying to do or to say.

As the spokesman for the State's position, I argued that David Mead made two distinct attempts at the same crime, the first unsuccessful, the second tragically not. Rich asked to briefly reply, His Honor emphasized "briefly" in his permission and Rich started to reargue his Motion to Dismiss. His Honor cut Rich off and reaffirmed he'd give that decision during trial.

Rich asked if matters of law during the trial would be heard outside of the presence of the jurors. The judge replied, "When appropriate they will be." Mauro didn't recognize the ruling went his way and lashed out, "The rules require it." It was going to be a tense weekend on both sides of the aisle.

Saturday morning I took the transcript and videotape over to Stormy's house. She was there with her two very energetic kids and their pet pot-bellied pig. Cute little fella, but as we stood in the yard talking, the porker found he had a taste for sneakers, blue jean cuffs and ankles, mine. Even though he was not being aggressive, just feeding, it hurt. Not wanting to make suggestions in front of the kids about this pet's potential for truck stop breakfasts, I did a hopping dance of avoidance while Stormy's kids laughed and laughed.

Monday was high-speed confusion. I finished the final draft of my proposed juror *voir dire* and a rough draft of the end of trial jury instructions and made my final best guesses about when each witness would be needed. We had over seventy potential jurors coming in. It would take at least the first full day to choose the final group.

22

T Day

My wife wished me well and sent me off with a kiss. Each of the kids gave me a hug when I dropped them off at school. I dressed in the first of my three good-enough-for-trial suits. I was off to court.

When a big case gets underway, the people in our office give encouragement, back pats, winks, smiles and nods. Jill and Michelle beat me to the office, and I was there early. Soon the Stokeses and Pastor Davis were ushered from the front desk to the victim counselors' area. I took quick inventory of our load of exhibits, boxes of binders full of police reports, transcripts, financial records and other writings, then went to brief the victim's family.

We'd talked at some length about the procedures and time frames we were looking at, but it never hurts to make sure that there are no remaining unasked and unanswered questions. Unfortunately, the big one, will we win, could only be answered with speculation. Everyone was nervous, showed and admitted it. Badly trying to patch together conversation to ease the tension, we picked up our gear and walked to the courthouse.

The Office of Clerk of the Court called in the panel of potential jurors from whom would be chosen ten citizens. Since this wasn't a capital case requiring the popular cultural standard of twelve, eight citizens would meet to decide the matter and two others would be alternates. The alternates don't know they're alternates, seated in case one of the first eight is unable to carry on and hear the entire case, to be excused when deliberations begin.

The defense staked claim to the table next to the jury box, to the left as you faced the judge, directly in front of the witness stand. There's supposed to be advantage in proximity, but the flip side is that jurors are right on top of any and all whispering or paper shuffling that goes on.

The name of each member of the *venire* was drawn out of box and assigned a number by the clerks before they were brought up and seated in order by the bailiff. While His Honor waited in chambers, potential jurors filled the jury box, the benches behind the two counsel tables and the first rows of the gallery on both sides of the aisle. The clerk handed each side a list of jurors by number and both camps, with the court's permission, moved our chairs to the opposite sides of our tables to better view these people.

Pete the bailiff announced Judge Frederick's entrée. All stood as he strode to his bench and took his seat and Pete's gesture invited the rest of us to do likewise.

"Good morning members of the jury panel. Counsel. Is the prosecution ready to proceed?"

"Howard Lemcke for the State, Your Honor. The State is ready."

"Very well. And the defense?"

"Richard Mauro and Ben Hamilton for Mr. Mead. We're ready, Your Honor."

The judge nodded his head. "Members of the jury panel, this is the time set for trial in the matter of *State of Utah versus David Mead*. I'm going to ask you certain questions that bear upon your qualifications to serve as jurors in this case. And, when you are responding to my questions, I want you to stand and speak loudly enough so that we can all hear you. Let's first have you stand, raise your hand and take the oath."

Cindy stood, swore the potential jurors to answer truthfully the questions asked and gave them a short list of personal items to address in order: their names and occupations; their spouses' names and occupations. I use a form for this data, other information and my impressions and needed ten copies for this trial. These started "1 of 10—1st row, jury box" and ended "10 of 10—Their side, 3rd row behind rail."

The term jury selection is a misnomer: the actual process is juror elimination. As we moved through the process, each side identified *veniremen* to drop "for cause," those who weren't legally qualified, couldn't serve for good reason, were associated with one of the parties or witnesses or who announced they couldn't fairly hear the case. The other side can concede or contest a challenge for cause, but it's the judge's call. After challenges for cause, each side has six preemptory challenges to knock off a potential juror on the basis of gut feeling, as long as that gut isn't driven by categorical prejudice. After all the challenges for cause had been ruled on, only the first twenty-two remaining jurors have any relevance: eight jurors, two alternates and twelve preempts.

We moved quickly through our panel. Then I gave a brief outline of my projected case. Judge Frederick explained the duties of all parties including the jurors. No hands were raised when he asked if there were *venire* who wouldn't follow the law as given by the judge or the facts that arise from the evidence. "I will, at this time, ask the lawyers to introduce themselves and the witnesses they propose to call. We will begin, Mr. Lemcke, with you."

Rich Mauro had David Mead stand so the jury could see him clearly. Then he outlined the defense position.

His Honor read the charges and the penalties to the potential jurors and noted that the defense denies the allegations. A few hands raised after he asked if any of the panel knew any of the attorneys or witnesses. A couple of folks worked at the airport and knew witnesses, none to the extent that it might interfere with their hearing the case fairly. One had a cousin with the same name as Jack's wife, but it was quickly determined that the spellings, and people, were different. One remembered Rich's investigator from their college days. No *venire* stood in master/servant, debtor/creditor, employer/employee, partner/joint obligor or attorney/client relationship to any announced participant nor were adverse parties in lawsuits involving Mead or the State. Several had prior jury service and each told the nature and outcomes of those cases. Some said they'd give a police officer's testimony greater weight because the witness was a cop; a couple said they'd give it less.

A number of jurors had business commitments, travel, appointments or other problems that might interfere with their ability to serve if the trial dragged on for several weeks. I noted those on my sheets. No one announced any unasked reason why they wouldn't be fair to both parties. One of them felt that the statutory penalties were too light, another indicated a belief that if someone were criminally charged they're probably guilty. Several had read in the newspapers about the case, but none could recall any detail without prompting, nor had any made up their mind as to guilt. We went through some individual questioning of those, although not to the extent Rich wanted.

Rich asked Judge Frederick to ask several questions. How would they view a witness who'd been cut a deal on their own criminal charges in return for their testimony? Would the fact of the Meads' interracial marriage or the race of either bother any jurors? Were any small business owners who had to meet a payroll? Had any been through financial bad times? His Honor was fine with those. Had any paid employees "off the books" or otherwise engaged in creative accounting? I knew where Rich was heading. So did Judge Frederick. We didn't go there.

Then the same defense who fought tooth and nail to keep out David's alleged bad acts and conduct reversed direction. "Oh, Judge, I think the evidence in this case will show that Mr. Mead, during the course of his marriage, had an extramarital relationship. And, during the extramarital relationship there were certain allegations and other things that were alleged against Mr. Mead. And I'm wondering if anyone here has had a spouse or someone else that's had an extramarital relationship, and how they felt about that. Whether or not that would affect their ability to judge the evidence in this case."

To giggles in the courtroom, Judge Frederick asked,"Let me get this straight. You want me to ask the panel who among them have had extramarital affairs?"

"No, I don't want you to ask that question. I want you to ask whether they have been the victim of an extramarital affair. Someone—their spouse has had an extramarital affair."

"Well, I will ask the question this way. Members of the panel, are there any among you who are so abhorrent to the idea of an extramarital affair that it affects you emotionally, to the extent that you could not be fair and impartial in judging the evidence in the case, if that turns out to be the evidence? If so, raise your hand." One hand did.

Rich handed the marked up master to Pete, who handed it to the court, who looked the master over and called out the names of jurors numbers 2, 3, 4, 5, 7, 13, 16, 24, 33 and 37. A homemaker, assistant principal, retail manager, finance director, retired nurse, contractor, fire fighter and small business owner would decide the fate of David Earl Mead. A warehouseman and mail worker didn't know they were alternates.

Briefly the court thanked the *venire* not chosen and handed one a voucher so each would be paid $18.50 by the clerk of the court. The bailiff placed the chosen ten into the jury box by number. It wasn't quite noon when the panel was sworn and jeopardy formally attached to David Earl Mead. Before the jury was excused and led to the back corridors for a quick lesson on where jury room, bathroom and phones were found, Judge Frederick told them to return at 1:30 to hear opening arguments. They were admonished not to watch or read anything about the case, to discuss it with anyone including other jurors or to form any opinions before the appropriate time. We stood, the three women and seven men left and Judge Frederick asked if anyone had any last minute business. Seeing none, he'd see us at 1:30.

A frantic lunch hour, after a full day of jury selection took half of that time. As soon as we could, we excused ourselves from the Stokeses and hit the phones. Opening might take an hour and a half, max, I needed witnesses for today. We'd asked our people to be flexible and expect a call. The larger problem was that everyone would be moving up and our out of state witnesses with fixed airline reservations were set in cement, so we'd have to be flexible, too. "Sorry, Meesh," I said, "another weight on your yoke." Michelle's a pro; she understood; she'd get it done while I was off to the court.

We returned after one. Richard Mauro had several things he wanted to discuss before the jury returned and complained about the *voir dire*, the way the judge rephrased some of his questions and his lack of ability to follow up. When this was met by stern non-response, Rich moved to more fertile ground. Since Judge Frederick was still reserving his rulings on much of the defense's pretrial motions and, therefore, these were not yet ruled admissible, Rich asked the State be foreclosed from mentioning any contested matters during opening argument. His Honor agreed. I tried a weak response but three words out of my mouth a crash startled the courtroom.

"Your furniture is falling apart, sir." I looked on as the bookshelf near the clerk collapsed. "Apparently there's a shelf in there that has fallen on the lower shelf." A second crash resounded, "Actually it's fallen on the floor." Everyone except His Honor laughed. He told me to cut to the chase and do my opening quickly.

Opening statements are an important part of a trial where first impressions are made. Opening sets out where the sides are going, what the jurors can look for, gives a proposed context to upcoming evidence and is often referred to as a road map for the case. There's an opening line I always use, so I'm never lost for what to say first but, without being able to mention the contested evidence, what would I say next?

All present, including Judge Frederick, stood as Pete brought the jury in and sat them in the box. A number of the people from my office and the defense bar were there along with the families, reporters and curious onlookers. His Honor read the charges without comment, then added, "You may present your opening statement, Mr. Lemcke."

I walked to the podium with thin notes. "Thank you, Your Honor. Your Honor, Mr. Mead, Counsel, ladies and gentlemen of the jury, again my name is Howard Lemcke. I'm a Deputy District Attorney and I represent the State in this matter.

"What we're going to go through for probably the next two weeks is one of the most important ceremonies that our society has to offer. It is a ceremony in the limited sense that it is done under some very strict rules and guidelines. The people in it have specific roles to play.

"As the judge told you, you are the finders of fact; he is the trier of the law; the defense counsel and I are advocates of a position. The witnesses will come up and under certain rules give testimony.

"It is not a ceremony in the sense that the outcome is preordained. The only outcome that is preordained is that you will decide the case and that decision will be yours and yours alone."

I expanded on Judge Frederick's explanation of procedure and reminded the jury of one other thing that he'd mentioned: what lawyers say isn't evidence. If the answer to the most grandiloquent question is "No!" then the evidence is the "No!" and not what was presumed by the question. Any argument not supported by evidence may mean that someone is not being straightforward.

I told the jurors what we charged David Mead with, walked down the list of the witnesses I would call and those things I knew they'd be allowed to say. It's poison not to acknowledge weakness up front, so I finished, "We will tell you through our evidence how, in fact, everything in this case focuses—the entire situation that David Mead is in focuses—right at August 15. We are going to show you through an entirely circumstantial case, because we have no one who saw David Mead kill his wife. We have no confessions of David Mead that, in fact, David Earl Mead did cause the death of his wife, Pamela Camille Stokes Mead, having failed a few weeks earlier to get it done through the instrumentality of Jack Hendrix.

"We will show you, through admittedly sparse physical evidence that deals with the wound and how the wound must have taken place, that Pam Mead got into the pond that night and drowned through the devices of her husband, the defendant here.

"That, ladies and gentlemen, is the case you are going to be listening to and that is why the State thinks that we have enough evidence here that you will find for convictions in these matters. Thank you."

"All right. Thank you, Mr. Lemcke. Mr. Mauro."

The defense began. "Mr. Hamilton will be doing the opening, Your Honor."

"Very well, Mr. Hamilton."

Ben would open, Rich would close, no surprise. Ben rose, walked to the podium and addressed the jury. "You are going to hear a lot of people testify in this trial and there's going to be a lot of time that you're going to be sitting there listening. One of the things that you're going to hear, as Mr. Lemcke has already indicated, was that this was an accident. Pam Mead's death was an accident! All the physical evidence at the scene indicated it was an accident. All of the people at the scene believed that it was an accident." He was off to a fast, emotive, effective start.

I scribble notes during the other side's presentations, arguments or examinations, put down quotable lines and potential responses. A promise un-kept or a claim unproven in opening will find its way into my close. If my opponent says one of their witnesses will give certain testimony and elects to duck that point on direct, I'll start cross with "Did you know that the defense, in their opening, told us that you'd say . . . Is that true?"

Ben hit on the character issues on Winnie and Jack and pushed the concept that the defense would emphasize the events and discoveries the day Pam died and that "the government" would talk about any day other than that day. He spoke of Baron the dog, without setting out specific theories, Pam's difficulties in walking, and asked if anyone knows how they'd react to finding their life partner suddenly dead.

Jill nudged me and pointed with her eyes at the defense table: the David Mead Charm Show was underway. Still concentrating on Ben's opening, I looked over to see poor David, hankie to his face, crying. Our defendant had turned wonderfully emotive: when I was up talking about the State's case, David was mightily indignant with arms folded, brow furrowed and lips clenched; as Ben spoke about how Pam had been taken, the widower was overwhelmed with sadness. It's amazing how red eyes can get when rubbed with the sewn corner of a hankie, but not generate tears. David was building eye contact with at least one juror.

Ben finished, "In our system of government we have what's called the presumption of innocence. It's not 'yeah' or 'yes or no,' I'm going to sit here completely unbiased. No, you have to start with a bias! You have to presume in your heart that David Mead is absolutely not guilty of any offense. He is presumed to be innocent, right now! Nothing Mr. Lemcke has said should convince you otherwise! And nothing I have said should convince you otherwise until you actually sit down and hear.

"Our system is set up so we don't put innocent people in prison. Our forefathers were wise enough, the Founding Fathers of this country were wise enough, to say 'It is reprehensible, it is abhorrent, it is just plain ugly to put an innocent man in prison.' And so they set up a burden of proof, the highest burden available, proof beyond a reasonable doubt. And they made it even harder by saying that there is also a presumption of innocence. So not only do they have to prove it, but they have to overcome your initial belief that this person stands as an innocent but accused man until that government proves beyond a reasonable doubt that he is guilty. That's what we ask of you—to presume David's innocence. Think about the evidence in terms of innocence. Make the State meet its proof with their circumstantial case."

The main act was about to begin.

23

The State vs. Mead

His face serious and somber, the judge turned to me. "Call your first witness, Mr. Lemcke."

I took a deep breath; we were underway.

"Barbara Wayne."

Ms. Wayne was a neighbor lady who lived on a small street, almost an alley, that ran behind the Meads' backyard, the neighbor that everyone has and is lucky to have. She works hard, goes to bed early, is concerned about the well-being of the neighborhood but doesn't meddle.

Pete stepped out into the hallway and escorted Ms. Wayne forward to the bar. His Honor responded, "Come forward, ma'am, if you will please, and be sworn." The clerk stood and raised her right hand. "Do you solemnly swear that the testimony you are to give in this case, now before the court, will be the truth, the whole truth and nothing but the truth, so help you God?"

"Yes," she nodded.

There are a number of theories on how to set out a case for a jury: start with one of the more spectacular witnesses and grab the jury's attention right off the bat or build in crescendo with the big witnesses at the end. This case was an oddity, entirely circumstantial, with a lot of fragments of circumstance to fit together like a jigsaw puzzle; mine would have to be a long presentation requiring thoughtful and comprehensive examination by the jurors. I always hope to seat the most intelligent, articulate jury possible. In *State v. Mead* it would be critical. I didn't need to build in elements to keep it interesting—this case would hold their interest—but I needed to keep it organized. I chose to build the case calmly in logical chronological progression, starting with the discovery of Pam's death then forward. I would call Winnie, Jack and Stormy to bring flashbacks and give context to later events. That day I would have the opportunity to call only those witnesses who set the scene at the Mead home the night Pam Mead died. My aim was to send the jurors home that night wondering how this terrible accident that stole a bride from her husband's loving arms could ever be a murder and wanting to hear what came next.

In response to my question about her memories of the fateful night Pamela Mead died, she began, "I was awakened in the night with screaming."

"About what time?"

"Well, I don't remember exactly."

"After dark?"

"It was after dark. It may have been around midnight. I don't remember exactly."

"What did you hear, as best you can recall?"

"I heard screaming. It sounded—when I was awakened by it—it sounded like it was a woman calling for help." It went on for a while, for minutes, not just seconds, or hours. She called 9-1-1 but wasn't about to go out and insert herself into an unknown situation.

Rich used the cross-examination as an opportunity to make a good impression on the jury. Working to make everything clear and understandable, he brought out a poster-sized aerial photograph of the neighborhood and asked Ms. Wayne to step down from the witness stand and mark her house, the Meads' and other relevant landmarks. It was good technique and it was helpful.

Mauro asked the witness if she'd heard anything earlier that night. She had not. Specifically, fighting? Arguing? Struggling? Could Ms. Wayne normally hear things at night from her window? "Yes, but that night the air conditioning was on and it was loud."

The State had no further questions and the witness was excused. The bailiff escorted her out of the courtroom.

Next Barry Baxter, another neighbor, went over his memories of August 15.

"You saw somebody?"

"Somebody."

"When they came out of the backyard, where did they go?"

"They went into the back of the house and it turned out to be David. And I met him at the front door. And he was in quite a state of hysteria."

"Tell us what you observed of David Mead at that moment."

"He was on the floor, kind of leaning against the doorjamb, as the door opened. And he grabbed me and stood up, and we ran out to the back."

"You say he was on the floor? Laying on the floor on his knees?"

"He was on his hip laying against—if I recall—laying against the doorjamb. His legs were pulled up underneath him and he was kind of slouched there against the door—supporting him there—the jamb. And he grabbed me and he said—and he said, 'Come on!' We went to the backyard and he was mentioning Pam by name." It wasn't coherent, but it was about Pam.

David had almost been in full sob during Baxter's testimony about trying to revive Pam but, after a point, grew tired of rubbing the corner of the hankie into his eye. The young woman whom Jill had once encountered wearing her skirt as a top was there lending support, as were several members of

David's family. At least one female juror was making eye contact with Mr. Mead bordering on fondness; several were almost leaning in his direction.

Dave led Barry on a run through the house, out the back door into the darkness. The further they ran from the house and what little residual light that came from there, the darker it got. When they got to the doghouse, near the fishpond, Barry could make out the outline of a person on the ground.

Baxter was familiar with the Meads' backyard. There were lights back there, floodlights, just not on. He went over to the form and recognized his next-door neighbor Pamela Mead. With knowledge of CPR, Barry tried to resuscitate her, but working to ventilate her he found a blockage in the airway. Mrs. Mead was cold and bloated. He'd seen her a few days before and she hadn't seemed bloated.

Baxter, shown a photograph of the pond, identified it and went on to discuss the pond's description.

Later in his testimony, Baxter described how high the brim, the edge of the pond, came on David Mead after the grieving groom jumped in; it came to the bottom of his rib cage as he stood upright. He didn't fall when he went in, though it was very dark and hard to see. Mead was very agitated and pulling bricks and rocks into the pond in a swimming motion, not slipping and sliding, maintaining his footing pretty well.

The police arrived within minutes, then more cops who seemed to take charge and ask questions. They all asked questions, a lot of questions. Baxter felt the Meads were a happy couple and there was no sense of foul play or that this was something that David had done. There was defensiveness among the neighbors that David, who'd just lost his wife, was subjected to questioning. Pam was a good person, just a sweet wonderful lady.

The witness observed that the Meads were constantly working on one home improvement project or another. The fishpond was about the only project in the backyard and David had been working on it for some months. He showed it to the neighbors when he thought it was finished, but the pond leaked and David had to reset the plastic lining.

Ben finished up a brief cross, "Did you have any reason,

at all, to believe that this was anything other than an accident, based on what you observed that night?"

"That evening, no. Or that night, no."

On my redirect I asked, "Have you since changed your mind?"

"I have reconsidered . . ."

Ben cut in, "Your Honor, I'm going to object to this. Without foundation we don't know what the basis is."

Judge Frederick responded, "I'm sure the witness would be pleased to tell us. But, at this stage I think, Counsel, he's answered the question. He has changed his mind."

Once again, my turn, "Okay. What are the factors that went into changing your mind between then and now?"

Angrily, "Objection, Your Honor. It calls for speculation. There's no foundation for this."

With chippy, feigned indignance I answered, "This is the foundation!"

"Well, the objection, I'm going to sustain. We're getting into an area here, which is in the province of the jury to determine, not a witness, at this point. Counsel."

Frustrated at being foreclosed from what he wanted to say, Barry Baxter broke in, "Your Honor, may I—I was interrupted in that answer, when I said I'd changed my mind."

"Well, if you wanted to add something to that answer that 'I changed my mind,' without going into the details of what changed your—what you changed your mind to or what it was that went into changing your mind, then certainly you may say what that was."

In a moment of silence Baxter pursed his lips, turned first to stare at the defendant, then to the jury and said firmly, "I was going to say I changed my mind insofar as I no longer have a certainty of his innocence and I'm more than willing to wait out the process to see things . . ."

Excitedly, "I'm going to object to that and move to strike, Your Honor!"

After Baxter, I called another neighbor, Hank Rider, who had also gone to the Mead house to find David screaming and the frightened dog, Baron, "going nuts." Hank Rider, looking for how he could contribute, grabbed Baron's chain in an attempt to restrain the dog. But Baron, upset at his master's distress, struggled until his collar pulled over his head and sprinted off into the darkness. Hank remembered David falling on the ground and clutching Pam's leg before the widower stepped into the fishpond screaming that "it was the damn pool that killed her."

He had been there when the police arrived.

Ben Hamilton crossed this witness as well and asked him to describe Baron. "A very husky, solid animal. Big and beefy. I recall one time I cut through their backyard to visit, like I did occasionally, and he was friendly. But he jumped up on me—just, I guess, to greet me—and he almost knocked me over." Hank said he was about six foot and two hundred pounds. When Ben asked Rider how big Pam was, the witness flinched at guessing the dimensions of a woman. Required, he estimated five six and one thirty. Ben wanted to intimate that Baron was quite capable of knocking Pam down.

Ben had done his homework and asked what Mr. Rider was doing earlier that evening, knowing the witness would answer that he and his family worked late that evening in their backyard painting wood to side a garage. They were out back and would have seen or heard any commotion or struggle near the fishpond. Hank went to the defense's aerial photo and marked his home and garage.

My re-direct examination consisted of re-asking if the witness could have heard the sounds of a fight? He could. But could he hear the sound of someone being hit in the back of the head with a brick, being lowered into and held under the water? Ben calmly objected, noting we had no foundation about what a brick hitting a head sounds like. His Honor found that a fair objection and Hank Rider's testimony was at an end.

Next I called Officer Sam Tausinga, massive in his dark blue Salt Lake City Police Department uniform. Sam remembered getting the call from dispatch that night. He and another officer, each in his own car, were sent to investigate screaming that had been the cause of several calls to 9-1-1.

Sam had tried to calm David down while Mike dealt with the body and the other two men. David wasn't responding well but Officer Tausinga kept up the effort while Jensen radioed for a supervisor. When Jensen forced the decision for David Mead to get out of the pond and David agreed, Sam lifted David up, out and over to dry ground. He wrapped a blanket around the wet widower and put him in a police car out of the wind. Sam stayed around to help with security after supervisors and detectives arrived, maybe another hour or so. He never questioned or spoke with the defendant.

Rich had no cross-examination. Next I called Mike Jensen.

Mike could hear the screams as he drove towards his call. He wasn't given an exact address so he followed the noise. He saw Pam beside the fishpond and David standing in it screaming, cursing, pounding his fists, pulling at the rocks but holding his stance. Jensen asked Mead to get out of the water and explain what was going on before the request escalated into demands that went unanswered. When the cop held out a can of chemical mace and threatened its use, the grieving Mead responded in a "pretty immediate" fashion. David started to become hysterical again and was handcuffed by this officer who'd walked into an emotional situation where the only certainty was death.

Once again, Rich Mauro didn't cross-examine.

Ken Farnsworth, who had left the Medical Examiner's Office and went to work as an investigator for the AG about six months after Pam's death, testified that he put on surgical gloves and examined the deceased for rigor mortis, livor mortis and external injuries. Ken explained terms to the jurors, telling them that rigor mortis was the progressive stiffening of the joints after death and livor mortis or lividity was the gravity-driven pooling of blood into the lowest portion of the body. The first was useful in determining time of death, the latter how the body was positioned after death. Neither was obvious, but there was blood at the back of Pam's head indicating a scalp wound. He also noticed Mrs. Mead's orthopedic shoes and was told of her recent surgery.

Ken Farnsworth took the temperature of the air, eighty-one degrees just after 2:00 AM. The water was sixty-seven. He took two measurements of the internal core temperature of the decedent twenty minutes apart to note the direction and amount of change. The first was eighty-four, the second showed little change. The body was wet, only dirty where it touched the ground; bags secured with rubber bands were placed over Pam's hands to protect them. Her clothing showed no evidence of trauma.

A conversation with Detective Candland confirmed no history of violence with the Meads. The ME's investigator took other measurements and some photographs. No conclusions or theories leapt forward. Everything at the scene appeared entirely consistent with the conclusion that Jill Candland was forming, that this had been a terrible accident.

Then Rich led Ken Farnsworth through his observations or, better, lack of observations, of outward trauma to Pam's body or clothing, unit by unit, piece by piece, occasionally interjecting that, had they been observed, such trauma would have indicated a struggle or fight. Ken had not observed these or noticed any of the red flags that indicate a struggle or make Pam's death appear a homicide. Rich knew he'd asked enough questions and I had no re-direct examination.

Another officer, Michael B. Roberts, who had been the supervisor in homicide at the time, told the jury that all unexplained deaths are initially assumed to be, and are treated as, homicides until the investigation reaches a different conclusion. A crime scene can be any size, from square feet to square miles depending upon the unique circumstances of the crime. Normally these decisions take place after consulting the Medical Examiner, the District Attorney and the law.

Mike Roberts saw David Mead in the back of the police car, wrapped in the blanket, his face distorted from crying. Given his condition, it was impossible to delve into anything with David. The supervisor accompanied Jill Candland through the Mead home, looking for evidence, and noticed the fishpond was well on its way to being destroyed from Mead's flailing. Except for damage to the pond, everything was consistent with what the cops were being told, more by the neighbors than by David Mead, that this was a horrible accident that befell a young couple.

I asked Mike about the investigation that took place in the days afterward.

"The following day we began to get information from other witnesses that took us in a different direction than the information we had the night before."

I let the answer hang there and passed the witness to cross.

A moment later Rich Mauro zeroed in on Jill's demotion: "You're not the case manager for the case?"

"No, sir, I'm not."

He brought out that she'd been transferred back to the patrol division.

On re-direct I said, "Lieutenant, was there any particular reason, given the information you had that night, to secure the scene or prevent people from going back in there?"

"No, sir. We had no specific reason."

"All right. Okay. Are they—Counsel asked you about Detective Candland's transfer. Do you know who the current president of the police union is?"

"The current president?"

"Yes."

"I believe that it's Ms. Candland?"

To low chortles of jurors from blue-collar backgrounds, I told His Honor Frederick I had no further questions of this witness, nor further witnesses for this day. It was 4:55, the judge felt this was "fortuitous," admonished the jurors to avoid news accounts or discussions about the case and told us to return at nine o'clock.

Rich, Ben and David exchanged smiles and pats on the back. The first day of testimony behind them, the State's witnesses for the most part seemed to be agreeing with Ben's opening contention this was a terrible accident. With facial demurs to the press that they couldn't talk during a trial, they left little doubt the defense believed the State hadn't laid a glove on them and had real bounce in their steps.

The Stokeses made the same observations and were upset. "Why did you put on witnesses that didn't seem to be advancing our cause?" Jill intervened on my behalf, asked the family to trust me, reassured them I knew what I was doing but cast a private look that hoped I did. They said they'd meet us at court.

Jill, too, was worried about the momentum of the case and

I told her first thing tomorrow morning, she'd take the stand and begin to steer the course towards home. She found her car, agreed to meet in my office about eight thirty and left without fanfare.

After a check of notes, voicemail and e-mail at my office, I decided which needed immediate attention and addressed them before heading home to a family with questions arising out of the news coverage. I picked out a shirt and tie to wear with my second suit and slept poorly as questions that might have been better asked ran through my head.

24

A Heated Exchange

The morning of the second day, Wednesday, October 21, started with forgotten business: no one had invoked the Exclusionary Rule. Although the jurors were already seated in the box and the judge told me to call my first witness, Rich broke in and asked if he could. His Honor started the day irritated. "Certainly."

I wanted Jill to stay at the table and the Stokes family to remain; Rich agreed, asked that his investigator and David's mom stay and announced he wouldn't call Mrs. Mead, even though he'd announced her the day before. The judge repeated the invitation to call my first witness and I called Jill.

She stood, walked before the clerk, was sworn and took the stand. Jill D. Candland told the jurors she was a Salt Lake City Police Officer assigned to uniformed patrol on the graveyard shift following eight and one half years as a homicide detective, one and a half as a burglary detective and five years in patrol. Seventeen years down, three short of the magic twenty for retirement.

The witness related to jurors how she was called out to the

scene of Pam Mead's death to become the "case manager"—
or detective in charge of an unattended death—to find several
uniformed officers already present. David Mead was sitting
in a police car wrapped in a blanket and hysterical. The
detective spoke with the widower only long enough to
express her sorrow at his loss. Sgt. Mike Roberts arrived
about the same time. There were neighbors talking softly in
small groups.

I had the witness take some time to educate the jury about
the duties of a case manager, the nature and structure of a
police report and the steps and people required to "process"
a scene, then had her describe her observations of the fishpond. She told us of stagnant water, bare ground, loose rocks
and bricks, dog droppings, the fact that it was a slightly
uphill walk from the house and how she found Pam's body.

The former detective said because there was little or no
light available she called in portable floods. Ken Farnsworth
arrived and she noticed a sack of fish food, a small fish tank
skimmer and a trickle of blood near the body. Jill Candland
told the jury about checking the house for the negative evidence and the genesis of the precaution.

She covered how she looked for signs of struggle near the
pool, found none, examined each rock and brick but discovered neither blood nor hair. Although she was never able to
meaningfully deal with the widower, Jill gathered the information that came through the other officers and stayed in the
Meads' backyard until three or four o'clock in the morning.
"There were no indicators. All of the evidence was consistent
that this was a tragic accident."

The testimony turned to the next morning when Candland
called Chris Ahern at the airport and confirmed David's alibi
before she joined Todd Grey at the medical examiner's table.
During that procedure she relayed to the examiner what evidence the police and Ken Farnsworth discovered and applied
that to the observations of the examination. Jill called
David's brother and was told he was still distraught. She
understood and asked that David give her a call after the
funeral to answer a few questions and wrap her case up.

As I took my witness into a chronology of the following
days, I glanced at the defense, who looked ready to pose

objections. On August 18, Angela called and told the case manager about a friend named Winnie.

Rich broke in, observing that Jill was referring to her notes in forming her answers. The judge asked the witness directly, "What are you looking at?"

Confirming, "Notes."

His Honor turned to Richard Mauro. "Okay. She's looking at notes."

"Okay."

My turn. "Why are you reading your notes rather than going off the top of your head?"

Jill shook her head. "It has been four years."

We moved on into what Angela said that Winnie said that David said about how Pamela would die. Rich objected on hearsay, but I said that this wasn't for the truth of the matter asserted. His Honor, growing irritated asked me, "Well, Counsel, I assume that this . . . Miss Winnie . . . is going to testify?"

"She is." But I was admonished to step carefully through what may cross the bounds and took Jill cautiously through a meeting with Winnetka Walls on the nineteenth, a call from Jane Dryer of Pennington, a meeting with the Stokeses just after the funeral and a call from Patrick Anderson about interviewing David around the twenty-fifth. I avoided filling in the details of the incidents that took place before the interview of David Earl Mead.

As I moved into that area, Rich jumped up and asked to *voir dire*. It seems not only had the micro cassette recorder worked poorly that day, but after Detective Candland took that tape to a police stenographer who transcribed the tape, the original tape came up missing. Mauro pounded a series of questions, each asking if the tape was missing. Jill kept calm, but when Rich asked if she was a case manager, she almost laughed back that she was a patrol officer. Rich raised his voice. "You are now!"

"Just a moment! Ma'am. Mr. Mauro, you established that there was a tape that is not available, or lost?"

"Yes."

"Okay. Mr. Lemcke, go ahead."

The witness, entertained by the last skirmish, related that

David told her he came home from work around eleven o'clock and found his young wife floating facedown in the fishpond. She asked the defendant about the insurance and learned that, in December 1993, it was Pam's idea the Meads take out $250,000 Pennington life insurance policies. David recalled working on the pond for a few months before Pam's death and filling it with water about four days prior. Although the business was in Pam's name, David ran it. He'd gone to work that night at eight thirty and returned home around eleven. When asked what his job was, Mead responded it was cleaning planes. He'd done that alone that night, although he'd hired a guy named Tom. I asked what Mead had to say about this Tom; Rich came back into the fray and objected again because of the missing tape.

His Honor Frederick ruled the witness could refresh her memory from the transcript and testify about what she recalled. For the benefit of the jurors we ran through a series of short questions to emphasize the interview was transcribed, the transcription was provided to counsel, civil and criminal counsel. David and his attorney were present and would surely recognize if any portion of the transcript of his own statements wasn't correct.

After all that, Jill answered that David told her he'd hired someone named Tom—David couldn't remember his last name—who never showed up.

Jill asked David about Winnetka Walls and was told Winnie was a woman David had been seeing for about five weeks prior to Pam's death, nothing serious, and he'd broken it off. "I asked him when was the last time he spoke to her, and he said 'Yesterday.'"

In feigned surprise, "Yesterday? From the interview?"

Perky, "Yes!"

"But he said at that point the relationship had been broken off?"

"Yes! And he said it was nothing serious!"

The defense wasn't enjoying this nearly as much as we were. I started my next questions, Rich brought up more objections about the missing tape and Judge Frederick held his ground. I had my witness tell the jury how she'd questioned David Mead to gauge his reactions to who could have done this to his wife. He answered "No one. She had no enemies." Asked who among their circle would be above suspicion, he responded by listing some names. When asked what he thought ought to happen to the person who did this, the answer was a list of punishments, but he never did react by asking what Jill meant by "did this."

After going over Mead's background, Jill Candland told the jury how her interview took David Mead back to the events of the night of Pam's death. Jill said she was told David left for work about eight o'clock, but Rich interjected and corrected her that it was eight thirty. Momentarily taken aback, she dropped back in time to David relating how the Meads went for a walk earlier that evening, how Pam, coming off bunion surgery, needed the exercise and a little support. Before he left for work, David kissed his wife goodbye—she was in the living room at the time—asked Pam to clean the fishpond or feed the fish and left for the airport.

Slowly, methodically, I set questions to lead Jill through how she came to encounter the witnesses I would call. The witness told the jury about the steady dialogue among herself, Todd Grey and Greg Skordas until the change of administration, and me after that. We briefed them on the process of screening a police case with the DA and the timing runs from the Mead home to the airport and back over the doomed Sixth North Bridge. When we got to Anne Sulton and the Stokeses' civil suit as the basis of our decision to put the criminal investigation on hold, Rich objected.

We haggled briefly about relevance. Jill listed the evidence—including the financial records, David's several statements and Bill Morgan—that came out during the federal trial, I announced I had no further questions and His Honor called a ten-minute recess.

Rich came back from the break with his batteries charged.

"Now, Detective Candland, you are no longer in the Homicide Division? Is that correct?" He asked a number of questions about Jill's demotion and transfer, including showing the witness a copy of the discipline letter she'd received.

Rich went into only the detail that the offending conduct was alleged to be mishandling evidence; he wasn't going to go into the substance.

Then changing directions, Rich asked a few questions about Anne Sulton and the pile of documents from the civil trial, hinting at foundation objections when Anne took the stand, then a series about Angela and Winnie, with emphasis that Winnetka Walls never claimed to be an eyewitness to the killing. Mauro asked a few more about the scene and made the witness repeat there was fish food and a skimmer but no measurements made, no weapon found and no one told to stay out of the backyard.

When Rich got to questions about Jack Hendrix, the adrenaline kicked back in. The defense's attack on Hendrix's credibility as a witness, the only witness either possible or necessary for the count of solicitation, was underway. Jill met with Jack at least seven times. She didn't remember transporting prisoner Hendrix between jails, but if the booking sheet said she did, she assumed it was true. She knew Jack had a criminal record, a long one, a bad one, but never specifically pulled it. The then detective did talk Jack Hendrix into testifying against his cousin, David Mead. She didn't promise him anything; she really couldn't. She must have promised him he wouldn't go to prison? She didn't have the power to make or keep that promise but did write a letter on Jack's behalf to the board after he went to prison.

Again Mauro needled her. "You are a homicide detective or you were at that time?"

"Yes."

"And, you want to know whether the witnesses are going to be reliable?"

"Yes."

"And a professional homicide detective would want to know if the witness is going to be accurate?"

Candland hesitated, pursed her lips and wrinkled her eyelids while considering the question. She cocked her head to one side, then the other, and responded in the tone of a question, "I don't know if there's any way of knowing that."

Richard Mauro started to wind up his cross with a series of questions about the history of the investigation of David Mead over the past four years. Yes, the cops and the DA wanted to wait out the civil trial and see what shook out and no, there were no eyewitnesses to Pam's death. None came out during the federal case, no murder weapon was ever found, not at the scene, not during the intervening years, not during the civil case.

Then Rich walked up and handed Jill a copy of the letter she wrote to the board for Jack Hendrix. "I am handing you what's been marked as Defendant's 15. Do you recognize that?"

"Yes. This is a copy of the letter that I wrote on November 4, 1996, to the Chairman of the Board of Pardons on behalf of Jack Hendrix."

"No further questions!" Rich walked back to his table. I know the technique of leaving a witness holding an exhibit, the damning exhibit, with nowhere to put it, and the counter-technique. When the court asked if I had any redirect examination, I directed a question to my opponent, "Is this being moved as an exhibit?"

"I am not moving to admit it at this time."

"I will."

His Honor was amused. "Any objection to 15? I presume not."

"No."

I know how to rub it in. "And, Your Honor, I would move the two photographs. I believe they are 12 and 13."

"Any objection to those?"

"No."

"Very well, they are likewise received."

On re-direct I questioned Jill to bring out that the letter of reprimand she'd received was not the subject of litigation and that she'd been a union official for sixteen years and became president in June of this year.

Re-cross was brief and a bit angry. "And are you taking the position that the allegations that Captain Danker and Police Chief Ortega are making against you are false allegations?"

"Yes."

"That a police chief and a captain are wrong?"

Perky, "Yes!"

After that he went back to the pond issues.

"You didn't bring anyone out from the crime lab to

examine the rocks and bricks with any substances to determine if there was blood?"

"What kind of substance would that be?"

"Luminol or any substance like that?"

"No," she answered quizzically.

"Nothing further."

My turn was so short I wouldn't need the podium. I just stood up behind the table, "Would luminol work on something that's already been thrown in the water?"

"No."

"By the time you realized that a weapon had been used, what had happened to the pond?"

"The pond had been dismantled and filled in."

"Nothing further." I stayed on my feet as Jill left the stand and held her chair as she sat back down beside me.

After a short recess allowed everyone to catch their breath, Chris Ahern took the stand. Now the Lieutenant for Internal Affairs, Chris explained to the jury that he had been the Police Liaison to the Salt Lake City Airport the August Pam Mead had died. Ahern knew of Valley Ground Service but didn't know David personally. He explained the liaison's duties and told the courtroom about the call he got from Jill Candland the morning after Pam's death. He initially confirmed David had been at the airport, but that was based on a computer-monitored perimeter that required magnetic cards to pass through unmanned gates. Ben objected that Chris Ahern was not the person in control of the airport's computers nor the single keeper of the airport's records. Further, the Police Department Liaison had not kept any tape, disc, printout or physical record of what his search discovered. Therefore, he lacked the foundation to testify, couldn't satisfy the Best Evidence Rule and, if he did, it would be hearsay. His objection was upheld.

Afterward I asked Chris what he observed of the records of the night Pam Mead died. He couldn't remember the date, except that it was the date Detective Candland asked him to check. The records showed that David Earl Mead, or at least David Earl Mead's airport access card, entered Salt Lake City Airport through Gate #13 at about the time in question. Then I approached the witness and placed a poster-sized sight plan diagram of the terminal buildings at SLC International on an easel between the witness and the jury.

I spent a while discussing the diagram.

On cross Ben hit the lieutenant with questions to reaffirm his point that no record was kept of the data observed. Chris admitted his memory, like everyone else's, is imperfect, but he did go back and forth several times in his telephone conversation with Jill about each point while he held the printout in his hand.

On re-direct Chris told the jurors he actually read from the printout. When I asked him what he would have done if his information contradicted, rather than confirmed, Mead's alibi, he replied "I would have kept a hard copy. I would have asked the people in charge of the computer system to, you know, duplicate the information that was there or to store it in a way that was retrievable beyond the normal time limitations of computer retrieval."

Then I showed the entire video of Kevin Harris's deposition. This viewing, in equal segments broken by trial day two's lunch hour, would be a rare opportunity to sit back and relax just a little and observe Anne Sulton, Patrick Anderson and the late Kevin T. Harris.

The screen lit up with Kevin seated at a table. Anne's or Patrick's hands occasionally came in from the side. The witness, looking thin and weakened, sat in a gray mock turtle top, hematite bracelets and loose necklaces as Anne moved him through normal questions of introduction and identity. Anne's questions concerning knowledge of, and opinions about, David Mead and his guilt had been edited out, along with those portions of the tape that dealt with Winnetka Walls. The presentation in court started with how Kevin met the Meads some two years before Pam's death, introduced by a mutual friend who learned they were neighbors. Kevin went on about how his friendship with Pam grew and they became running buddies, hanging out, going shopping, particularly enjoying yard and estate sales. They both refinished furniture. They'd have dinner at each other's home and, although Pam's work schedule as a flight attendant made their activities somewhat irregular, Pam became Kevin's best friend. Kevin didn't think that there was a better person in the world then Pamela Mead.

About midnight on the night Pam died, Kevin came home to a message on his answering machine from a mutual friend: "There's been a bad accident. Pam is dead. I'm on my way to Dave and Pam's now." It took Kevin less than two minutes to get there and see the completely darkened backyard cordoned off by yellow plastic tape. The floodlights on the corner of the house weren't turned on

On the screen Kevin Harris recounted that those were usually on in the evening if anyone was outside, and they illuminated most all of the backyard where David built the pond. That night they just didn't work. Kevin Harris, awash in the shock of events, wanted to do the right thing. "That night— it was the next day after the first burglary—the floodlights weren't on, so I went and got money and I bought some floodlights to put into them. When I got there, I realized that the floodlights had just been . . . They weren't screwed all the way in, so I screwed them in and took the floodlights that I bought back."

Anne Sulton asked Mr. Harris, "So the floodlights were operational? They simply weren't screwed in?"

"Right."

"How high off the ground were these floodlights located?"

"I had to stand on milk cartons to reach them."

Anne asked Kevin about the pond and he told the camera that day, and the jury this one, that the fishpond was David's project; Pam hadn't been involved. She would have told Kevin. He probably first saw work back in June, digging. After the hole was dug, David lined the pond with plastic and rocks and filled it, but when the water leaked out it was necessary to redo the lining. David and Pam came by on their walk the day before she died. They told him, "We got the pond fixed. You have to come by and see the pond."

Kevin Harris would never see the fishpond, wouldn't go there before the night of August 15, and that night he wouldn't have walked up there even if the police would have permitted it. The next day he did go by, only to see David's brothers shoveling dirt into the hole, on top of the rocks, bricks, plastic and whatever was there and thrown in first. We edited out Harris's conversation with David's brother about if this should be done before the Stokes family arrived, but the jurors heard Kevin remark to one of the brothers that he hoped the Meads were insured and his answer, "I don't know. I hope they are, too."

As we came upon the noon lunch break, Jill signaled me with elbow and eye to look at the defense table, where David Mead was fast asleep. The same man who'd been in full-blubber sob a few witnesses before couldn't stay awake to watch his wife's dearest friend speak from beyond the grave. The defendant's posture was noticed by the jury box; Ben noticed the noticing and woke Mead with little fanfare.

After an all too brief lunch, we resumed. Anne Sulton took Kevin into several areas: his impression at the time of the funeral was that David was treated badly by Pam's family; he'd heard about the break-ins and the robbery and figured out that David and Winnie were more than just acquaintances; he described the dimensions of the fishpond, but admitted he'd never measured it. Kevin had occasionally worked for David and VGS but didn't know till he spoke with the Stokeses at the funeral that the business was in Pam's name. She always referred to it as David's.

The witness spoke from the screen about Pam's surgery a month before her death. The day before she died, when the Meads came by on a walk, Pam was crouched over and walking on her heels, so Kevin teased his best friend about looking like a little old lady taking tiny steps in her enormous boots. She was holding on to David and walking on the sidewalk very carefully.

She confided in Kevin that shortly after the surgery she was in a lot of pain, but she was the kind of person who was determined to find a way to get into her front yard to water the plants. Kevin hadn't seen her in the backyard since the surgery. It was a mess with bare ground, dog droppings, pebbles and fallen fruit.

From here the tape of Kevin Harris's deposition took on a herky-jerky character from the editing to excise where the questioning delved into what Kevin knew, or heard, about Pam and David's relationship and finances. The jury did hear that Pamela Mead may have confided in a good friend the extent of physical pain but never the emotional pain, if there was pain, in her marriage; that stayed at home. She could be very private.

The last public pronouncements of Kevin Harris were in response to a few questions from Patrick Anderson. Kevin felt that David was still a friend and thought that the Meads were a happy and loving couple, always talking about what each was going to do for the other. Kevin used to tease Pam about her cooking. She told Kevin that "David would eat it, because he loves me," so Kevin was giving her cooking lessons.

The lights came on in the quiet courtroom, the tape was received as an exhibit and the TV/VCR cart was wheeled from the room.

25

Medical and Other Truths

Todd Cameron Grey, Chief Medical Examiner for the State of Utah, took the witness stand, recited his credentials and took the time to educate the jury about the duties and responsibilities of the Office of the Medical Examiner, the distinction between a coroner and an ME, and the protocols of autopsy. Over his career Todd had performed about thirty-five hundred personally and supervised or participated in close to eleven thousand.

With a demeanor exuding both experience and confidence, Grey related to the jurors his initial observations of the foam plug in the airway, the wound to the back of the head and the abrasions to the elbow and abdomen.

The examination hadn't found defensive wounds, which he defined for the jurors, nor tissues under the fingernails indicating a struggle. I borrowed a defense technique and had

Todd report, one part at a time, the absence of any injuries to the other portions of Pamela's body to bring out how absolutely improbable it was that she fell on a pile of loose rocks and bricks and injured only the back of her head.

I took the doctor into the content of his conclusions. The cause of death was drowning, the initial manner of death was accident and Todd changed that conclusion twice. The witness told the courtroom that during this time he got a telephone call from Jill Candland to the effect that the detective had learned Mr. Mead had a mistress and told his mistress he'd kill his wife. Since this suggested the possibility Pamela Mead's death might not be an accident, "on the nineteenth, I changed my certification of the manner of death from accident to pending. Which means that I wanted to wait and see if we could get more information to clarify what was going on in this case."

We detailed evidence brought to the ME's attention before his second amendment to head off accusation this change was only based on the unsubstantiated statements of Winnie and Jack. Todd told the jurors he learned about the insurance policy, the mistress, the cousin, the in-laws and statements of others, including David finding Pam floating facedown.

He told the jury that a body of a recently drowned person typically does not float at all: it sinks. Were the victim obese or wearing blousy clothing, it might or might not. Someone in a swimming pool can do a "dead man's float," but that person is alive with lungs full of air. Pam Mead's hyperextended lungs were full of water.

The doctor told the jury that the time to initiate floating is also a function of temperature. "Putrefaction," the process where a cadaver decays, hosting bacteria that generate gas by digesting flesh, causing a body to bloat and float, is as nasty a concept as it is a word. The warmer the water, the sooner putrefaction begins. In a warm bathtub, water above eighty degrees, it could start within a few hours, but sixty-seven-degree water would not lend itself to rapid putrefaction. If Pamela Mead's body was in the water from eight thirty until discovered at eleven, two and a half hours, Todd wouldn't expect floating. There are some rough formulae that can determine, or at least estimate, time of death from the rate the body lost temperature; however, these are inexact and subject to several variables. Todd couldn't fix a time of death with any precision but estimated Pam died closer to eight thirty than eleven o'clock.

The Office of the Medical Examiner did a toxicology screen on the decedent's blood and tissues. All tests were negative; no drugs or alcohol were detected.

We returned to the wound on the back of Pamela's head. In the doctor's opinion it was not a potentially lethal wound in and of itself; however, it was indicative of a blow that could daze a person, knock them unconscious or render them so helpless that, were they to wind up in water, they wouldn't have the control to save themselves or could be held under with very little force.

I asked the witness and Detective Candland to come into the well and stand in front of the jurors. As they came out, I asked Todd about Pam's hair and how it might affect the blow. He noted Pamela Mead was an African-American female with fairly thick, tightly curled hair that had been styled with some thickness and would have provided some cushioning but, obviously in this case, not complete protection.

Jill, Todd and I were in front of the jury box, I held the brick from the clerk's bench and we went into our act. I had Jill stand obliquely facing the jury, placed Todd behind her and offered him the exhibit, "Doctor, the brick."

Officer Jill Candland looked back over her shoulder at the two men behind her and, with a nervous giggle, asked that we proceed with caution. This request, heard by those close by, but not the reporter, got the response, "We're your government; trust us," and a few small laughs from jurors.

Dr. Grey stood behind the lady cop and demonstrated how an attacker with an upright victim would need to wield the brick to produce the damage observed in Pam's autopsy. He swung his arm up, describing the motion as a topspin tennis hit. Then I had Jill bend over at the waist, bending her knees slightly until her torso was parallel to the floor, and asked the ME to demonstrate how in this circumstance he would strike the blow, which came somewhere between sidearm and overhand in a motion easy to associate with attack. Jill waited in pose and asked if it were safe to stand up.

Todd returned to the stand and I wound up direct, "And then, Doctor, you changed your conclusion a second time? What date was that?"

"That was on the . . . I initiated the paperwork on the twenty-eighth of September."

"And what did you eventually change your conclusion to?"

"I certified the manner of death in this case as 'homicide.'"

"And the cause of death was still…"

"I still felt that this individual died as a result of drowning. But the circumstances leading to the death indicated that it was the result of the actions of another person."

We took a short break and Richard Mauro came back in top form.

Rich hit piece by piece at those observations that supported the defense theory of the case, from a vantage point where Todd knew of nothing but the body. Point by point we went through clothing, to learn that no buttons were missing or anything torn, before we moved to Ken Farnsworth's investigation and report. The courtroom was dragged, point by point, through every aspect of those and of Ken's credentials, followed by assurances that Ken was a fine investigator.

Rich produced several more pictures of the pond and made the point the rocks and bricks in the collar were irregularly placed, some even propped up on top of others, edges pointed into the air. Mauro went to the condition of Pam's post-surgical feet, introduced a photo of the pins and swelling and had the State's expert testify that these would be extremely painful. Todd remarked that he wouldn't want to walk on those feet and stated that leaning forward, as in the State's recent scenario, would be very painful. He conceded that there was no indication those pins were deformed or displaced indicating that Pam had been dragged before or after she died.

On cue, Ben went to the side of the defense table and retrieved a white, almost featureless foam head, the kind used to display wigs or sunglasses, and handed it to Rich. Rich handed it to Todd, along with a black magic marker and asked the ME to draw the wound on the mannequin. Dr. Grey asked for a ballpoint pen so he could draw a finer line. After that was done, Todd asked if Rich would like the witness to indicate the face on the head, Rich said that was fine, Todd took the magic marker and recorded "FACE" in huge black letters across the shallow depressions that hinted of eyes. Jill and I weren't alone biting our lips to contain a laugh.

Rich kept his cool and used the head and brick to question Todd Grey on possible scenarios that would create a superior undermining wound and had Todd admit that, at first blush, it seemed possible Mrs. Mead fell backwards and struck her head on the edge of a brick. The witness admitted his first amendment was made without exhumation, re-autopsy or any new physical evidence. The information Winnetka Walls provided Detective Candland had not changed the wound to the head, had not changed the abrasion to the elbow and had not changed the abrasions to the abdomen. The amendment was not based on new, scientifically observable evidence and Dr. Grey had no way to know whether or not Winnetka Walls was telling the truth.

During that last line of questions, Rich walked over to the defense table, picked up a sheet of paper marked as an exhibit and, while he continued to question Todd, handed it to me in a courtroom courtesy to allow the opponent to see which exhibit the witness is referencing. In a case with lots of documents, it's easy to lose track. It was a copy of the un-amended death certificate. Rich was back at the podium. I pulled my reading glasses down, took a longer look and saw something, slid the certificate to Jill and pointed at a corner. She caught my meaning in an instant; we exchanged glances and I slid the paper to the front corner of our table.

Rich retrieved and moved it, handed it to the witness and it was received without objection. Todd looked it over and conceded he'd checked the box labeled "Accident." One question and one answer at a time we learned there were other boxes not checked that read "Natural Cause," "Suicide," "Undetermined," "Homicide" and "Pending Investigation." Rich asked and received permission to publish the exhibit to the jury and placed it on their rail.

From there the defense questions took the ME back to

communications with Candland that culminated in the meeting at the PD with the cops and Greg Skordas. Rich asked the same series of questions he'd just asked about what Todd knew about Winnetka Walls, this time about Jack Hendrix. There was still no new physical evidence.

Rich paused and walked back to the table where Ben set out the transcripts of this witness's prior testimony. In the prelim, Todd only mentioned Jack and Winnie's statements as underlying his changes. In the civil trial Wally Bugden had led him through several hypothetical scenarios, one where Pam fell backwards, struck her head, was knocked semi-conscious, fell into the pond and drowned and another where Mrs. Mead was knocked into the pond by the dog, struck her head and drowned.

Rich produced a plastic baseball bat and a two by four and asked the doctor if either could cause the sharp edge wound observed. No and yes, but in any event it wasn't the head wound that killed Pamela Mead; it was the drowning. There is no place on the autopsy forms to record witness believability, nor prior inconsistent statements, nor motives to lie.

Rich concluded by making Todd confirm that when he was asked in prelim, "If we take out those two witnesses, it is consistent that this case was an accident as opposed to a homicide? Isn't that correct?" He answered, "On the scientific information alone, that is a possible conclusion. Yes." To press a point Rich leaned forward. Exaggerating the force on the toes by not bending his knees, he rocked onto the balls of his feet and asked if this would put pressure on the toes? He went on to query, had Pam done that, would it put pressure on her vulnerable toes? Todd agreed to both and the cross-examination was over.

I got up and handed the photos of the rock collar to Todd Grey, had him look at those, took them back, put them on the jury rail and had Todd come off the stand into the well. I put the brick on the floor and asked the ME, if someone fell backwards onto a pile of rocks, what sort of marks would he expect to see on the rest of the back of the body? He would expect to see a lot of abrasions and bruises from the very irregular surfaces of the rocks and he did not find those. On the other hand, if someone fell outside the collar, striking only their head, where would their body be? On the ground, entirely outside of the collar of rocks and not in the water. Had the examination revealed any marks consistent with being struck by a dog so hard that Pamela Mead was propelled entirely across the fishpond hitting only her head as she reached the far side? It had not.

With the photo and the witness at the jury rail, "If somebody were to have snuck up behind somebody else, who is bent over—'Honey, why don't you look down at the fish?'—and hit her over the back of her head, would you have that kind of wound?"

Rich broke in. "That's leading. I think that he can ask a hypothetical . . ."

"It is leading."

"Hypothetically, Doctor, were somebody to come out and say, 'Come on, Honey, bend over and look over the rocks . . .'"

"I object."

"'. . . and look at the fish . . .'"

"I object to that part of it."

His Honor Frederick asked, "What part?"

"'Come on, Honey.'"

"Well, Mr. Lemcke, forget the 'Come on, Honey.' Just state your hypothetical."

Never miss a chance to ask the question that lays out your theory. "Take the victim—have the victim bend over to see the fish, take the rock and hit them over the back of the head like so . . . would you have the wound you found on the head?"

"Yes."

"Were they to tumble into the water, perhaps scraping their abdomen on the way down, would you have the scrapes you found on the abdomen?"

"That would be consistent with what you've described. Yes."

"And were they to go into the water in a dazed condition, would they drown, particularly if there was someone there to make sure that their face didn't come up?"

"Yes."

Still in the well, next to our jurors, I took care of one last piece of business and handed Todd the original death certificate still lying on the jury rail. "Doctor, I would also like you to look at the exhibit just entered and tell us, sir, the date that you certified that."

"This was signed by me on the sixteenth of August. It was accepted by the Health Department on the seventeenth."

"All right. And would you look at the bottom of it and tell us the day that someone went down to the Health Department and made sure that they had this?"

"That date is stamped August 17."

"So somebody went down to the Health Department and made sure that they had a certificate of death that same day?"

"That's what it appears. Yes." He returned the document to the rail as jurors passed the paper around and pointed.

His Honor motioned and Todd returned to the stand. "And these are typically the sorts of things that are sent to insurance carriers?"

"That would be one piece of documentation an insurance company would ask for. Yes."

"Counsel gave you a couple of hypothetical scenarios about this, that and the other thing. But he never asked you what you thought of the probability, or possibility, of his scenarios."

"That is correct."

"What do you think of the possibility or probability of his scenarios?"

"I don't think that his scenarios adequately explain the lack of findings on Pam's back and other portions of her body, if this was a tumble-over-backwards-and-fall-in-the-pond event."

I felt he completely missed the connection Doctor Todd Cameron Grey made with the humanity of Pamela Camille Stokes Mead, but I turned him over for re-cross.

Rich came back and asked Todd if he'd ever known of people who'd fallen backwards, struck their heads and died—no questions included 'by drowning.' Mauro hit briefly on the notion that neither David Mead nor his brothers had anything to do with filling out the death certificate and concluded by referring to my hypothetical, asking wouldn't her face be bruised if she were knocked forward striking her face on the plastic or the rocks. The doctor agreed that she would be and that he found no such bruises.

Re-re-direct examination was brief enough to take place from the table, "If Mrs. Mead's face hit the water, she wouldn't have those marks? Would she?"

"I would not expect to see any marks."

"Nothing further."

Rich replied, "Nothing further, Judge."

"All right. Doctor, thank you, you may step down. You'd better go while you have a chance."

"Don't need to warn me twice, Your Honor."

For my last witness of the day, I called Bill Morgan to testify in this second contest. Mr. Morgan took the stand and told the jury about his VGS employment.

Morgan said he and his son stayed at the airport the night of August 15 and never ran into David Mead. I started to ask the witness why he decided to come forward during the civil trial so long after Pam's death, but Ben objected on the irrelevance of Morgan's motive, the judge agreed and direct was over.

Ben drew this witness and, very directly, attacked his credibility: "You don't like David? Do you?"

Mr. Morgan made the mistake of trying to spin things into a better light, instead of just laying out the unpolished, unattractive truth. "I have no feelings about David, one way or the other."

Ben seized the opening. "David fired you? Didn't he?"

"There was a mutual understanding that I would quit. I wasn't happy with the working arrangements out there."

I saw the need to break this rhythm. "Your Honor, I thought counsel objected to this gentleman's motives as being irrelevant?"

"Well, you just haven't had a chance to respond on rebuttal."

Ben took control of Morgan and made him admit that he was fired in an angry incident preceding several months of unemployment. Hamilton pulled from the ex-employee that he and David Mead never hit it off and there were a series of problems with Morgan's work.

My voice was steel-edged as I concluded.

"Were you out there that night?"

"Yes."

"Was David Mead out there, when you were out there?"

"No."

"Nothing further, Your Honor."

It was almost four o'clock and I was out of witnesses for the day. I'd talked with Judge Frederick and the defense about this possibility the day before, so His Honor told the jury that they got a lucky break and were to return at nine the next morning.

The emotions of this evening had evolved from those of the day before. Backslapping and congratulations on Team Mead's side of the aisle were less robust, the eye contact Mead cultivated with jurors had grown tentative, posture shifted from outreach to upright, there was less fear in the eyes of the Stokeses and Jill found her competitive sense of humor. Everyone recognized that the case was being steered into the State's desired direction; not to say that a sense of cocky confidence had entirely shifted to our side of the room, but we were in gear.

26

Blows to the Prosecution

I was worried and concerned. Nine o'clock in the morning arrived without our reaching Winnetka Walls, my next witness. Then, at about a quarter after, Judge Frederick reminded us that, first, we had a jury waiting, but further, we had motions pending and invited Rich to briefly state his motions still remaining under advisement.

Rich Mauro started out with his objection to Matt Jenkins, expressing concern that Matt would be drawing conclusions based on incomplete records and couldn't provide an accurate picture of what was really going on. David Mead wasn't the world's best businessman, but also not the worst, and to extrapolate sweeping conclusions about David's finances and intentions was inherently unfair and prejudicial under Rule 403.

The defense went to what Mauro characterized as "the Stormy matters" with the position that the call Pam overheard was too remote in time and too inexact to be meaningful. He pointed to differences in detail of Stormy's statements to sell the entirety of her testimony as unreliable. David's visit to her workplace should be excluded as distant from the time of Pam's death, not relevant to Mead's state of mind and nothing more than bad character evidence to poison his cause.

Starting with my trump card, Matt Jenkins, I carefully and logically took His Honor through Matt's analysis of Mead's poorly kept records, how this affected his expectations and lifestyle, the lifestyles of his blood family and, most importantly, his inability to pay a hit man absent insurance proceeds.

I argued that the dealings of David Mead with Stormy, before and after his wife's death, were relevant and admissible. The overheard call may well have been the genesis of the year of the perfect husband and Mead provided Stormy with detail about motives of his heart and wallet that valued VGS more than his bride. The confrontation in Stormy's office was proper to impeach David's statements denying knowledge of Stormy, the same sort of evidence as flight, evidence of a guilty heart.

Judge Frederick is not a man of faint heart when it comes to ruling. I had no sooner finished than he moved into his rulings, explained his interpretation of Rules 403 and 404(b) and how he would apply them in this case. His Honor noted that this was an entirely circumstantial case and, given the State's underlying burdens, the absence of alternative evidence and that testimony would describe unseemly conduct but not to the extent it "would to any degree rouse the jury to an overmastering hostility toward the defendant," the testimony of Winnetka Walls, Jack Hendrix and Stormy would come in.

Just as I was starting to feel better, despite the fact that

Winnie was nowhere to be seen, Judge Frederick turned to the testimony of Matt Jenkins and suppressed it. It would only serve to confuse or mislead the jury, because Mead's motive, by the State's theory, was for the insurance proceeds. However, were David Mead to take the stand and testify that his finances were all in good shape, I could use Matt in rebuttal.

As the rug was pulled out from under my feet, I watched in panic as the "Matt Jenkins Light and Magic Show" flew away. A couple of weak inroads were quickly shot down; the folks across the aisle enjoyed it and deserved to for winning a well-framed motion. Rich asked with flourish if the court wanted him to draft an order. When Judge Frederick started to direct the bailiff to bring in the jury, Rich asked to deal with Pam's hearsay statements and David's conduct after Pam's death.

The jury was still waiting, but I had no witnesses and we went back to motions. With Stormy's testimony about the overheard phone call coming in, I didn't need the hearsay, or to call Mary beyond providing the time frame for Stormy's call. Rich agreed to stipulate to the dates when Pam returned to the Springs.

Rich was concerned we'd put on the Stokes family's observations and run those through Supervising Special Agent Mary Ellen O'Toole's analysis to profile his client as someone who staged a homicide; that CV was still having an effect. Judge Frederick, ever direct, cut in "And, do you propose to call this witness from the FBI?"

"No, Your Honor."

Turning to Rich, "So, that renders it somewhat moot? Doesn't it?"

"I believe so."

"All right." And with that, the absence of a witness and a calm absence of irritation or anger, Judge Frederick called a further recess. Jill and I got on the phones and Mrs. Hendrix walked in. I'd hoped to put on Jack's mom, Jack and then Jack's wife as a group, but this would maintain the sequence even if it were broken. Hopefully Winnie would show up and it could be broken.

Some time around June or July that year Mrs. Hendrix got

a call from David asking about how Jack was doing, to be told his cousin was "up and down." My witness told the jury that although Jack wasn't incarcerated, he was on drugs. David told Mrs. Hendrix he wanted to help her son and had some work for him. Could he have Jack's phone number? Mrs. Hendrix thought that this was odd: David and Jack weren't close and when Jack was on drugs, he wasn't close to anyone. She agreed to pass along David's message. Mrs. Hendrix knew Jack was staying with his girlfriend and didn't feel comfortable giving out her number.

In cross-examination Rich attacked the witness's son and asked if Jack, just out of jail, was living up to the conditions of release to stay off drugs, attend AA meetings and look for work. The sad witness didn't know: when Jack was on drugs he wasn't close to anyone. She conceded that, in the past, Jack had done some work for the Meads and VGS.

When Mrs. Hendrix stepped down, there was still no Winnie, Jack nor Jack's wife. His Honor asked me where we were and I told him we had the remainder Hendrixes on the way. In a continuing and unexpected calm, Judge Frederick called yet another recess. As I stood at the table alone, wondering what was going to happen to my no Matt, no Winnie case, Jill came in and announced that Winnie and her mother just walked up the courthouse steps.

Ms. Winnetka Walls was an unhappy witness, her dark mood emphasized by eyes set straight ahead and lips pursed hard as she walked past Jill and me without a word. Eye contact with Winnie's mom revealed that only Winnetka Walls knew what Winnetka Walls was about to, or not about to, either do or say; I wouldn't know one second sooner than anyone else. She was sworn in, took the stand and sat staring unblinking, at the defendant. His Honor let the opportunity to admonish the tardy witness pass without comment of any sort.

There was no sense trying any juror education or acquaintance, so I got right to the point. Within seven questions, Ms. Walls answered that she'd met the defendant in August of '92 and they became lovers. By April of the next year, she learned that David was a married man, but by then she was in love with him. She told a very focused jury she was still in love with him. I started to ask the witness about the apartment David was providing during Pamela's lifetime when Ben objected, asking for specifics on times and payments. Judge Frederick questioned "Specific times of payments of the rent?"

"Yes."

I restarted a question, "Over what period of time . . ."

Ben interjected, "It's not relevant to anything, Your Honor."

Ignoring the interjection, "Over what period of time did David pay the rent or help you pay the rent?"

"Your Honor," Ben came back in angrily, "I believe I also made an objection as to relevancy."

"The objection as to relevance is overruled. Let's have foundation with regard to the time frame of the rent payment."

I started questioning times. Winnie was answering forthrightly in a strong, almost clipped voice, but as she listened to my questions she was mouthing something to the defendant and he was responding in kind. She never took her eyes, never took her stare, off David Earl Mead and her hard stare was answered by his attempt at baby-face plea.

You learn a few things in law school, you learn a few things in practice and I learned something from my third grade teacher. "Ms. Walls, I noticed that you were just mouthing something back and forth to Mr. Mead. I'm afraid I'm going to have to ask you to share that with all of us."

"What I said?"

"Just now, to Mr. Mead."

Never losing her focus on David, she almost shouted, "Why?"

In mistaken belief the witness was responding to me with a question of her own, I asked, "Why what, ma'am?"

This time she shouted directly at the defendant, "Why did you do this? To me?"

Everyone snapped to attention. Juror eye contact with the defendant shrank into occasional glimpses reserved for the train wreck we're told not to stare at.

We went through the arrangements on rent before I started questioning about the vacations she took with David Mead.

Ben objected on relevance: "This has nothing to do with August 15." Overruled, His Honor would "entertain examination of the nature of their relationship."

Ms. Walls told us about Mexico, Hawaii and the West Coast. Ben objected on foundation, giving me the opportunity to have the witness tell the courtroom about Mexico before Pam died, Hawaii after and several trips to the coast on either side of that event. With calm strength born in sadness, she described how she fell in love with David and sought to make him hers alone, her efforts to force Mead to make a choice, the Christmas '93 ultimatum, the incident at her parents' home, the videotapes and what she threatened to do with those videotapes.

We covered how Angela brought Winnie down to the PD, the interview with Jill and the robbery the night Hendrix and cohort burst in on Mead and Walls. Ben placed frequent objections on the table, disrupting my rhythm.

Ms. Walls acknowledged the handwritten and notarized statement she wrote and told the jury how David moved her to Southern California on very short notice when the civil discovery process got hot and heavy. She testified he told her what to write, took her to the notary and took the sworn statement back to Utah with him. She admitted some of the things she told Jill weren't true and some of the affidavit was, but there was mostly truth in the former and falsehood in the latter. Together we led the courtroom through the saga of being found by Action Jackson, the subpoena, taking the Fifth, being named in the federal lawsuit and finally seeing the light through begrudging eyes.

During the several conversations where David promised to resolve the problem, Mead said it would look like a robbery gone bad, a nasty slip and fall; he would have an alibi. He had jocularly used the term murder at her parents' home. Never in so many words, but Mead told Walls Pamela would die. Question and answer bogged down: Winnie couldn't remember, there had been a lot of conversations. Jill as librarian handed me transcripts of Ms. Walls's prior recorded statements. I brought each of the tabbed entries to the stand, had her read the passage, refresh her recollection, then take each question. Ben worked at keeping my technique within parameters he approved; sometimes His Honor agreed; sometimes he didn't; sometimes he got irritated with each of us.

I came to David's visit to Winnetka earlier this year and Rich and Ben looked at each other in surprise. Team Mead knew about the visit; the client just never briefed his lawyers and there was shock the State knew. Ben pushed a series of objections but Judge Frederick recognized, among other things, the defendant recently violated his conditions of pre-trial release, allowed it was relevant and he wanted to hear it, too. We heard about the proposal without a ring and David's concern about Winnie's upcoming testimony. When I asked if, by marrying David, Winnetka became unavailable as a witness, Ben interjected she didn't have the qualifications to give a legal opinion and the judge agreed. After clarifying the nasty spill Mrs. Mead was scheduled to have, direct was over.

Ben knew where he wanted to go, pulled out the handwritten letter and gave it to the witness to confirm she'd sworn to tell the truth, the whole truth and nothing but the truth. That letter was a sworn statement that said what Ms. Walls told Detective Candland was a lie and the declarant was sorry she said it.

The cross invaded Winnie's emotions as Ben asked her to recount the times she felt scared, screwed up, depressed, in love, used, angry, happy or betrayed. Ms Walls would pause briefly, appear to take herself back to the moment and allow her body language, countenance and voice to display that feeling. She rode her roller coaster of the heart in front of the whole world, but held strong.

She was made to admit that she gave David Mead many ultimatums, almost constant ultimatums, and he kept her on the line with excuses that were just lies. She revealed her pain when, after Pam's death, David's brother, not David, called this young woman to tell her that David couldn't talk to her and didn't want any contact for some time. She wasn't allowed to console and comfort the man she loved.

Hamilton took the questioning back to the several and contradictory statements of the past four years. He seemed, I felt, to imply Ms. Walls lied to the police out of spite, lied in federal court out of fear of the lawsuit and was being forced by subpoenas to testify and lie today. She was reminded how she and her family suffered pain and ridicule over events now laid bare, but Winnetka Walls was visibly annoyed.

"You also indicated that if 'I'm forced to testify, I will serve my own best interest'?"

"That's what I'm doing today."

Loudly, "That's what you're doing today! That's right!"

I jumped in, "Your Honor, is counsel testifying or is he asking questions?"

"Counsel, allow the witness to finish her answer and she'll allow you to finish your question, I presume."

"And you're doing this in an effort to keep you and your family from suffering any longer?"

"Yes!"

In turn, I went back to the notarized letter, handed it back to the witness, referred to Ben's cross about the majesty of a notary public and asked if her testimony before a federal judge was under oath and her testimony at the prelim and here before Judge Frederick and these very jurors empaneled to gauge her credibility. I reminded her that she took the Fifth in the civil deposition. "What part did David have in suggesting you take the Fifth Amendment in that deposition?"

"Objection! Your Honor, her taking of the Fifth is her own decision!"

The court knew where I was going. "No. That's not the point. The question is what part, if any, did the defendant play in that decision. Overruled."

"Your Honor, it also goes beyond the scope of cross."

"It is beyond the scope. Sustained."

I ended by asking Winnetka's motive for going with Angela to the police station. She said it was anger, but also fear. Her emotions were very confused.

On Ben Hamilton's re-cross, the witness conceded that she wasn't so fearful of the defendant; she did go back to him. He repeated that subpoenas forced her to testify and that today, under the force of subpoena, this witness would serve her own best interest.

Winnetka Walls left the stand without even a glance at any other player in the drama, straight out the door and through the press to find someplace where her memories, her thoughts and her pain could be hers alone.

I'd never seen Jack Hendrix wearing store-bought clothes or with unchained hands, but there my next witness was, looking good in his own duds, walking in with his wife through the front door. He'd won parole a couple of months back, married his longtime girlfriend and evidenced his new-found, faith-based self-control through a regular job and day to day conduct. He took the stand while his wife, still banned by the Exclusionary Rule, was sent to wait outside. Even though Jack's transformation was remarkable, I asked, "Are you a convicted felon?"

"Yes."

"How many felonies have you been convicted of?"

"Three? Four?"

"Have you ever been to prison?"

"Yes."

"You're currently on parole?"

"Yes."

"How many times have you been to prison?"

"Two parole violations and two sentences."

"You had some paroles that hadn't worked out well, and . . . Are you a drug addict?"

"Recovered."

"What is, or were, your drugs of choice?"

"Cocaine."

"When did you become an addict of cocaine? When did you first start using cocaine?"

"Nineteen eighty three or 1984."

"How heavily?"

"A lot," he said heavily. But he perked up: "I'll have three years of sobriety in February!"

Jack told the jury, who now, I could see, all were riveted on his testimony, about the several facets of the perfect husband, that in that fateful summer, recently out of jail, living with his girlfriend, Jack got a call from his mother asking him to phone David. He told of the meeting, the first gift of cash and coke and intellectual exercise of how much would it take for you to kill that led to an offer of $30,000 on the life of Pamela Camille Stokes Mead. Hendrix told him "yeah," he wanted into the coke. David and the whole family were well aware of Cousin Jack's history of being imprisoned by gray walls and white powder, but they exchanged the second gift of 8 C's and 58 g's. Besides killing his wife, David even wanted Jack to help out in the drug trade.

Jurors got a brief course in the lurid and brutal details of the life of a junkie on a binge, how much cocaine goes into each injection and how many injections can go into one user with resources. They learned how his girlfriend kicked Jack out, how the newfound friend was dragged away by her parole officer and how Hendrix kicked in Mead's door to steal what he could after the gifts ran out.

Mr. Hendrix told how, in a moment of clarity, he called his mother, learned of Pam's death and that David was staying at a brother's. He realized the home was vulnerable, went over after dark to right where David said the money and jewelry were kept. Rich interposed an objection to break my stride, which reminded me to ask whether during the prior meetings David had noted that in the burglary-gone-bad scenario some theft would make the scene look authentic, Pam wouldn't need her jewelry anymore and there was this water cooler bottle full of cash. Hendrix just followed the suggestions, got the stuff and bought more dope.

His Honor called the lunch recess. Our side was feeling pretty upbeat and exchanging observations when Ben asked for a private moment. Ben Hamilton was more than a little unhappy about being surprised by Ms. Walls's revelations of Mead's visit. I told him it wasn't my fault his client hadn't let him in on those travels, but Ben said angrily, "You sneaky bastard!" and stormed away. As a lawyer, I accepted that as a compliment.

Another working lunch, coordinating a process further complicated when Judge Frederick canceled the "Matt Jenkins Light and Magic Show." I managed not to spill the lunch I didn't eat on suit number three.

Since good evidence can't be mentioned too many times, I used my first questions to take Jack Hendrix back to the first burglary at David Mead's home and the water jug full of money David identified as worth stealing. Touching briefly on the other burglaries and the notion that Pam's jewelry went away with Jack's cocaine companion and the PO, Hendrix told the jurors how he went to David's home to console the widower and learn where the two cousins stood in terms of the drugs not paid for by the deed not done, "and then he told me he figured I would have used it. I asked him if I could somehow make it right with him and then he said that he was a suspect in the murder and that they wanted him to take a polygraph test and that he denied it." Denied what? He continued, "The murder," David's words.

I asked Hendrix if Mead said how he'd pay his hit man and Jack told the jury about the proposed trip to Vegas with the whims of Lady Luck pre-determined in the amount of $30,000 from the insurance policy David said was for $250,000.

Jack Hendrix told the room about the armed robbery he and his confederate pulled on David and Winnie. After the highway patrol caught the robbers that night, swimming in drugs, confusion and fear, he called his sister and set out the whole story. He asked her what he should do, was told she'd make some calls and find someone. That someone was first Detective Wade Wayment and later Detective Jill Candland.

The testimony moved through a litany of Jack's cases, charges, sentences and what he was getting for testifying here. Little doubt the defense was going to cover in excruciating detail Jack's history, so I chose to touch the benefits the witness had and had not received. Asked what deal he got on the robbery, Jack said one to fifteen years for the robbery, one to five for the gun and a ten thousand dollar fine, just because. He didn't get a plea bargain for this or make any promise to testify when he pled on the robbery. He didn't testify in person in the federal case but gave a videotaped deposition in a room down the hall from his cell. What consideration did he get for that? Nothing. For testimony at the prelim? For his testimony today? Nothing, he was already on parole and said he felt badly about all that had happened.

When I finished my examination, I handed Hendrix over to the defense for cross-examination.

Rich surprised me with his first question, "Mr. Hendrix, David Mead passed the polygraph test? Right?"

After being reminded to speak up and not just nod, "Yes."

"You knew that he passed with a plus fifteen?"

"I didn't know the numbers."

An interesting tactic to bolster his client, since polygraph results aren't admissible. After that Mauro sought to push the witness further down the path of ill ease about testifying against his cousin with a short series of questions to remind Jack that David and the Meads had been kind to and done favors for Mr. Hendrix in the past. Then Rich moved to questions about the witness's dealings with Jill, Anne Sulton and his own family.

With questions that were very well crafted, Rich was impeaching Jack with detail from transcripts and soon had Hendrix nodding rather than answering, doing so well I needed an opening.

"Your Honor, if counsel is going to testify as to what is or is not true, perhaps he ought to be sworn. I don't believe that's a proper form of a question."

"The characterization that it's true? Counsel, I think that's a legitimate objection. It mischaracterizes the testimony. If you're simply comparing the testimony of two different occasions, you can say 'the same' or 'not the same.'"

That briefly broke the flow, emboldened Jack to hold his own but turned the questioning combative. Mauro asked about small differences in the sequence of people in David's would-you-kill-so-and-so-for-this-amount-of-money enquiry and Jack responded, "Yeah. But, sir, it was a long time ago. When you try to think of a conversation like that, how do you remember, exactly word for word, what was said?"

Hendrix made a point that, despite defense contentions to the contrary, he was trying, struggling to tell what he knew and he'd not been drilled by others on a story.

The attorney for the defendant questioned the witness with points well taken during the cross: David spoke of bringing his cousin into the dope business and never explicitly said that the cash and coke were a direct payment for his bride's death. David never specified a way Pam was to perish, provided a weapon, map of the house, schedule for the would-be hit man nor primer on the condition of the lights.

Then Rich walked to the defense table, picked up the copy

of Hendrix's rap sheet, walked back to the podium and started one at a time, with each variation in spelling, to go through the aliases. Jack admitted that aliases were a device he used to get out of trouble. If he had warrants, he lied to the police and told them he was someone else. Jack knew it was a lie, told the lie, was convicted of felonies, had been to prison and burglarized David's home after Pam's death, three times.

Rich brought Jack into the events between his arrest for the robbery and when he eventually went to prison, other incidents in that period of time when Jack was briefly out of jail before he committed other offenses, got caught and his lawyer got him a plea bargain. Some charges like the burglaries were never filed, but Jack pointed out the cops weren't aware he'd committed them. A judge sent Jack to a hard-core, no-nonsense drug rehab; he failed, came back before Her Honor and went to prison. Some members of my community would be shocked that the doings over this period of time represent a systemic norm, not the aberrational, gift-wrapped package the defense portrayed.

At one point Hendrix objected. "Well you made me feel like—you made me look like I'm lying. And I ain't telling one lie here, guy!"

"Mr. Hendrix, I'd never do that," Rich countered.

"That's what you're trying—to make me look like I'm lying! And I don't even want to be here! And all I'm trying to do is tell the truth! And you're trying to twist everything around!"

Mauro grew frustrated and read from transcripts rather than using question and answer. Judge Frederick, who saw I was just sitting back, reveling in Hendrix's sincere humanity and Rich's dilemma and not pushing valid objections, broke in.

Rich's questioning now focused on contrasting Mr. Hendrix's potential and actually served sentences.

Rich took Jack through a series of questions seeking to impeach the witness's sincerity about getting off drugs through a history of failed attempts, drew the questioning to the day the judge sent Hendrix to the joint, pointed out that I was the Deputy DA who covered that hearing and passed along a recommendation for one more chance.

His Honor asked the defense attorney, "How much more examination?"

"I have just a few more questions, Your Honor."

"You heard it folks," Judge Frederick shared with the jury. "Maybe more than a couple. But not many more."

"Objection. Breach of promise."

Rich responded with a smile, "This is what gives lawyers a bad name." He asked Hendrix about Jill's letter to the Board of Pardons, followed by a few questions about Jack's total time served and how much of it was spent as a fire-fighter, and cross was over.

"Mr. Hendrix, hi. At the beginning of cross-examination, counsel asked you, 'And you know that David passed a poly-graph?' Do you remember him asking that question earlier today?" He nodded. "In fact, David talked to you about pass-ing the polygraph? Didn't he?"

"Yes."

"What did David tell you about preparing to take the poly-graph exam?"

"He told me that he went to the library and got books on it. That he had . . ."

"On how to what?"

"About polygraph tests. And that he had known more about the polygraph test than the guy giving it to him."

"Did he use a police polygrapher or one of his own? Did he hire one or use a cop?"

"He paid for it."

"Okay. And you took a polygraph test?"

"Yes."

"And you passed it?"

"Yes."

I had two other points to make. For the first I walked Hendrix down in front of Mauro's notepad and asked why he didn't give identical answers in each session. Wasn't he asked identical questions? I asked him if other people he knew got plea bargains, Rich objected and it was sustained. I referred Jack to the now admitted PSR, which contained a summary of Jack's co-defendant in the robbery's plea bargain.

"And he didn't testify in this case? Did he?"

"No."

"But he got a plea bargain?"

"Yes."

"How unusual is it for people to get plea bargains?"

Rich Mauro's objection was sustained.

"Did David Mead ask you if you would kill, or find somebody to kill, his wife?"

"Yes."

"Are you getting any plea bargain, any benefit, for standing in here today, looking your cousin in the eye and telling the world he paid you, or wanted you, to kill his wife?"

"No." All the skills and tricks of the lawyers aside, in the end it would be, and it should be, whether or not the eight jurors who would deliberate on this case believed Jack Hendrix for the real and, as all of us are, flawed human being he was.

27

Intense Moments

I wanted Hendrix's wife's testimony to put a little context and corroboration into what Jack told the jury, since I had little doubt David would take the stand and charm his way through a competing version. The defense had attacked and would continue to attack Hendrix's person as not worthy of belief, rather than undermining the content of his statements.

She took the oath and told the jury of her six years with Jack, before and after their wedding. She remembered the summer of Pam Mead's death painfully well. Jack was not doing well, in and out of jail, begging friends and neighbors for joints, then one night walked in with lots of money and drugs. She wasn't a druggie and the sight of hundred dollar bills and large quantities of drugs frightened her. She held a full time job, and a few days of watching Jack shoot up pushed her over the line. She kicked Jack and what remained of the drugs and money out of her home.

I asked if Jack explained where the drugs came from and Rich objected on hearsay. The witness told the courtroom what happened since those events, confirmed that she took him back, they were married and Jack had been clean and sober for several years. I asked about the genesis of Jack's newfound strength and Rich objected on relevance.

Rich's cross-examination was brief and again went to Jack Hendrix's credibility as a witness. Jack's wife confirmed that in the summer of Pam's death, Jack had history and skill as a burglar, robber and thief. David wasn't Jack's only potential source of resources.

Afterward I called Jack's attorney from 1994, whose good humor and endearing personality effectively mask a tough and successful lawyer.

Then, after a brief off-the-record sidebar conference to ensure that everyone was on the same page of His Honor's pre-trial rulings, Stormy was called. With Winnetka Walls and Jack Hendrix just behind us and the tactics of Stormy's cross during prelim not yet ancient history, the courtroom parties, spectators, reporters and the witness braced for the Second Battle of Stormy. But Rich and Ben are attorneys who know the craft, know a jury would forgive them for beating up Winnetka Walls and wouldn't forgive them for not beating up Jack Hendrix, but beating up Stormy could be a different matter.

Calmly we went into the story of how Stormy first met David Mead at a nightclub in '92 and ran into him again. She told how she went to his home, movies, lunches and began dating him before learning there was a Mrs. David Mead and dropping the relationship.

Our courtroom learned how Mead called Stormy at her work in early '93 and confided he was an unhappily married man. She told him, "If you're unhappily married, don't be married; get divorced!" He responded by explaining how the financial problems with the aircraft cleaning business and the financial backing of his in-laws would cause that business to wind up in Pam's family's control following a divorce.

"And did he say anything else?"

"At one point in the conversation he said that he would—that it would be better to kill her and get the insurance money."

The questioning then took an attentive jury to David Mead asking Stormy to hold on, how she waited until David picked up the phone and told her that Pamela was "freaking out." Pam had been listening on the extension and was on the front porch throwing things.

"I asked if I could talk to her and he said, 'No.'"

"Why did you want to talk to Pam?"

"Because during our conversation, we had talked about the fact that we had dated. And I just wanted her to know that it was done and over and . . ."

"Did you have any particular sensitivity to her situation?"

"Yes."

"What's that?"

"I was married and my husband cheated on me."

When I moved into Stormy's impressions of David's body language and her feelings of intimidation on the day he visited her new workplace, Rich started objecting. Judge Frederick said it could come in but was fair game for cross. Stormy told us how, after Mead left, she grew frightened, took personal precautions and sought counsel.

One of the things about a vigorous and aggressive cross-examination in a previous proceeding is that a sincere witness will go home, think about that situation and remember more details.

"Did David—What did David tell you about the distinction between civil cases and criminal cases in this instance?"

"That there was no criminal investigation. The Stokeses had initiated a civil case for the money. At the same time he mentioned that he'd excavated the pond out of his home, the next day."

"He told you he excavated the pond?"

"That he had it excavated. Yes."

In continuing surprise, "That he had it excavated?"

"Yeah. And he said that he jumped into the pond upon finding . . ."

Rich interrupted, "Well, I'm going to object on foundation. I don't know what the foundation is for this. She's jumped into a conversation that I'm not aware of."

Judge Frederick knew a valid objection and a vein of evidence worth mining: "Let's make sure where this is transpiring—this conversation—Counsel."

I led Stormy by question and answer back through the details and the sequence of the declarations Mead made in her office.

We briefly covered when, why, how and to whom Stormy came forward in the fishpond case, and Stormy was given over for cross.

Rich used Stormy's previous testimony to imply that she felt David was just being jocular in the suggestion he ought to kill his wife, but Stormy had been impeached before. Rich handed her a transcript, asked her to refresh her memory and asked about David's tone of voice during "the insurance question." Stormy corrected the lawyer and told him her prior testimony concerned David's tone of voice announcing his wife was on the extension and upset. Mauro grew irritated and pulled out a videotape of her interview. It turned out to be the wrong one but the right one was found and played.

The defense ran the witness through a syntax of questions about her original lack of concern. She didn't call the police, didn't seek out the investigators and didn't contact the plaintiffs. But she had since talked to the detective, talked to the DA, talked to the Stokeses and watched lots of news. Stormy disagreed on watching a lot of news.

Re-direct consisted only of having Stormy confirm that, when she referred to David Mead's jocularity, it was when he talked about Pam's reaction to the phone call, not when he talked about killing her. Stormy stepped out of the courtroom unscathed.

Afterward I called another neighbor, Todd Ryan, whom David told that Pam overheard a telephone conversation between Mead and Stormy.

"And did David tell you what Pam overheard?"

"He said that he said, on the phone to Stormy, that, you know, he was wanting to get together with her. But he couldn't because Pam was in town, and, you know, he was kind of tied down." Todd Ryan paused; his face turned hard; his open expression facing me became a stare at his old neighbor. He took a breath and in a strong voice continued, "And he said we ought to—'I just wish we could knock the bitch off!' "

When we finished with Todd, it was a little after four thirty and I had stipulations but no witnesses to end this most intense day of trial yet.

The judge had his regular Friday calendar in the morning and asked everyone to assemble at ten o'clock. We were in recess and looking into a Friday without the Matt Jenkins Light and Magic Show. The folks on our side of the aisle, not knowing what enormous stock I put in that now missing element, walked out with more spring in their step while our opponents seemed to lack a little energy.

His Honor's Friday morning calendar ran a little past ten while the *Mead* parties waited in the courtroom gallery and the jurors in the back. I wore good suit number one and had three brief witnesses scheduled. If I couldn't get Matt on, it would be a short day.

David Mead's kid brother was the first. He also worked for Valley Ground Service and brought forward the history of VGS, about when the brothers' mom formed it in the early 1980s under another name till David took over the company a decade later.

The younger brother testified he was there and participated in the destruction of the fishpond. The widower's brothers dug a trench to allow about half of the water to drain downhill before plastic, rocks, bricks and the dirt from the spoil pile went into the hole. There was a brief effort to rescue the fish, but that was ineffective and abandoned. No one told them to do it; they just did. I asked if he was aware the defendant, in deposition, said he ordered the pond destroyed, but the defense kept it out as lacking foundation.

Richard Mauro crossed, asking David's brother how he learned his sister-in-law passed away, how the family gathered around David at his stepbrother's house and how David just curled up and cried. Mauro asked Mead about the decision, which the witness still remembered as the brothers', to fill in the pond. Neither the police, nor anyone else, told them to preserve the pond. The lawyer handed the witness one of the photographs taken at the scene that night and the witness agreed the photo showed the fishpond and neighborhood children on street bikes gawking across the police tape.

Mauro detailed family concerns about the cost of the funeral and David's expressed anger at himself and the fishpond for their roles in Pam's death.

In my brief re-direct, not followed by re-cross, the brother admitted that before Pam's death there had never been any family concern or discussion about the safety of the pond. The younger Mead was followed to the stand by his equally ill-at-ease stepbrother.

I took his stepbrother directly to the topic of the bank account he held with David, the defense objected vigorously and I assured the court I was headed down a relevant path. Judge Frederick reminded me he held the VGS finances irrelevant and I proffered that, given some leeway, I'd show it wasn't for business purposes. After hearing about an account the younger brother, who was the business manager, wasn't aware of, where $30,000 went through in a lump, His Honor saw the State's point.

The stepbrother testified that David talked about his marriage, the possibility of divorce and that he could lose his house and business in a divorce. I started to ask about David Mead's emotional investment in VGS; the defense objected, but the judge overruled.

"What would you describe was his sense of ownership? Like you said, the family business goes back to his mother. Describe for us what he told you he felt."

"I mean—I mean—He worked the business for many years. I personally felt that he felt, like, very strongly about the business. I mean, he worked hard for it. But I am not sure that we ever had a discussion about how he felt."

His stepbrother ran into difficulty remembering what was said, so I picked up the transcript of the federal trial. "Did you say at that time, 'I mean, we lost the business when the airline moved out'?"

After objection and hesitation, "Yes. He lost the airline business."

The re-direct was swift. "Was this one of the sources of disagreement, that David kind of liked to go out and do things—with other women?"

"Going to clubs or whatever, yes," agreed the stepbrother, conceding that although he'd introduced Dave to Winnie when Pam wasn't around, the get-togethers continued even when the wife was around.

I had three reasons to call Pam's mother Sinie: to fix the time frame of her daughter's retreat to Colorado Springs and Stormy's overheard phone call; to give her some actual participation in the process—victim families often feel they've been kept on the sidelines, marginalized; and to give the jury a chance to meet her and sense the humanity of this woman and her family.

Mrs. Stokes well remembered how she learned of her daughter's death. She was already at work that morning. It was still early, probably about seven thirty, when Pam's sister called. She cried and called David to be told he was heavily sedated and couldn't talk. She spoke to his stepbrother, who told her Pam fell into a fishpond. Sinie told the jury she told him that she didn't believe it and Rich Mauro interjected gently that this wasn't relevant. Quietly, I agreed but told our judge it provided context to something quite relevant, what Mrs. Stokes did next, what she told his stepbrother she wanted. Sinie told him she wanted to see that fishpond; the Stokeses were headed for Salt Lake and they wanted to see that fishpond.

I handed her the defense exhibit of the initial, un-amended, death certificate and had her explain to the jury the steps the Department of Health requires to obtain copies.

Finally, I asked Pamela's mother if she had a picture. Her daughter handed me her mom's purse and I carried it to the witness. Sinie reached inside and retrieved the folded photo of the young couple taken around the time of their wedding. I took it, left it folded and stood where the jury could see the witness and the photo, the mother and the daughter, the real human beings the fishpond case was all about. There was no cross.

It was just past eleven and there was good time left for presenting witnesses and evidence to the jury. I told Judge Frederick we needed to talk; he called a recess and invited us back into his chambers. We met in there without a reporter, off the record, a good chance to take off suit coats and robes for a few minutes and relax.

His Honor asked me what I had and I explained my witness dilemma with the out-of-staters and the rest of this Friday set in my mind for Matt Jenkins's analysis. I took one more shot at trying to convince this jurist it ought to come in, given what we heard about the emotional connections of the defendant to his business, but he cut me off and reaffirmed his decision.

Before we broke, Rich brought up one more issue. "Judge, I'm wondering if I shouldn't get a polygraph expert."

"Why?"

"Because Hendrix told them David beat the poly by studying for it. I think I ought to bring in someone to tell them that can't be done. I don't want them to dwell on that. I don't want Mr. Lemcke pounding on that in his close."

"Howie, you're not going to argue that? Are you?"

"No. But I don't want to be foreclosed from arguing it if Rich is going to tell them 'he passed the poly.' Besides there isn't a result that's in; all we have is David telling Hendrix that he passed."

"All right. If neither of you is going to bring it up in argument, there's no problem. You don't want to bring in an expert on an inadmissible technology. Even if you called him, it would just make them dwell on it. I'll give them a clarifying instruction if you want."

"I guess you're right and I guess that a clarifying instruction would just highlight the issue, too. I don't want a clarifying instruction."

We went back out into the courtroom and let everyone know the score to a general sense of relief among those swimming in our little caldron. A lot of lawyers will say you need to send out the jurors for a weekend on a strong note and we did, just not the note I'd originally planned.

28

The State Peaks, The State Rests

Monday mornings are never easy, but some are more memorable than others. I was trying to gather my thoughts and my packages when Pam's sister Mary Stokes walked into my office with a huge grin and a large stone menorah, gray and square. Mary held it like a trophy, "Look what I found! I had to show you!"

"Is this the one? Where did you find it?"

"In a store, here in town. I'm sure it isn't Pam's, but it's identical. Can we use it?"

The lawyer's sneaky mind ground on. "Maybe not as evidence, but we can use it. Oh yeah, we can use it!" The Stokeses headed for the courthouse with the menorah.

I sat at my desk in suit number two, signing a few papers when Michelle stuck in her head and announced the Fairfields were there. "Send them in."

I was still head down in paperwork, saw people enter out of the corner of my eye, finished signing a pleading, started to stand up, looked up, dropped my jaw and stood there staring like a dolt. The Fairfields are straight off the pages of fashion magazines, an interracial couple like the Meads who are tall, lean and know how to wear clothes and carry themselves. Gayle Fairfield may well be the second or third most stunning woman I have ever seen. After overcoming my initial dumbstruck reaction, I introduced myself, we talked over the day to come and I worked at not embarrassing myself further.

The weekend was good for everyone and the courtroom seemed to have a feeling of energy. Jill and I set up our papers and properties and waited for the judge. I walked over to Mary Stokes, who handed me the menorah with an almost ceremonial flourish; I took our prize and set it on the front of our table facing the defense. It was solid and heavy with distinct edges, clearly capable of causing a superior undermining wound.

The defendant saw the statuary and became unsettled. He took his attorneys by the sleeve and said something to them while gesturing with his eyebrows toward the State's table. The lawyers walked over and Ben asked, "What's that?'

"A menorah. Isn't it pretty?"

"So—a menorah? Why a menorah?"

"Yeah! You know, Judah Macabee, the cleansing of the temple, that little bit of oil that lasted many days."

"What's it doing here? Why do you have it here?"

"Hey, you never know, miracles can happen."

His Honor's entrance put an end to Biblical history. The Stokeses knew what reactions to look for at the appearance of the icon and our little scripted, overly formal handover. David's continued disquiet was rewarding. I wondered if, just maybe, this symbol of how the Macabees were given what they needed to light the good work might aid our quest to illuminate this room.

Gayle Fairfield took the stand to attentive stares and talked about her friend Pam Mead. The witness had been a flight attendant with Pam and they'd get together when Pamela flew through Denver. After she started working as a Pennington insurance agent, Pam told her the Meads were thinking about life insurance and asked what Gayle had to sell. The two talked off and on over the next year.

In October of the year before Pam's death, the two couples met in a Denver area restaurant and agreed on a policy. The deal wasn't finished or bound, because the papers weren't completely filled out and no money was exchanged. Around Thanksgiving Pam came by the Fairfields' office with the completed applications and a check.

That next August the Fairfields were on vacation in New Mexico when a call came by voicemail. Would they call David Mead in Utah? It was an emergency. The witness couldn't get through to the widower, was directed to one of his brothers and told of her friend's death. David's brother said he held a policy and power of attorney and wanted to know how to cash the insurance in, to cover funeral expenses. As I started to question about what else she heard, Ben began a rapid-fire string of objections, "Objection as to relevancy, Your Honor."

"I don't know what the answer is. Overruled at this point."

"They wanted to make sure . . . They asked me if I was certain that no one else could get this information."

Ben crossed with a series of questions about whether it was the happily married Pam who was the Mead interested in insurance. Mrs. Fairfield considered that, agreed that it was true in the early stages, except for the time the Meads were separated.

When Gayle's husband got on the stand, I gave him a copy of the application for the Pennington policies. Warren told us that, although his wife is listed on the policy as the agent, he did most of the work on the deal and almost exclusively dealt with David Mead over a period of months, largely over the phone.

We talked about the meeting at the Denver restaurant and Warren explained how the policy applications were signed, even though the paperwork wasn't completed and the money wasn't available, due to a Colorado requirement that the applications be signed within the state. To the witness's knowledge this and acknowledging the amount were Pam's only participation in the process. The application and check came in around Thanksgiving and the final papers were overnighted to David.

Ben crossed Warren on the details of the policy, emphasizing David Mead's expressed concerns for the continued well-being of the business and Mead's hobbies that included scuba diving and rock climbing. The witness confirmed the two couples discussed the Meads' plans to have children and repeated that the policies had passed scrutiny of the underwriters.

Maybe I wasn't going to have Matt Jenkins, but I still had Anne Sulton. Anne introduced herself, her relationship to the Stokeses and to the case, gave a brief description of depositions, interrogatories and transcripts and moved into the transcripts. Although Rich Mauro made a yeoman's effort to break in and out, and then objected that the results were too broken up to be meaningful, I was able to have Anne recite to the courtroom questions and then answers that David Earl Mead addressed in other settings. One of the big problems with telling lies is keeping track of what lie was told to what person and hoping they never compare notes.

Among the things Anne noted, "Defendant Mead recalls arriving at home and finding that Pamela was not in the house. Defendant Mead recalls calling a couple of Pamela's friends to see if she had gone to visit anyone. After leaving messages with Pamela's friends, defendant Mead decided to check in the backyard to see if Pamela had fed their dog, Baron. Upon walking into the backyard, defendant Mead observed the fish food sitting on the edge of the pond. And it was at that point that he walked up to the pond and discovered Pamela facedown in the pond."

We learned that when questioned in a different setting, Mead stated a man named Tom—David didn't know Tom's last name—was supposed to help David out at work but never showed up.

The jury learned Mead told Pennington, "As soon as I saw her in the pond, I jumped in and I started screaming. I struggled. I don't know how long. There was a lot of blood. I remember trying to push her out of the pond. It was so slippery."

We went on through the recitations of questions and answers and heard David's contentions that he phoned 9-1-1 and after realizing his wife was dead, "jumped into the pond in a hysterical rage" and started tearing up the pond, although he doesn't remember a thing until he was "hauled out of the pond by a police officer." He requested his brothers dismantle the pond, "had the pond buried."

When asked to identify "all women dated by David Mead" proximate to Pam's death, he listed Ms. Walls, two others—he didn't know either's address or one's last name—but not Stormy. I had Anne expand upon how hard and often the civil plaintiffs asked about the mysterious Stormy. Anne testified about finding Winnie in Southern California and Rich won an objection on relevance. We did get in Mead's statements that he dated while he was separated, traveled with Winnetka to Las Vegas and, when asked about paying her rent, "that he has assisted several people with rent, including friends and family, during the relevant period of time."

As I led the witness to one particular transcript citation, Rich came in before my question and exercised good sense damage control. "Judge, again we'll admit that Mr. Mead made pornographic videos with Ms. Walls."

I handed Anne Sulton a copy of the buy/sell agreement detailing how David Mead re-acquired VGS, but put it in Pam's name, and a copy of the loan agreement with Mary. Rich objected on relevance and a three-way haggle erupted. The court wins all haggles, but the parties sometimes get to speak their piece.

Judge Frederick proffered, "I suppose that the issue at the moment has to do with whether or not these agreements ought to be received in evidence. If there is a dispute, at least on the face of the document, about the legal ownership of the business, then I suppose I ought to allow them to be admitted."

Rich responded, "I suspect those documents are accurate. The issue is whether Mr. Mead ran the business, and he did. That's what the issue is."

"The issue, Your Honor, has been all along why murder was a more acceptable alternative than divorce to Mr. Mead!"

"I am going to allow the witness to lay foundation for 30 and 31."

"Then, Your Honor, we will stipulate to their admission." Again, wise damage control by a good attorney to limit discussion about tough evidence.

Then I asked Anne about a call Mead made directly to her unlisted home number during the civil trial.

"What did he propose to you?"

"He told me that, if I dropped the lawsuit, he would return the body to Pam's family." Anne sat silent to allow the courtroom to contemplate a husband's love, and then continued, "It sent chills down my spine."

"I have nothing further, Your Honor."

"Objection! We want to reserve a motion! Your Honor, can we take . . . ?"

"Your objection has been noted, Counsel. You may cross-examine the witness."

About a minute into an angry cross, Judge Frederick called a recess. The jurors left and Richard Mauro exploded, "At this time we move a Motion for Mistrial, Judge! The question was asked of Ms. Sulton that she received a phone call from Mr. Mead. I will state for the record—we weren't aware of the phone call! I suppose Mr. Mead could have told us, but we didn't receive any discovery on the phone call."

Rich told the judge that under the rules the defense objection should have been made outside of the jury's presence, it was improper to bring up David's offer to settle the civil case in his criminal case and Anne's last statement about the chills in her spine was objectionable as irrelevant and prejudicial.

Anne was still on the witness stand. I rose to respond, thanking the defense for pointing out that if they didn't know about their client's offer to the plaintiff, it was because their client hadn't bothered to tell them. I made the point that all of the things Anne was pulling out of the civil transcripts were things that contradicted David Mead's representations to others. The whole offer to sell the body was a clear contradiction of the loving husband theme the defense brought out as recently as that same morning.

I admitted, giving a faux scolding glance to my witness, that Ms. Sulton's chilled spine comment was objectionable and should certainly be stricken.

Judge J. Dennis Frederick wasted no time in ruling to deny the Motion for Mistrial, joined our agreement to strike Anne's last observation and instruct the jury not to either take into account the statement or consider David's prior inconsistent statements as anything except that. The defense declined, not wanting everything dredged up one more time. We took a short break. Ben dropped another "Sneaky bastard" as he walked past but wouldn't look at me.

Rich had done his homework, had his own set of tabbed transcripts and took the witnesses to passages where David Mead told others he had no fear of losing the business in a divorce: Pam had no interest in it. She didn't want to dump lavatories. Rich moved to Mead's admission that Winnie often asked, begged and threatened him, but he offered a string of excuses to put her off and continued to play games, including telling Ms. Walls he ran over Pam's feet with a car.

Briefly, Rich had Anne go back over David's version of finding his wife in the fishpond, how he noticed the fish food, walked up to find Pam floating face down and saw her back and shoulders.

Rich bore in on the detail David provided about Stormy: He couldn't remember her last name. They had never had sex. She was about five foot two with long brunette hair. He gave some description of her children, thought she lived out in Tooele and might work for a video distributor. David provided the plaintiffs detail; they were just never successful in locating Stormy. Rich finished his cross-examination by having Anne relate David Mead's thoughts that the reason Pam left him was her pain in knowing her husband discussed family matters with "Miss Stormy."

My re-direct was short. "You mentioned that—in the direct examination—that the defendant never came forward during the discovery process to let you know that he had found Stormy. When you were questioning him at the federal trial, how did he tell you that he had, in fact, found Stormy? And gone in and talked to her?"

"He never mentioned it."

"Although he was being questioned about Stormy during a federal trial?"

"That's correct," and with that Anne Sulton's work on the other side of the witness stand was over.

I recalled Jill to the stand for some clarifying questions. Then, after clearing up a few loose ends, I felt we'd done all we could to bring the truth about Pam Mead's death to light. Subject to making sure all the appropriate exhibits were moved and admitted, I said, "The State rests."

29

The Defense Speaks

It was after eleven o'clock, but early enough that His Honor
Frederick wanted the defense to call their first witness. At the
close of the State's case defense attorneys routinely make a
Motion to Dismiss claiming insufficient evidence that,
granted on rare occasions, serves as a preview of what they'll
argue in close. The judge gave the defense the right to make
that motion after they called witnesses and Ben Hamilton
took Mary Stokes by surprise, calling her as his first witness.

The defense had the same problems scheduling witnesses
and told their people to be ready for that afternoon. Since
Mary Stokes was in the courtroom, even though she was
unhappy being called by lawyers for the man she truly
believed killed her sister, they did.

Ben handed her the loan agreement; she confirmed that
the loan was paid off, that David continued to pay even during the Meads' separation and paid it off before Pam's death.
I had no cross.

Since Mary was the only witness available, Judge
Frederick sent the jury to lunch and asked Rich to pose his
motion. Rich rose to the task and told His Honor the solicitation of homicide count could not stand. The court ought to
dismiss that charge because the State hadn't proved David
Mead intended to have his wife killed when he dealt with
Jack Hendrix. Hendrix felt Mead wasn't being serious and
said so four times in deposition. It was too distant in time and
too ambiguous in its intent. Wasn't David just trying to estab-
lish a drug ring? What was the substantial step that took
place?

His Honor Frederick should dismiss the homicide count.
Winnetka Walls and Jack Hendrix weren't worthy of belief,

the big insurance policy wasn't even in effect during the overheard phone call, Dr. Grey changed his mind based only on the statements of Walls and Hendrix and there wasn't any evidence or witness directly bearing on August 15, 1994. The State hadn't met its burden.

Judge Frederick responded that he was persuaded that there was a sufficient showing to warrant jury consideration of both counts and would we reconvene at one thirty? We said our goodbyes to Anne and the Fairfields and went off to prep the afternoon.

When we returned attorney Kevin Kurumada was standing with the defense. Rich informed the court that Rich wanted Kevin to testify he advised Winnie, at the time his client, to take the Fifth on the deposition and that she told him she'd lied to Detective Candland. Kevin, however, intended to invoke attorney/client privilege. Team Mead felt Ms. Walls waived that privilege by testifying, so Kevin, as an officer of the court, had a duty to come forward.

I countered there was no record to correct: Ms. Walls testified that she took the Fifth and that not all of her original statement was true, she'd been thoroughly and vigorously cross-examined on those points and it's not proper to call a witness simply to have them invoke a privilege in front of the jury.

Judge Frederick asked Kurumada if he'd invoke and Kevin said he'd serve his client and her privilege. His Honor reminded the defense that Winnetka Walls was the owner of that privilege and, absent actual consent, Kevin Kurumada was not to be called.

Douglas G. Meacham was a case worker and psychotherapeutic counselor at the Utah State Prison; Jack's co-defendant in the robbery of David and Winnie was an inmate in his portfolio. Doug wasn't acquainted with Jack Hendrix.

I asked for a proffer of what this witness had to say and why it was relevant. Rich wanted Meacham to testify about where, how and for how long the co-defendant was serving his sentence, because I had asked Hendrix if his co-defendant got the same deal and same treatment.

"I never asked that question!"

The judge let Rich ask Meacham where the co-defendant

was housed and when his next parole date would come. Mauro did, to take one more swing that Jack got a sweetheart deal, and waited for my cross.

"Mr. Meacham, do you have any identical prisoners?"

"No. Not even identical twin brothers."

"So, the co-defendant would have a different prior record than Mr. Hendrix?"

"There is a certain degree of generalization that can be made, based on type-of-offense, degree-of-offense type sentences. But everyone is a unique situation."

"So, the co-defendant may well have a much different prior history before committing these crimes than Mr. Hendrix?"

"Very easily."

"And the co-defendant may have conducted himself much differently in prison than Mr. Hendrix?"

"Also very easily."

"So, when the co-defendant gets out—is that considered separately from Mr. Hendrix?"

"There will be no overlap between the consideration of release for either of them."

The look on Rich's face showed that he knew he got little mileage out of Doug Meacham. He called Edward Paul France, Ph.D. For ten or fifteen minutes, before we moved to his work on our case, we were treated to the detail of Dr. France's CV. Wally Bugden provided France copies of the ME's report, Todd's civil deposition, photographs from the scene and the autopsy.

Rich had a poster-sized note pad for the doctor to write down his points as he testified; I objected that it was duplicative but the judge waved me off. The expert's work had three components: he evaluated the scene of the accident; he explored the dynamics of the fall to define how a person in that environment could or could not fall; he tried to match the injuries to the event in order to reach his conclusion about the consistency, or inconsistency, of an accident or homicide. He was a good witness who used the word accident often, death seldom and murder or homicide only when accompanied by a negative and told the jury he tried to gather as much information as possible about the environment the victim found herself in at the time of the accident.

The witness observed the rocks and bricks forming the collar about the fishpond did not appear to be fixed. The loose nature of those stones might have formed an uneven surface that would lend to a slip and fall, exaggerated by the condition of Pam's feet, her balance impaired by unnatural footsteps.

He looked into the possibilities Pamela fell backward, fell face first or was struck and propelled into the water. Considering gravity and rotational components, he reasoned Pam's head was traveling thirteen to fifteen miles per hour at the instant of impact; he didn't specify which scenario. Rich asked if the doctor could quantify the resulting force and whether or not there would be sufficient force to cause specific injuries. I objected on foundation: this wasn't a medical doctor. His Honor agreed and Rich built foundation.

Dr. France participated in studies where cadavers were struck in the head to produce skull fractures, read about military experiments on forces causing changes in consciousness and supervised a student project that studied head injuries in aerial free-style skiers. He wasn't a doctor but his master's degree included study in physiology. Rich took him back to the scenario of Mrs. Mead's head traveling at thirteen to fifteen miles per hour and asked if the doctor had an opinion about her particular injury.

I objected, asked to *voir dire*, handed him his CV, asked if he were a medical doctor and he said he wasn't. My reading of his CV was that he had attended conferences on head injuries; had he ever been a presenter? No, but was once invited to. I renewed my objection that this was beyond his expertise.

The judge asked if Rich had a physician witness. He did, "Like the medical examiner. But the medical examiner isn't a biomechanical engineer."

His Honor understood the distinction, why a physician can talk about the medical implications of the blows and this biomechanical engineer about biomechanical engineering.

Frustrated, Rich moved France's CV as a substantive exhibit, I chose not to object on relevance, it was admitted and Rich placed it on the jury rail. A few jurors briefly thumbed the stapled inch of documents, then ignored it.

The doctor talked about how the "directionality" of the head wound helped him look at the dynamics and the positioning of the fall, when he took into account all the marks on the body and the final position of the body. Rich asked if Dr. France formed an opinion whether these were more consistent with an accident or a homicide. I objected, was overruled and, unsurprisingly, heard that the expert the defense hired was of the opinion Pam's death was an accident.

"Because, as I examined the evidence, it explained all the dynamics from the initiation of the fall: the contact with the head; there was an abrasion on the right elbow—back of the right elbow; and then the final rest position of a face-down position in the pool were all consistent with falling back into the pool, hitting on the back corner or the far side with the head. The elbow contact indicated that there was a rotational component that would take the body and move it into an upside down position."

"When I examined the scenario which involved a homicide, I found a lack of injuries to the front facial features, which I would expect if someone was hit and propelled across the pool onto the other side. An impact with an object that would have created the damage to the head, in my estimation, would also have created velocity for that body to move that individual, not only into the pool, but also onto the other side, with at least the forehead and the upper face region. I didn't see that evidence."

Rich broke in, "that last statement was a mouthful," needing a bit of incremental explanation. I lusted to cross-examine Edward Paul France, Ph.D. He continued on to tell the courtroom about a brick traveling at twenty-five to forty miles per hour transferring momentum sufficient to toss a human body across an entire pond. Alternately, we learned of a fall with its victim similarly sailing across to the distant shore, requiring a complete rotation of the body before impact, what a competitive diver or gymnast would refer to as a half twist. There was a bird's-eye-view diagram added to the sketchpad with red and green marks for perceived probable positions of standing and impact. We heard the words *diagrammatically* and *angulation* used in conversation.

Rich wound up his direct showing Dr. France an upward arm swing to beg an opinion that such a blow wouldn't be very accurate and would be difficult to control with the exact force needed to produce Pam's injury. Bending over to allow a side-slung blow, another hard swing to control, would have been painful to her feet.

I'd done my homework, too. The good doctor's report for the criminal defense team had morphed from the one prepared for Wally. If Todd Grey's amendments were an issue, I ought to return the favor. I'd save violations of the laws of physics and common sense for my close, but I was going to have some fun with the vaunted CV.

"Doctor, let me give you your CV back if I might. Apparently you have three academic appointments?"

"Actually, some of those are not current right now, so they would be past appointments."

"So, the CV you've given us isn't necessarily accurate?" I can do theatrical and transparent feigned surprise.

"No! I would say that it's accurate. It just needs to be updated and I haven't done that."

"So, you didn't give us an updated one?"

"I haven't produced one yet! I gave you the most current one I have."

"And you show four different jobs?"

"Yes."

Incredulously, "So, you have seven jobs right now?"

The witness launched into a short dissertation of how some of the company names are really different titles for the same entities or some appointments are where "every once and a while they will call me to consult." Team Mead seemed uncomfortable as their expert witness's temper rose.

"And you've done a lot of work on braces?"

"Yes. Most of my published work relates to knee bracing."

"Uh huh. A lot on carpal-tunnel syndrome?"

"One or two papers."

"Some on tissue fixation?"

"Yes."

"Have you done papers on slip and fall?"

"No. I have not."

I asked him about his proffered scenario for a homicide. He described, "And she would have been bent over. And there would have been an impact to the back of the head with an object, such as a brick, which would have caused her, then, to be propelled into the pool."

"By the blow?"

"Yes. By the blow."

"Or, perhaps by the assailant?"

"Could you elaborate on that for me, sir?"

I would do that, just a little later. "Why do you think that she was standing alongside the pool when she was hit?"

"Because there was no evidence of any blood or tissue outside the pool. Whatever would have happened, from a homicide standpoint, had to be localized, in the pool."

"It did?"

"I believe so, because there was no other evidence surrounding that pool."

"As a basis for your opinion, were you told that when the police arrived Mr. Mead was in the pool, pulling rocks and bricks surrounding the pool into the water?"

"As a basis of my opinion, that makes no difference. I mean, I saw that, but it makes no difference to me."

In an incredulous tone, I asked, "So, if Mr. Mead were to have taken the brick, or the rock, that had the hair or the blood or the tissue transfer on it and made sure that was the first one that goes into the pool, that wouldn't affect your opinion?"

"Would it affect my opinion?" After verbose equivocating that would do my profession proud, "So, yes. I think it would affect my opinion."

We moved to his opinion about the head wound. "You said that it would be difficult for someone to make this particular type of wound in a homicide scenario?"

"And match up all the other evidence that I reviewed. I'm not saying it couldn't be made by a brick."

"In a homicide scenario, would it be the object of the killer to make this precise wound or to kill his victim?"

"I would expect, in a homicide scenario, you want to kill the victim."

I picked up a copy of Dr. France's expert report, his first expert report prepared for Wally. "And you did a report?"

"I did."

With a smile, I handed it to the witness. "Uh huh?"

A little startled, he responded, "Yes. I did. I'm agreeing with you."

"And the summary of your report said—is it true it says, 'Based on a biomechanical analysis of the evidence reviewed, it is currently my opinion that the accidental slip and fall scenario is consistent with many of the facts of physical evidence available and cannot be dismissed as a viable possibility for explaining Pam Mead's death'?"

"That's correct. You read that . . ."

My voice continued the rise it had started during the last question and the tone became accusatory, "So, we have a viable possibility and now you are saying it is a probability?"

"I think the evidence, as I look at it, would lend more support to an accidental death."

"What other homicide scenarios have you considered?"

He spoke of Pam standing upright next to the pool and being struck. I asked if he considered a scenario where someone stood alongside Pam, hit her over the head and put her into the water while she was dazed. The witness went back to the lack of gore on the stones; I went back to physics.

"Well, you gave your scenario, Doctor, that, in fact, the momentum imparted from a brick as a weapon would be imparted into the body of Pamela Mead and cause her to surge forward?"

"There would be some horizontal component to the motion."

"Right! And what if there were somebody there, who had just hit her with a brick and then took her and pushed her into the water, would that change her momentum?"

"No. It would not."

After I responded completely incredulously, "It would not?" I invited the witness down into the well. We picked out a colored magic marker at the defense's sketchpad; I had Dr. France indicate where he felt Pam was standing in his accident scenario and draw in a stick figure of how he thought Pam landed while striking her head, at between thirteen and fifteen miles per hour, of course. We covered in more detail where she must have stood, how she slipped, translated, rotated and impacted. We talked about the collar of rocks.

I walked with the expert to a spot about ten feet in front of the jury, where, with the wave of a hand, I described on the floor an imaginary collar of rocks and bricks surrounding a six foot diameter pond. The two of us, side by side, not hand in hand, walked a circular path within that ring as we talked. He confirmed it was his opinion that Pam Mead walked from her house to the pool, then stepped at least two steps into the ring of loose rocks. She must have been turned sideways, on the inside of the collar, tangent with the edge, then walked a circular path, slipped and twisted and struck the back of her head on stones on the far side of the fishpond.

"So, she would have been walking inside of this collar of rock?"

"Or stepping along the collar."

The doctor and I walked together during the next questions, two steps ahead toward the imaginary center of the pool, then turned right and walked in an arc to our left to neither walk into the pond nor out of the collar, "At least two steps in and walking around it?"

"Yes."

"Sideways? On those loose rocks? In her orthopedic shoes? With the pins coming out of her toes?"

"That's right."

After the defense's expert witness confirmed he changed his opinion over the life of the fishpond case, from slip and fall couldn't-be-dismissed-as-a-viable-possibility to probability, I asked about the abdominal scrapes. He knew only David Mead saw Pam floating facedown in the pond and those scrapes were consistent with her being removed from the pond over the rocks. Even though I asked, he offered no opinion on whether the loving husband dragged Pamela Mead out of the fishpond by her feet or her hair. As faces grimaced considering those possibilities, I turned my back on the witness, walked back to the State's table and left him standing alone in front of the jury. Jill and I exchanged small smiles.

The re-direct examination of a witness after a tough cross,

called rehabilitation, went on for a bit about rotational components and the like. Dr. France inserted specific injuries and the lack of others into his hypothesis and restated his opinion. I asked one group of questions on recross, more to beg questions than get an answer: after Pam walked up onto that ring of stones, in the dark, on injured feet and turned sideways, was she walking clockwise or counterclockwise? His Honor called a short break as Edward Paul France, Ph.D., left the stand and the courthouse with less swagger than when he arrived.

Rich Mauro called David Mead's stepbrother back to the stand and asked if he ever had a telephone conversation with Mrs. Stokes where she asked him not to fill in the fishpond. He had not. I didn't cross-examine.

Ben Hamilton called the stepbrother's wife, who testified that a few weeks before Pam's death, she ran into the Meads out for an evening walk, talked with Pam, heard that David had just made his wife a present of clothing. Pam and Dave seemed very happy. On cross, she confirmed this was shortly after Pam's surgery; David was pushing Pam's wheelchair.

"Was David being the perfect husband?"

"What do you mean? He was just the David I always knew."

Another Capitol Hill neighbor testified he saw the Meads on their walk the night Pam died. He couldn't recall if Pam was using a cane but she needed assistance just walking, hanging on to David. Between ten thirty and eleven that night he got a telephone call from David Mead asking if he'd seen Pam or knew Kevin Harris's phone number.

On cross the neighbor told us that when he saw them the evening Pam died, the Meads were walking on a flat, solid sidewalk. He'd never gotten a similar phone call from either of the Meads in the two years he'd lived nearby.

The defense also recalled Hank Rider, another neighbor the State had called.

The night of Pam's death the Riders were working on a project, painting some boards out by their garage, heard nothing unusual, nothing over at the Meads'. I had no cross and Hank gave way to his wife.

She testified she had been on the painting project the

entire time; Hank had to work on his thesis. She saw David
Mead leave home between 8:15 and 8:20, waved and shouted
small talk before David, his normal friendly self, drove away.
They painted until well after dark. Normally she'd hear conversations from the Meads' backyard, but she neither saw nor
heard anything that evening, no backyard arguments.

Ben told the judge the defense was out of witnesses for
the day, Judge Frederick asked how many they had left and
Rich answered that they only had two, Dr. Kris Sperry and
John Mead, each flying in that evening. Judge Frederick
called the evening recess and told the jurors to return at nine
o'clock the next morning. I felt drained and needed the
evening with my family away from this traumatic case to
refuel.

30

A Formidable Roadblock

The next morning started with a phone call from the Bureau.
SSA O'Toole and her crew wanted an update, I filled her in
on the events of the afternoon before and she asked if I'd gotten the fax. I hadn't, but Michelle walked in with one. The
FBI wasn't ready to publish yet, but had a rough draft of an
article about profiles of staged and insurance fraud homicides. Better late than never, I'd read it whenever the jury
went out. With good wishes from back east, we headed to
court.

David's older brother was the first witness of the day. The
older Mead flew in the day after Pam's death to find David
curled in a fetal position, extremely emotional and only
barely able to participate in important decisions. It was this
brother who made the decision to get funeral arrangements
underway.

After David confirmed that Pamela had insurance and

provided his older brother with the documents, the brother looked those over and called the local claim service. He wanted to provide for funeral services so he called Pennington on Wednesday, or maybe late on Tuesday. He was instructed to call the Fairfields, the agents who sold the policy, phoned and left a message on their voicemail.

When Gayle called, Mead's older brother said he'd be staying a few days and serve as the contact person. Gayle said she'd process the claim and the brother, thinking this was no one else's business, asked Gayle not to speak to anyone else.

He was aware of the burglaries at Pam and David's home and stayed there a few nights because of those. Rich asked his witness about filling the pond, "Did David participate in any of those discussions?"

"No. I told David what my decision was after I made my decision and I instructed my brothers to dismantle the fishpond."

He told the jury he was the person who sent Detective Candland the flowers, signed David's name and used David's credit card to thank her for the compassion she showed dealing with the family.

I started my cross-examination with the insurance policy. "Gayle Fairfield testified she found the call on her answering machine on Tuesday." He wouldn't "discredit" that but remembered talking to another agent and telling her only to talk to him. I asked if he recalled emphatically telling her not to talk to the Stokeses. He didn't; a brief review of prior testimony refreshed his memory of the demand, but he still disputed whether it was emphatic.

He testified he asked that the money arrive quickly out of concern for David's ability to pay for the funeral, though he wasn't aware of David's finances. It was none of his business and he understood David was doing fine.

We met Kris Lee Sperry, MD as Rich Mauro took the Chief Medical Examiner of the State of Georgia through his impressive credentials. Dr. Sperry is a man of great renown, often giving commentary on television coverage of notorious cases. I stipulated to his qualification as an expert, but a good attorney like Mauro wasn't about to let that get in the way of gilding this lily.

Doctor Sperry reviewed the original autopsy, Ken Farnsworth's report, the photographs from the scene and the autopsy itself, the toxicology and other laboratory results and Dr. Todd Grey's civil transcripts. He formed opinions on this case and those were that the cause of Pamela Mead's death was drowning and the manner was accidental. Kris was an extremely credible witness who calmly explained to an attentive jury the procedures for arriving at findings about the cause and manner of human death. It's unusual to use outside or investigative information as to cause of death; that almost always comes from the autopsy. Manner of death, however, requires an ME to "generate a more comprehensive or bigger umbrella" of input. A pathologist will frequently take into account the circumstances, the investigation and elements that may be found, or may be missing, at the scene.

The witness addressed how he reached the conclusion of accident, and well up his list was the absence of other injuries indicating attack by another or attempts at defense by the victim. The fatal mechanism of drowning in an environment that appeared so conducive to bad footing was important and the condition of Pam's feet heightened that. Rich handed Dr. Sperry the foam head and they discussed the wound drawn by Dr. Grey. The Chief Medical Examiner of the State of Georgia was at all times complimentary of the work of the Chief Medical Examiner of the State of Utah. In a very non-derogatory and professional manner, Kris Sperry built his case: they were two professionals who disagreed on a conclusion.

This doctor told the jurors that the head wound appeared more consistent with the force typical to a fall than to an attack—not a fatal injury, but certainly one capable of rendering someone unconscious or dazed, unable to extricate him- or herself from a dangerous situation, like a fishpond. It was a "pattern injury" that indicated the sort of object, like a brick in this case, that impacted the victim.

He felt the elbow injury was indicative of a fall and the abdominal abrasions consistent with being dragged out of the pond. A couple of the jurors squirmed on that, perhaps recalling my quandary to Dr. France about which handle David employed.

Georgia's Chief Medical Examiner also felt the absence of other injuries was significant: based on his experience an attacker often not only leaves "defensive wounds" on his victim's hands and arms, but frequently will repeatedly and brutally attack the face. That was not present here.

Rich then took his witness into a discussion of staged homicides. Dr. Sperry had seen those; they're very difficult to get away with because there was always something out of place. Like setting up a string of dominoes or a house of cards, if everything isn't perfect, they all fall down. There's always something that doesn't fit.

Mauro handed the doctor the brick and asked him if the brick were capable of causing the injury that took place. He agreed, but it would be difficult to achieve precisely the wound Pam received. If the blow weren't hard enough "you'd have a fight on your hands," and most people attacked with blunt instruments are hit over and over again until they stop moving.

The expert had dealt with people who died accidentally falling from a standing position, often people who were intoxicated or otherwise unable to maintain their balance. There was nothing here Dr. Kris Lee Sperry saw as inconsistent with an accidental death.

This was a serious expert with professional observations and conclusions that needed to be worked with rather than assaulted. One thing about an honest pro, they give honest answers and, asked the right questions, they become assets. I abandoned the tack of going after the "reasonable medical certainty" and steered in other directions.

Dr. Sperry agreed with me that, as a state ME, he almost always testifies for the prosecution, but today he was a privately funded expert for the defense. When he as an ME receives a case, and a body, his duty is to gather and marshal all the evidence and determine what conclusion the evidence supports. As an expert for one side in a lawsuit, wasn't his duty to marshal all the evidence that supports the client's conclusion? He disagreed: his duty is to review the available evidence and generate his opinions. If his conclusions favor the person employing him, he'll probably wind up in court; if not, they won't buy him a plane ticket. Dr. Kris Sperry will give an honest opinion, based on the information he is provided. The information he worked with here was provided by the defense, first by the civil lawyers, the rest by the criminal defense team. He didn't obtain evidence on his own or call Dr. Grey. He'd like to some day, but they were on opposite sides in a lawsuit and it wasn't a good idea.

After he once again told us he had no problems with Dr. Grey's work, the witness said he didn't know what additional information Todd had and it would depend on what that was to determine if it might change his own opinions. Kris Sperry was not told the specifics of how David Mead, before his wife's passing, announced to four separate people he would cause her death. He hadn't been told David hired Jack to kill Pam, that his wife would have a nasty slip and fall, that it would be easier to get someone to kill her for the insurance or that David ought to knock the bitch off. The defense expert knew there was a new insurance policy but not the details. He hadn't been told that the liner of the fishpond was covered with rocks and David stood steadily while picking up and moving stones.

These wouldn't change his underlying opinion, but "I mean, does it raise the suspicion level? Yes."

The doctor commented on blows struck against a victim standing upright, so I repeated that examination assuming a victim bent at the waist. We talked about defensive wounds and the witness conceded that, were the victim taken by surprise, as example struck in the back of the head, mounting a defense and receiving defensive wounds would be unlikely. He also felt that most people who slip and fall try to catch themselves and, in the accident scenario, Pam landed on a pile of rocks but her nails remained long and smooth. He agreed Pam did not have the sort of additional bruising he'd expect on someone who fell upon stones, but she had dark skin and bruising might not have been obvious.

"In a homicide scenario, is the object to put a three or four centimeter cut to the back of someone's head, or is the object to kill them?"

"In the vast majority of them, the object is to kill them, at any cost and with any effort available."

"All right. If somebody were trying to set this thing up to look like an accident, they would probably not go to the multiple blows you've been talking about? They would probably try one blow?"

"If one were going to do that, I think that more than one blow would be a red flag for the pathologist. Yes."

I heard the magic words. "And there are such things as red flags?" My level of conversational questioning became more intense.

For a while, the witness joined in, "Of course. I mean, in most homicide scenarios, you know, the level and degree of severity of the injury is off the scale, if you wish. I would say, in a homicide scenario, this small amount of injury that appears is almost . . . Well, I wouldn't view it that way. That just isn't what people tend to do if they set out to kill someone else."

"Now, you are familiar with scenarios, particularly in sexual situations, where one person hates another and wants them dead out of hate?"

"Yes! Yes."

"And, in fact, usually those are extremely brutal?"

"Overkill is the term that's often used. Yes."

"Lots of wounds to the face typically?"

"Face! Much more severe injury than what is necessary really to kill the person. Yes."

"'Cause they're just getting their licks in?"

The doc brought us back to proper courtroom jargon and pace. "Well, it's a phenomenal outpour of emotion that's focusing on this one individual. Yes."

I matched his tone. "Well, what about a homicide where the motive is not emotion or hate, but it's money? You don't see that kind of outpouring of violence? Do you?"

"No. Usually not in those scenarios. No. I would say overkill would be unusual where that is the sole motive."

"Now, you were talking about staging and you were cross-examined in the federal trial on staging?"

"Yes."

"And, as I recall, you've talked about red flags there?"

"Yes."

"And you were cross-examined about the FBI's list of red flags in an insurance-related staging death?"

"There were some questions asked me about that. Yes."

"And you said that you recognize those?"

"I know of their existence. I cannot quote them to you. It's not something I've looked at in a long, long time."

Rich objected that his expert wasn't familiar with these criteria; I said I was only asking him to look at these in terms of his experience. The judge always gets the last word: "That's the vein I took it. I don't think the witness is being asked to comment on the credibility of the FBI's list. I think he's simply making observations based upon his own experience."

With the jurors hearing once again those three glittering initials of our culture, FBI, we moved on. Physical evidence is removed prior to police arriving? Yes, I can see that. Offender may alter evidence by collapsing, falling, removing or destroying evidence after police arrive? I can see that, too. To individuals close to the offender and victim, it may appear that their relationship was improving? I don't have enough knowledge to comment on that.

The doctor repeated that Pam endured a significant blow to the head that would have caused some degree of dazing, even unconsciousness, very reasonable to assume it sufficient to allow another to put the victim into a body of water and hold her head under, with little effort, until she drowned.

Re-direct came swiftly and Georgia's ME said that he's free not to testify if he doesn't agree with the position a client requires. He agreed a witness who lied would distort a finding, if the pathologist relied on the lying witness.

Rich asked where the face and body would go if a person, while bending over, were struck in the back of the head with a brick. Dr. Sperry said it would be downward, possibly forward, face-first into the rocks, but Pam sustained no facial injuries. If she were held under the water, there might have been other bruising, but none was found.

The witness, who never personally amended a manner of death finding, talked about my list of FBI profiling criteria and what would make the house of cards of a staged homicide come down. Inconsistencies are what make everything fall apart.

I had a one question re-cross: "Doctor, you know how Counsel talked to you about when you see red flags and the house of cards comes tumbling down. In such a scenario, after the medical examiner and/or the detective realize that the house of cards cannot stand, what is the normal consequence in a homicide scenario? Isn't that when someone is charged with murder?"

"Yes."

"Thank you."

"All right, Doctor, you may step down, sir."

"Thank you, sir."

"And, while you have a chance, you'd best go."

"I'll get while the getting's good. Yes, sir."

"Any further witnesses, Mr. Mauro?"

"Kevin Kurumada, Your Honor."

We'd been waiting for David Mead, but Kev wasn't much of a surprise. He had gotten hold of Ms. Walls, who said it was okay for him to testify. He told us that when he first met with Winnie, she told her attorney she'd lied to the police. When Ms. Walls told Kevin about the deposition, he advised her to take the Fifth. Kurumada went with her to the deposition and she did invoke.

I showed Kev the hand-written notarized statement and asked if that lined sheet of paper, torn from a pad and signed "before the majesty of a notary public" was the work product of his law office; it wasn't. I asked him if he was aware of her many statements or that his client testified to this very jury that there was truth and lie in each of her statements. I pointed at the jury and asked a witness neither hostile to my person nor cause, "And within your range of expertise as an attorney, you're aware that these folks, right here, are the ones who are going to judge whether or not what she told them is the truth?"

"Yes. I believe that is true."

He left the stand and Judge Frederick asked if the defense had further witnesses. All eyes were on David Earl Mead. Was he going to testify? Rich stood. "Judge, we rest."

"Any rebuttal, Mr. Lemcke?"

"Your Honor, the State will have no witnesses on rebuttal."

There was a certain ceremony for the defendant to make a record that he's aware of his right to testify in his own behalf but chooses to follow the advice of his attorneys and not testify. In my gut I wanted him to take the stand; we were well armed, had the FBI scheme ready to go, reams of transcripts of prior statements to confront and impeach and I was on a roll. But two very good lawyers at the defense table made the wise choice.

It was only about eleven o'clock. Judge Frederick sent the jury out for lunch and brought the parties back into chambers where we worked on the final jury instructions and double-checked that all evidence was admitted. I told Jill and the Stokeses I'd meet them at one thirty; I needed to be alone and firm up my thoughts on closing argument. I went back to my office, turned off the lights, closed the door and my eyes.

31

Closing Arguments

The troops gathered for closing argument with handshakes, pats on the back, words of encouragement and confidence on both sides of the aisle. Despite certain mystique about closing as an apex of trial, there are rules everybody works to stay within, but still push the envelope. I couldn't talk about the internal finances of VGS, but I could get into David's feelings. Rich would have to walk softly on the loose stones of Dr. France's medical conclusions.

The afternoon started out with instructions to the jury read by Judge J. Dennis Frederick. There were thirty-three numbered instructions—some as short as a single sentence, others more than one page—that defined the crimes, detailed the duties and set forth the protections and presumptions that the

Constitution provides a criminal defendant. They set forth the law of the State of Utah on intent and actions, explained motive is not an element, distinguished direct and circumstantial evidence and reminded the jury that statements of lawyers aren't evidence at all.

They opened with, "You are instructed that the defendant, David Mead, is charged by the Information which has been duly filed with the commission of Criminal Homicide, Murder, and Solicitation of Criminal Homicide. The Information alleges: . . ."

They ended with, "When you retire to consider your verdicts, you will select one of your members to act as Foreperson who, as Foreperson, will preside over your deliberations.

"Your verdicts in this case must be either:

"Guilty of CRIMINAL HOMICIDE, MURDER, a First Degree Felony, as charged in Count I of the Information; or

"Not Guilty of Count I, CRIMINAL HOMICIDE, MURDER, a First Degree Felony; And/Or

"Guilty of SOLICITATION OF CRIMINAL HOMICIDE, a Second Degree Felony, as charged in Count II of the Information; or

"Not Guilty of Count II, SOLICITATION OF CRIMINAL HOMICIDE, a Second Degree Felony; as your deliberations may determine.

"This being a criminal case, a unanimous concurrence of all jurors is required to find a verdict. Your verdicts must be in writing and, when found, must be signed and dated by your Foreperson and then returned by you to this Court. When your verdicts have been found, notify the Bailiff that you are ready to report to the Court."

With that His Honor signed and dated the packet of instructions, showed the jurors the four pre-printed verdict forms and noted only half of those should be signed, dated and returned. Then he turned to me. "How much time do you need for argument and how do you chose to split that time?" I took a deep breath, thought and announced an hour and fifteen minutes and I wished to divide them at fifty and twenty-five. He said he'd warn me when I had two minutes left. Rich said the hour and a quarter would be fine, although he didn't believe he'd need that much.

"Mr. Lemcke, you may proceed."

"Thank you, Your Honor. Your Honor, Counsel, Mr. Mead, ladies and gentlemen, in a case as long as this, with as much evidence as we've gone over, there's always a question of where do I begin . . ."

I looked at the jury, letting my eyes quickly roam their faces one by one. Then I went on.

"I want to start with something kind of recent, something from yesterday. If you remember, David Mead's stepbrother's wife came in here and she told us about the one time when she saw David wheeling Pamela around in the wheelchair. And I asked her, because of the other things that came out, if it seemed to be a perfect marriage. And she said, 'Yeah, it was the David we always knew.' Well, it was the David they always knew, but not the David they thought they knew."

"We've brought in our witnesses in this case in somewhat of an order of how they became involved in the case or, actually, how they became involved with Detective Candland. You first heard from Barbara Wayne, a lady who was a neighbor to the Meads and who heard wailing that night. She thought she heard a woman in trouble. She did. She phoned 9-1-1. She did not go down to the scene."

With that I addressed witnesses in order of appearance and how the testimony of each played into the fishpond case.

"Now, Detective Candland—the now defrocked Detective Candland—was the case manager!" Jill's laugh was an octave or two above jurors' chuckles as we walked through Jill's odyssey at David Mead's house and into the next morning, discussing how at first glance the scene looked like an accident. "All she had to do was to interview David, clean up a few things, close the case and move on."

I recalled the call from Angela, Winnie's revelations large and small, sad and spectacular, true and otherwise, discussions with Todd Grey, the message from Jack Hendrix. More meetings with Todd Grey led to Greg Skordas, Anne Sulton, Mary Stokes and the provocative conversation about Stormy. I highlighted the insurance policy, civil lawsuit, an affirmative decision to wait out the depositions and interrogatories and a man named Bill Morgan, the same man who, while listing employees who did work that night, did not remember seeing David Mead.

Then I touched on how Pam's friend, the departed Kevin Harris, found the light bulbs, plural, unscrewed, noted the pain Pam suffered when he saw her walking with difficulty one day before she died. Kevin also saw the bottom of the fishpond covered with rocks, not the slippery plastic of the defense expert's hypothesis.

After that I went to Todd Grey, who did the autopsy and changed his opinion twice. I brought up that Dr. Sperry had no qualms about Dr. Grey's work in the autopsy, just one of his conclusions.

Pausing a moment, I looked around to see if the jury was with me; they were. Seeing their eyes fastened on me, I went on. "Winnie. Winnetka Walls. Well, you were here. It was like pulling teeth: Winnie showed up an hour and a half late; answers that came from Winnie, each one came out late. We always had to go back and refresh her recollection. Winnie told us she still loves David. You remember that little tête-à-tête when I had to do my best third grade teacher imitation and say, 'I'm sorry, Ms. Walls, would you share that with the entire class?' and heard 'David, why did you do this to me?' "

Ms. Walls told several stories, hired Kevin Kurumada, took the Fifth and signed the document I mocked, but I reminded the jury that the only measure that counted was if they believed she told them the truth in this trial.

I surmised that none of the jurors wanted the old Jack Hendrix to be their next-door neighbor, but commented that the new Jack Hendrix had been rather straightforward with them about what he was and what he'd been. "No one contradicted Jack's testimony. His mother and his wife corroborated parts of it, as did details of Mead's situation that could have only come from Mead. The perfect husband for a year, David would have an alibi, a big insurance policy his stepbrother who kept the books never heard of."

I asked the jurors "Where would you go to find someone to kill a spouse. Church? PTA? Your junkie cousin Jack who just got out of prison?" This jury met Jack Hendrix. Was he clever enough to create this story and hold it together for four years? In the end, did this jury believe what this witness said in this trial?

"You heard from Stormy. Stormy is a remarkable witness, a truly remarkable witness, if you think about it; she ties everything together. Plus the fact that she—you know, if you meet her—she's kind of a normal person." Where again, other than from David, would she get the detail? Even the detail she doesn't remember, the dates of the concerts, fixes the start of the year of the perfect husband. David didn't know her in the civil case, but knew how to find her to keep her from coming forward.

Then I walked the jury back through Todd Ryan, who heard the chilling words, "knock the bitch off."

David's younger brother kept the books, found the Pennington policy, knew about Bill Morgan, how David's stepbrother introduced Winnetka, warned her to keep her distance, was a signatory on the account but didn't know what went through it, entered the airport through the airline package office, was there when Pennington was phoned. "David talked to his stepbrother about losing his home and VGS in a divorce."

"Two minutes, Mr. Lemcke," the judge let me know. I took a quick, deep breath. I had more than two minutes of evidence left to cover. I pushed into how the Fairfields' versions of an insurance deal contrasted with David's and "Make it quick. Keep it quiet."

The scenario presented by Dr. France—the witness who changed his mind—required us to believe Pam walked out to the pond, up onto the rocks, then turned and walked sideways to feed fish. She must have tripped and struck her head on the far side of the pond, at least six feet away from where she fell.

"Your time is up, Mr. Lemcke."

"Can I cut into my rebuttal?"

"Go ahead."

"I'm going to have to," I said, taking another deep breath. Time pushed me even harder. One of the few built-in advantages the prosecution enjoys is the ability to split the time of our closing argument and reserve a portion to rebut the defense, a precious commodity that needs to be guarded, and mine was slipping away. I reminded the jury the last people who saw Pam walking saw her doing so with assistance on a flat sidewalk. "This woman, who screamed in pain at a puppy's touch, had to maneuver alone, on loose rocks, in open-toed sandals, in the dark, after walking uphill on bad ground to fulfill this expert's vision and feed a few bucks' worth of goldfish?"

David Mead's oldest brother told us he was the one who decided everything, despite David's statements to the contrary. He wanted to see the pond but had others dismantle it and never walked out the back door to look. He was worried about David being able to pay for the funeral but had no idea about David's finances.

Finally, Dr. Sperry agreed with Dr. Grey about everything except the manner of death and admits he was not provided all the facts. He conceded the object in a homicide would be to kill the victim, not cause a particular wound, and talked about those FBI red flags we read off one at a time. "That list was this case!" Dr. Sperry said how hard it would be to stage a homicide, a house of cards where something will come apart, the cards will fall and someone will be charged with murder.

Now I finally had come to the end of all I'd planned on saying and felt so strongly.

"We have charged David Mead with soliciting Jack Hendrix to kill Pamela Mead. And when that went awry, he, by his own devices or devices other than Jack Hendrix, came back and caused the death of Pamela Mead. The witnesses, the evidence interconnect. And I think, ladies and gentlemen, you will look at it and you will see that the evidence is there to find the defendant guilty of these charges. Thank you."

I sat down. Every other thing I might have said spun through my mind. I got supportive looks from Jill and the Stokeses, but I worried about compressing my thoughts at the end and having too little time for my rebuttal.

His Honor called a ten-minute recess.

When David Mead returned to the defense table, Rich took over. "Thank you, Your Honor. On August 15 of 1994, Jennifer Rider saw David Mead going to work. She saw him bound down the hillside, get into his car like he always did, drive away and leave for work, like he always did. Nothing was different that night. David Mead arrived home at about eleven o'clock and he called Kevin Harris. You heard about that. He left a message on Kevin's voice machine."

Rich played Mead's message asking if Kevin had seen Pam. "Ten minutes later you heard Barry Baxter describe how David was crying and how he was sad and how he was pleading for help." Rich pointed at the aerial photograph of the neighborhood. "And you heard how Hank Rider came down through this alleyway with his flashlight, because he had never heard a scream like that. And Hank said that there's no way anyone could fake that. And they went into the back-yard and they saw David screaming for help and crying for help and begging for someone to please help him with Pam, because Pam had died in the pond that was in the backyard.

"The police came out to the scene and they saw Dave. And Officer Tausinga and Officer Jensen, they described that David was crying and that he was despondent and that he was distraught. The police reached their conclusions. They did what they had to do: they picked up evidence. Mr. Farnsworth was there and Sergeant Roberts was there. Ms. Candland was there and all the police were there. They did their investigation. They did everything that they needed to do and they reached a conclusion that it was an accident. They went to the medical examiner's office the next day and reached the same conclusion.

"The prosecutor doesn't really want to talk a whole lot about August 15, because August 15 is the day that this accident occurred. When Winnetka Walls came down the road, some time later, nothing that she said changed any of the physical facts that were developed on August 15. Nothing that she did changed the way any of the injuries were. Nothing she did changed anything, because she wasn't there and she didn't see anything.

"When the police talked to Jack Hendrix, in the Davis County Jail, for the first time—the first attempt—nothing he said changed anything concerning the physical evidence. Nothing he said changed anything on August 15. Nothing he said changed anything, because he wasn't there.

"When the police talked to Stormy just a few months ago, nothing she did changed anything. Nothing she said changed the way that this accident occurred.

"We heard one of the witnesses talk today about something that was a pretty powerful metaphor. He talked about dominoes. Let me tell you what the State would have to prove, to prove to you that David Mead is guilty. And they are dominoes. And dominoes are a good way of looking at them."

A central theme and/or analogy is a great way to hold a long argument together. Rich was off to a strong start and moved into rhetorical devices: David Mead, later David, had become the more familiar, comfortable Dave; Mr. Lemcke evolved into the State, the government and finally, they. Rich asked how his client could have set on their edges the dominoes of the perfect wound, just enough to stun, and getting Pam past his neighbors to the pond.

Rich shifted seamlessly back into his theme and reminded our jurors that witnesses, perhaps Winnie, Jack or Stormy, could lie, but physical evidence cannot. Everything gathered that evening could be scientifically tested. All the police experience on that scene didn't bother to pull out of the fishpond the bricks Dave pulled in. There were no red flags on August 15. Everything, or everyone, who came forward after August 15 could not be, maybe would not be, similarly scrutinized.

Mauro reminded the jury of Pam's condition, prone to slip and to fall, the fish food next to the pool, as if dropped during a fall, that little cut on her head and that big dog that jumped on everyone. Dr. Grey, the State's witness, called this an accidental drowning. There were no red flags in the physical evidence; the dominoes were all upright and steady.

"The neighbors saw nothing out of place. That terrible night they heard nothing before the accident, saw nothing unexpected after the tragedy, saw no tilting dominoes. Winnie, Jack and Stormy, who weren't anywhere near the fishpond, are the ones who say they know what happened."

Now he was full throttle. "What does that all mean with this change in the manner of death? . . . But you see what the problem is. He gets boxed into a corner because of the police.

What they end up doing, they end up going to the prosecutor and saying, 'God! There's problems with stuff other than the physical evidence and we want you to file this.' So, where does the medical examiner go? He goes to the police station. That's not a crime lab! The police, they don't show the ME evidence; there's nothing physical for him to re-examine. They talk to him about Winnie. He doesn't know if she recanted her testimony or changed her testimony or lied in any of her testimony. They didn't tell him any of that!"

Rich moved into how "they" told Todd about Jack Hendrix who "had a few problems in his life." Dr. Grey didn't test Jack Hendrix and only the statements of Jack and Winnie made him change his mind. "Is that what he did? You need to decide that. Let me suggest to you that that's exactly what he did in this case! It was good science that he had, and he exchanged good science for bad science. And that is what these people told you from the witness stand."

Dr. Paul France provided a reasonable alternate hypothetical scenario of slip and fall. This wasn't a static event; things and people were moving and Pam wound up in the pond where she drowned and died. Wasn't the thirteen miles per hour of a fall so much more logical, given the wound, than the twenty-five to forty miles per hour of a hard-to-control, impossible-to-predict, swing? How would you get exactly enough force to cause that wound and pull off the murder?

What made Dr. France's scientifically-based conjecture so reasonable was that the government hadn't defined a single homicide scenario of their own. "I mean, they've presented three or four different scenarios. And the reason that they have is because they flat don't know what scenario existed! They don't have an explanation; they don't have an explanation for you. And it's their burden of proof!" Dr. Sperry's analogy of dominoes set Dr. France's tile solidly on its end.

This courtroom heard through Anne Sulton about Dave himself: "He has cooperated. He has answered every question. He has provided them every business document." Dave had affairs, but that didn't make him a murderer. Rich expressed his fear that we offered a lot of evidence of Dave Mead, bad person, and a lot of little digs to cause jurors to write Dave off and convict him on that alone.

"But, you know, I hate to use this example, I mean we sort of live in a time where we have a president who had an affair. And let me suggest to you that he acted in many of the same ways David Mead acted, in terms of his honesty, in terms of what he said about what he did in the affair. But having an affair doesn't make you a murderer. And trying to make him look like a bad person doesn't change the dominoes. None of that changes the dominoes!"

We sat stunned as Rich moved on. He took his gamble, the zinger inserted to push his case over the edge. Jill grabbed my notepad and wrote, "Did he just say Bill Clinton is no different than David Mead?" I wrote, "David Mead has better taste than Bill Clinton."

The defense went after former Detective Candland, "an officer who the police say shouldn't be a detective anymore. There's no printout or paperwork from the Airport Police about Dave using Gate #13. How many times did Ms. Candland interview Jack Hendrix? Till he got her story straight? When she told you that she waited to screen the case until after the civil trial, what new evidence could she find? Anything except Bill Morgan?

"The government wants you to see Bill Morgan as 'the key to the case.' Bill Morgan was a disgruntled and incompetent employee who went through a bitter firing, with a motive to lie."

We heard all the reasons not to believe Winnetka Walls, how "heaven hath no rage as love to hatred turned, nor hell a fury like a woman scorned," the notarized recantation, the Fifth and the retaining of Kevin Kurumada.

Jack Hendrix was run over the coals of credibility in his absence. The charts were displayed. "Candland conducted all those interviews. Even after he went to prison, they helped him. I think that I heard the State say that Hendrix got nothing for his testimony. Freedom is not nothing! Being free and being out and being on the street is not nothing!"

Stormy was "an interesting person" angry at David for lying to her and her ex for cheating on her. If she had a sincere belief Dave was guilty, why didn't she come forward sooner? The most interesting thing about Stormy in Rich's construction was that Dave told her in 1992 he ought to kill

Pam for the insurance. The policies weren't in effect until early 1994. Where did she come up with this notion? Who interviewed Stormy? Ms. Candland! Is there a problem with Stormy's ability to remember over all these years? Was Dave misleading everyone about Stormy's identity? Hadn't he said she had lived in Tooele and worked for a video distributor?

Todd Ryan talked to Pam after the phone call. She didn't seem upset, frightened or scared, told Mr. Ryan the Meads broke up for a while but got back together.

The insurance policies were instigated by the Fairfields. Pam and Gayle started talking because Pam was worried about the business. The policy was only worth $500,000 in the event of an accident and Pennington put the whole $500,000 in the federal case's pool. Pennington thought Pam's death was an accident.

Rich wound down with the charge of solicitation to commit a homicide and referred the jury to the instruction that required them to find beyond a reasonable doubt. He said they only had Jack Hendrix's word and he said he thought Dave was joking. Jack said David just wanted Jack's help in dealing drugs. Jack said he never intended to kill Pam for those drugs or that money.

Mauro explained that proof beyond a reasonable doubt is the highest burden and standard in the law. His voice grew gentle. "This is a pretty important case. It's a pretty important case to David and it has been for four years. David has gone through a lot in four years. They've asked him questions. They've asked him for information. They've asked him for everything. He's given them everything that he had. He's not perfect and he's not going to stand here before you today and tell you he's perfect. And he's not going to stand here and tell you that he likes the things that he did. But he didn't kill his wife. And he didn't offer his cousin any money or drugs to kill his wife.

"Ben and I have tried within the last week to do the best we can, within the limits of our abilities, to demonstrate to you that the only just verdict, on both these counts, is a verdict of not guilty. That's your decision to make and, as I said, I know that you'll exercise that decision wisely.

"We've always said, from day one—and Dr. Sperry said it

best—that the dominoes have to fall. On August 15, this case was an accident. When the police talked to Winnetka Walls, this case was an accident. When they talked to Jack Hendrix, this case was an accident. And nothing that they did, or nothing that anyone said, changed this in any way. And today, this case is an accident. Thank you."

Judge Frederick was not given to wasting time. "All right. Thank you, Mr. Mauro. Mr. Lemcke."

My initial close had been calm, low key, almost pedestrian, but my rebuttal came with emotion. Sometimes the volume rises, the courtliness of language slips and choice of word, phrase or analogy returns a lawyer to his roots. Rich Mauro put on a strong, organized close; I had to up the ante.

"Thank you, Your Honor. Let me refer you right off the bat, ladies and gentlemen, to one thing that was said in Mr. Mauro's close when he was talking about Dr. Grey. He said, 'Well, you remember Dr. Grey and, oh, I think that I'll change my opinion because the police want me to.' That wasn't what Todd Grey said! The other thing they said, 'Well, gee, they didn't tell Todd Grey that Winnetka Walls had recanted.' She recanted two years later! If you're going to represent the evidence, the first thing you have to do is start by representing the evidence as the evidence was!"

I brought up dominoes and the difficulty of achieving a specific wound when the actual objective was to kill the victim. Rich said there wasn't insurance when Mead first talked to Stormy, but David recognized and remedied that situation to the tune of a half million dollars. The defendant answered every question; those answers just weren't true.

"The answer to whether what Winnetka Walls said had anything to do with the night Pam Mead died was in David's promise Pam would die, before the month was out, in a nasty slip and fall, while he had an alibi, and in his choice of the word *murder*. It has everything to do with that night.

"I never said Jack didn't get a deal; I said he got the benefit of what bargain he got long before he testified in this trial. The defense said he was uncorroborated, but what about his mom and wife, that $30,000 bank account David's brother and bookkeeper didn't know about and all the detail about David's home, business, marriage and wife's surgery?

There's one other concept: It isn't Jack Hendrix's state of mind—whether or not he intended to kill Pam Mead—it's David Mead's state of mind—whether or not to have Pam Mead killed—that's the question here.

"Did Pam tell Todd Ryan she wasn't afraid? She told him she was leaving her husband. Why didn't Stormy come forward and warn Pam? The day of the phone call she asked and Mead wouldn't let her. During the civil case, he found her and told her not to.

"There was cover-up when David pulled stones into the fishpond, had it filled the next day, couldn't remember Bill Morgan, couldn't remember Stormy, moved Winnetka Walls to San Diego and proposed to her, without a ring, this very year.

"There was no reasonableness in Dr. France's alternative hypothesis. Pam with her feet and protruding pins walking on loose stones, in a circular path, doing a back flip, hitting only her head on a stone on the distant shore. Is it reasonable she'd walk out there in the dark—because the light bulbs were unscrewed—uphill over bad ground, past the dog to feed the fish because her husband wouldn't be home for three hours? Goldfish don't starve in three hours! You can't starve goldfish! You feed goldfish by pitching the food on the surface, all of two feet! Why would anyone, much less someone who was physically hampered, walk up onto the rocks? Dr. France's scenario was silly.

"And we have theater, 'there was blood everywhere'—a great theatrical image; there just wasn't blood everywhere. Only David saw Pam floating facedown in that dirty old water. How many movies is that one in? But floating is extremely unlikely. What can you see looking down on the surface of water, in a dark pool, on a dark night? Nothing, just reflections, unless you know what to look for."

I suggested, "Think of David Earl Mead as actor. Who had David Mead fooled? Winnie? Not too hard. Pam? We don't know. How many family and friends as 'the David they always knew' in his 'perfect marriage'? And we know, full and damn well, it wasn't. There's a Bob Seger song, 'Running against the Wind' that says 'I wish I didn't know now, what I didn't know then.' And, ladies and gentlemen, you know now what they didn't know then, about David's 'perfect marriage.' "

This jury had been audience to theater: the heartbreak of day one, when David Mead cried and cried and the bailiff brought him tissues, became a nap at the table as poor, dear, departed Kevin Harris returned momentarily on video tape. They'd seen theater. Jurors nodded.

"Finally, ladies and gentlemen, one of the things Mr. Mauro told you—well, they don't have this scenario, they don't have that scenario. No, because nobody saw him do it. But if you go and set up a murder, is anyone going to see you do it? But think about what Mr. Mauro said, that we can't come up with a given scenario. We can't tell whether she was killed in the house, taken out in a blanket and dumped in the water or she's hit upside the head out by the water—over where David comes and says, 'Hey, Honey, stand over here and look at the fish.' No, we don't tell you that," I paused, "but, you know what the charge is—that he caused her death. And the ironic thing is that you can go in there, in that jury room, and you could have it, being there's ten of you here, five to five whether it happened in the house or out by the pool. Or three to seven whether or not he did it or had somebody else come and do it for him—and I can't tell you whether David finally had the baw—"

I caught myself and my breath and paused.

". . . had the backbone to do his own killing, or he used that $30,000 to get somebody else to do it for him. But if you, as a group, agree that he caused her death, then you have agreed unanimously on the charge here.

"What you have is a whole lot of evidence that interlocks. It interlocks from a lot of little pieces, like the patches of a quilt. And they tie together and they're bound together at the corners and on the edges. But it's there; everything is there. There's a lot of evidence here. It is not an easy case. It is not one where you can say, 'Yes—Joe was there—Joe saw him do it.' But it's not the case where Joe would be there to see him do it. Consider the evidence. We need to meet the standard of reasonable doubt on every element.

"On the solicitation, the only evidence you have—and you agreed, you promised, to decide this case on the evidence and not on speculation—is what Jack Hendrix told you happened. And it is corroborated by many other things. You have the killing. You have the red flags from Dr. Sperry—the whole profile of this case."

I turned and faced the defendant. Our stares turned to glares. "And she died and then the first thing he did was—we're going out to get the insurance. Yeah! And, in fact, he fooled everybody, but like President Lincoln said, not all the time, and like Dr. Sperry said, when the house of cards comes down because, in fact, you've left yourself some openings, that's when you wind up being charged with murder."

Again, I caught my breath and then returned my attention to the jury box. "Ladies and gentlemen, please look at the evidence. It's there. I will also thank you for your service. And that service is what the State of Utah will ask you for, a verdict just and true."

It was over. I walked back to the table but didn't sit down. The jurors were quickly sworn to the service of deliberation. It was after four o'clock on an intense day, so Judge Frederick excused the jury for the day, admonished them and ordered them to return at nine the next morning. In a personal ritual, I walked up to the judge, clerk and bailiff, shook their hands and thanked them. I walked over to the defense table, offered my hand and congratulations to Rich and Ben, as professionals, for the work they had done. I do this after the work but before the verdict so as to be neither gloating nor begrudging. Last, I stood before David Earl Mead. My norm is to hold out my hand and say that it's nothing personal. That day my hand wasn't extended to its full when I said, "Mr. Mead," a gesture in any event not accepted nor returned.

The courtroom relatively full of spectators was pin-drop quiet.

32

The Verdict

After going through the same mental gymnastics with the reporters gathered in the hallway, we started our vigil. I took
care of a few chores and went home and lay awake, going
over every detail, word and phrase used or left out.

The next morning I didn't have to put on a suit. Khaki
slacks, a shirt, tie and blazer would cover this phase of trial.
Judge Frederick had us show up at nine o'clock to be there as
the jury assembled, the two alternates were excused and
deliberations began. Rich took his exceptions on jury instructions and I walked back to the office to wait.

After a tense morning, I didn't feel like lunch. I had just
taken off my jacket and tie when Michelle stepped into my
office. Nervously I looked at my watch; it was only a few
minutes after one. "It's the court. They have a verdict." My
stomach. This was way too quick; there hadn't even been any
questions sent out by the jury. Hadn't I even made a dent? I
grabbed my blazer, cinched my tie, flew out the door, down
the block and into the courthouse. Jill and two extra bailiffs
were there. Ben came in after me; Rich got there without the
defendant, then Michelle as cameras and reporters set up
shop in the hallway. Neither the Stokeses nor David's family
had arrived. *What will I say to Mrs. Stokes if we lost?* I asked
myself. *What could I say?* His Honor took the bench with
minimal ceremony and asked about Mead. The defense
didn't know, but one of David's supporters walked into the
courtroom and said he was in the bathroom and would be
there in a moment.

Jill walked out to find the Stokeses, quickly came back
and said that they were across the street, up the block.
David's family wasn't far behind. David burst into the

courtroom to the judge's glare. As he pushed through the press, one of the reporters asked how he felt. Without stopping Mead replied, "I'm feeling very confident."

The judge told the bailiff to get the jury. I pleaded that the families were on their way.

"Mr. Lemcke, everyone that's required is present."

"Yes, Your Honor." We stood as eight citizens filed to their places, their faces serious. None looked at either our table or the defense.

"The jury has returned to the courtroom. You may be seated. Sir, you are the foreperson for the jury?"

"Yes, I am."

"Have you arrived at a verdict in this case?"

"Yes, we have."

"Would you present the Verdict Forms to the bailiff?" The bailiff took the forms from the foreperson and handed them to the judge, who, in turn, looked to see that only two of the four were signed and passed them to the clerk. "Members of the jury, I want to take this opportunity to express my appreciation to you for your service in this case. It has not been an easy case, but I have noted that you paid particular attention. And I'm sure that whatever your verdict is, it is a true and just verdict." He turned to the clerk, "Will you read the verdict forms please?"

I tried my best to show no emotion as the words were voiced. "*State of Utah versus David Mead.* Count I. We the Jurors impaneled in the above case find the Defendant, David Mead, Guilty of Murder as charged in Count I of the Information."

The reporters silently marked the moment. Rich slumped a bit; Ben turned his head, bit his lip and tightly closed his eyes. David Mead didn't flinch. "Count II. We the Jurors impaneled in the above case find the Defendant, David Mead, Guilty of Solicitation of Criminal Homicide as charged in Count II of the Information."

"Counsel, do you wish to have the jury polled?"

Rich did and one by one each juror stood and affirmed that this was, and this is, his or her verdict.

"Members of the jury, your service in this case is now concluded. The admonition I have given you about not discussing the case is now lifted. You can discuss the case with whomever you choose, but . . ." His Honor turned to me as I entered another personal ritual. "Is there some reason that you're standing?"

"Yes, Your Honor. What I was going to ask is that I would invite the jurors, as I am their employee, to call me at the District Attorney's office. There are things that I would like to discuss with each of them. In that way I can be a better employee."

Ritual to me was irritating to the court. "And that's fine. As I was saying, the admonition is lifted and you can discuss the case with whomever you choose. But, if you choose not to, you don't have to discuss the case with anyone. Again, thank you. You are free to go and excused."

We all stood and our companions of the past eight days returned to the community. "Mr. Mead, come forward, please, to the lectern here, with your counsel, Mr. Mauro and Mr. Hamilton." Seamlessly the bailiff moved behind the defendant while his two backups positioned themselves to block a run by David or a charge by spectators not yet present. "In light of the jury's findings, Mr. Mead, I'm going to take you, at this time, into custody." The defendant's hands were gently gathered behind his back and the distinct ratchet chatter of stainless steel handcuffs, first the left then the right, filled a room void of those who so deserved to hear this. "You have a right to be sentenced in this case in no less than two nor more than forty-five days from today's date. And, I presume Mr. Mauro and Mr. Hamilton, that you agree that a Presentence Report would be appropriate."

"Yes, Your Honor."

"We will schedule the matter for sentencing on . . ." he deferred to his clerk.

"December the fourth."

"Which is a Friday morning at nine o'clock, Counsel. And we will ask Adult Probation and Parole to contact Mr. Mead in custody and get the information they need from him for the Pre-sentence Report. And, if there's nothing further at this time, Counsel, we will be in recess."

The gavel crashed down, we stood and the judge, robes flowing, left to deal with other matters. David Earl Mead didn't glance sideways as he walked in front of the State's table and out through that heavy steel door.

Jill and I hugged without words and walked out of an empty courtroom to meet the Fourth Estate. Rich and Ben demurred and departed as the cameras pointed our way. It was just after one thirty and reflected sunlight sparkled through the glass wall. We took the expected questions, gave the expected answers, congratulated Rich and Ben—not there to hear it—on trying the case in a professional manner.

At the elevator, we saw the Stokeses waiting. A trembling family moved toward a lawyer with a barely disguised Cheshire grin. I looked toward the press, who had followed us. I owed them one for protecting Stormy during the prelim.

"Howie, what's going on? What's happening?"

"Mrs. Stokes, can you and your family come back to Salt Lake on December 4 when David Mead, who was just convicted on all counts, is sentenced to serve the rest of his life in prison for murdering your daughter?"

"Hallelujah!" The corridor exploded in happiness, hugs, tears, squeals and thanksgiving. Cameramen smiled as I tried to explain why the verdict wasn't held until the families arrived, which wasn't important now. Garfield Stokes is a soldier, trained to leave emotion to others while he bears the load, but I looked at a man with his eyes glistening. "You know, Garfield, now and again the army may lose a battle . . ." His face opened as he joined me, ". . . but we ain't never going to lose the war!" Two old GIs shared a long, hard, sincere hug.

Other people started to show up; lawyers of all stripes flashed me quick responses appropriate to their side of the aisle; I'd already said my piece and the cameras were interested in the Stokeses. I stood in the background and fell into warm adrenaline drain when one of the reporter walked over. "Howie, how do guys like Mead do it? You know, all those women? Pam? Stormy? Winnie?"

"Richard, I don't know. I guess that there are folks out there that can just charm the pantyhose off an octopus. I don't know, man. I'm not one of them." We had a good laugh. My unguarded remark didn't play on the dinnertime news, but it did lead at ten o'clock.

I returned to the background, when another frantic figure raced down the hall—David's mother. She dashed past me into the empty courtroom and within moments was back in the hallway frantically searching for someone no longer there. I wasn't the person she wanted to see, but there was no one else. I walked over and gave the news as gently as I could to another mother who loved her child. She gasped, put her hands over her mouth, pushed back into the courtroom only to encounter the bailiff, who was locking up, and, with a sob, she was gone.

33

Let Justice Be Done

Even the Mead sentencing did not follow the normal course. I got a call from the AP&P agent preparing Mead's PSR, who said David wouldn't cooperate and fill out his paperwork. There was an early escape attempt that got further than most, but that's not very far. Mead had been in and out of suicide watch and the mental health tier.

Ron Yengich called and said Mead's family approached his firm to handle the appeal; he was thinking about taking it and had a few questions. We talked and Ron talked to the other side before he did decide to take it. "Howie, David wanted me to find out if you were going to charge him with anything else, anything new."

I teased my friend Ron, "Like escapes? Or like drugs? Or like what, Ron?"

He responded to humor with a straight face, "Are you considering new charges?"

"No, I'm content to see him spend the rest of his life in prison for killing Pam."

"Okay. Thanks."

My word processor didn't even enjoy a rest. Rich

announced his contention the solicitation count was a lesser-included offense of the murder, which foreclosed David Mead from being sentenced on both counts. I put a law clerk on it, got in touch with Todd Brunker at the AG and timely got papers and cases to His Honor.

Just before Thanksgiving I received a very nice note from the Stokes family to express their feelings about what we'd all been through. I wrote back to brief them on the several situations heading into the sentencing and said a few clumsy thoughts about what they had come to mean to me.

The Monday before December 4, I got a memo from the Pre-sentence Report writer to Judge Frederick detailing how the defendant frustrated all attempts to get the PSR written. However, as of the date of the memo, David Mead changed his mind and now wanted to participate in the process. Could AP&P have a thirty-day continuance to carry this out?

Within the hour State's Objection to Continuance of Sentence was on Judge Frederick's desk and faxed to the defense. The expense of changing last minute reservations paled in comparison to one more cruelty heaped upon the Stokeses. I argued David's actions to manipulate the process waived, by conduct, any right to a PSR. When I got back to my desk there was a voice message suggesting that I shouldn't change those reservations. I didn't.

On Wednesday, December 2, another motion found my desk: "David Mead, through his attorneys, Richard Mauro and Benjamin Hamilton, hereby move to withdraw as Mr. Mead's attorneys in the above-entitled matter. A conflict of interest exists in the continued representation of Mr. Mead, because he intends to allege a claim of Ineffective Assistance of Counsel." It wasn't accompanied by a Motion to Continue, but the defense would ask that sentencing not go forward.

Judge J. Dennis Frederick didn't have a large calendar that cold, gray morning. We sat in our accustomed positions, Jill and I at the right-hand table with our supporters behind us, Rich and Ben back on the left side, before a smaller, tenser following while several bailiffs stood with Pete. The heavy iron door opened and David Earl Mead emerged. In a final scene of David Mead's over-acted four-year melodrama, the title character emerged without underclothing in a brand

new, crisp, starched, bright red Salt Lake County Jail prisoner jumpsuit unzipped to the navel, his hair in a short ponytail, and swaggered to his sentencing in a better stride than
I've ever witnessed in a leg-shackled prisoner.

"For the record, Counsel, this is the time set for sentencing. The defendant was found guilty of the charge of murder,
first degree, and the solicitation of murder, a second degree,
on the twenty-eighth of October of this year. I thereafter
ordered a Pre-sentence Report with the concurrence of
Counsel and Mr. Mead and have received a semblance of
such a report. Mr. Mauro, you've seen a copy of these memoranda?"

"And the memoranda from Mr. Lemcke. Right."

"And is there any reason known to you, Mr. Mauro, why I
should not proceed with sentencing at this time?"

"There is, Your Honor." Rich was subdued but made a
professional's best effort on behalf of an embittered client.
Richard Mauro and Benjamin Hamilton are really good trial
lawyers who can and who will put aside personal feelings
and affront and do their job. I may be in the business of
opposing with all my might their positions on facts, laws,
evidence or outcomes but not of denying their skill, passion,
integrity or humanity. "I made a filing to withdraw in this
case and I don't know how to approach that. There are some
questions that Mr. Mead may have about issues that may subsequently arise, either in appeal or by way of a Rule 23(b)
Hearing that deals with effectiveness of counsel. I have
explained to Mr. Mead what that is. I have also explained that
I am probably not the best person to talk to about whether or
not there is a viable claim to raise and I guess that it's my
view that we ought to give Mr. Mead the time to talk to an
independent attorney."

Rich told the court that an outsider needed to look at his
work; there were procedural steps that needed to be taken; he
didn't know how objective he was and wasn't comfortable
with proceeding.

"Mr. Lemcke, does the State have anything to say on this
matter?"

My position was that an ineffective assistance claim isn't
properly brought until appeal, which follows sentencing, and

a publicly-funded attorney may not withdraw until succeeding counsel is on board. There was also something to say to the judge, not for the judge but for Rich and Ben, "We think that it's proper to go forward with sentencing today. The claim of ineffective assistance under *Strickland*, or any other standard, is silly in this case. There was hardly a motion left unmoved or an objection left un-made. I have, literally, a carton of documents that go with the briefing of this particular case. There was effort. There was skill."

The judge agreed the only thing before him that day was to finish the case by sentencing the defendant and there were representatives of his victim who traveled from out of state to be heard. When His Honor started to address Mr. Mead's games with the PSR forms, Mead cut in, "I couldn't do it!" Judge Frederick ignored him and continued addressing the issue.

"Sir! May I speak in my own behalf?"

"I'll give you a chance. In a minute."

"I really—"

"In a minute. I will give you a chance. Go ahead, Mr. Mauro."

Mead stayed quiet while Rich addressed his concern about Jack Hendrix's testimony that David Mead claimed to pass a polygraph by studying: he'd wanted an expert on the difficulty of faking a poly but the judge denied the defense that witness.

As to the actual sentencing, Rich made the point that the defendant maintained his claim of innocence, even though our jury disagreed, and couldn't say he was sorry for deeds he continued to deny. Rich wouldn't replay evidence; he'd made his record on solicitation as a lesser included of murder. David Mead had no prior criminal history. The defense would submit.

"Mr. Mead, before I impose sentence, do you have anything to say?"

"Yes, I do, sir! Just on my own behalf." The David Earl Mead Show was on the air with tones of indignation and sarcasm that would make an exposed politician proud. "In regards to Mr. Mauro and Mr. Hamilton and the case they brought against me—or that the State brought against me and they defended me on—one point. In fact, I may have something to say, that this sentencing, I feel, is unfair." He had no idea of how important his PSR could be; his lawyers hadn't paid nearly enough attention to him after the verdict; he'd been in the suicide tank and mental health tier where it's hard to make calls.

"I should probably go with the fact that I am very disgruntled with the way I was defended. I can go into points, all the way through this situation, of why I feel I was ineffectively defended. I have a thirty-three page letter that only states a couple of the facts that I feel should—that should have been brought into evidence and I have a list."

As Mead waved papers, the judge told him not in this hearing, while Rich and Ben sat slumped without flinching as the abuse was heaped. "Ben Hamilton and Rich Mauro have not come to help me or at least to look at these documents and tell me whether I should fight it out or not. I'm pleading not guilty to these charges. I am not going to plead down." David felt this was a good time to halt the proceedings, talk to another lawyer and finish that PSR like the judge really wanted.

Then David turned and faced the gallery, knowing it included Pam's blood family and his own blood family. "I really do feel remorse that the Stokes family has not been able to accept this as an accident. I've suffered as well. I lost Pam. There is no one who mattered more to me and my family, and her family knows that. The only one Pam ever spoke to, that I know of, in an affectionate way was her sister Mary, and Pam and her, if you look at her, they have a lot in common in the facial features. Just to look at Mary, I'm reminded of my wife." The gaze cast into the Stokeses' section of the gallery was worthy of a '30s B movie. To this day I can't decide if it was meant to generate disgust or fear.

"I lost a person, too, in this battle and I've lost my entire family because of this. I cannot understand how the jurors, in a three-hour period, were able to go through all this evidence, all the testimony and all the physical evidence and convict me on three people's hearsay statements that are not true. They all have vendettas against me to lie in their own self-interest. Jack, to get back at me for that prison term he ended up serving. The other two people are spurned lovers. How can that end up convicting me on a murder charge, Your Honor?"

"All right, Mr. Mead. Does the State have . . . ? Well, let me first inquire if there are victim representatives that want to be heard."

"Yes, Your Honor. Mrs. Stokes," I summoned Pam's mother to the lectern. David tried to walk over to her, acting like he was seeking comfort, but the bailiff, his pals and David's attorneys knew better and pushed him over by the jury box. "Your Honor, this is Sinie Stokes, who is the victim's mother."

As Sinie turned to address David, he went into a series of theatrically phony facial expressions of shock, surprise, question and hurt, but Mead couldn't resist an attempt at some final, hurtful damage. As I stood next to Mrs. Stokes and watched David Mead mock his dead wife's mother, I realized that three professional degrees and sixteen years of daily dealing with the measured language of the law left me totally inadequate to describe my intense feelings about this man getting in his last, mean licks on the attorneys who'd fought for him, Pam's family, who once welcomed him into their lives, and, deliberately or inadvertently, his own family, who just happened to be in the way.

Despite his antics, now it was our turn. Mrs. Stokes carried the dignity I was on the verge of losing. "David, I'd just like to ask you, why? We accepted you into our family, we treated you like family, we cared about you, we loved you and this is how you repay us? You destroyed three sets of lives, the Stokes family, the Meads' and yours. And, why, because of greed? She gave you everything: she loved you; we did, too. And this is how you repaid us? You used her for financial gain and then, after you had what you wanted, you destroyed her. You no longer needed her.

"But one thing you didn't count on: you mistook our kindness for weakness. We're not weak and I want you to know, right now, we'll fight you to the end. Even when you come up for parole, you will have to look at me and my family again, because you took something from us that you cannot replace. All because of greed. And what did you do? You brought yourself down, lower than anything. My daughter was too good for you; she deserved better. And what did you give her? You repaid her by murdering her!"

As Mead made the largest flourish of facial antics yet, Sinie continued, correcting this phony ploy as only a mother could, "Yes, you did, David! You did that and I know that you did it within my heart, but that's okay. You walked around for four years; now it's time for you to pay. And I sat there and listened to you talk to the judge. You should have thought about that, but you walked around for four years and we had to suffer and fight and try everything that we could to make sure that you got what you deserved.

"Now it's time for you to pay and what do you do? You squirm! All I have to say about you is that you are a coward. She was struck from behind! You didn't want her to see you; you could not face her, but I am facing you now on behalf of her and my family. You deserve everything that you have coming!"

David face wasn't doing cute quite so well as Pam's sister came to the podium. "David, I told you in August of 1994 that I would make it my mission in life to find out what really happened to Pam. Now I know you murdered her in cold, premeditated blood. Your cold, calculating and selfish act is incomprehensible. My parents treated you like a son. You ate at their table! They trusted you; you were welcomed into their home. Pam was nothing but loving and supportive of you, but she was also naïve and you took advantage of that. You disrespected her, you abused her, you used her and, ultimately, you took her life.

"You can stand there and tell the judge what you will, but we both know the truth. You portray yourself as being a good person. You are not, David Mead. You are low-life scum unworthy of freedom or life.

"My family will never be the same without Pam. The pain and anguish that you've caused my family will never be forgotten. You have caused a permanent, physical loss to my family, but you have also opened up a spiritual understanding and awakening in me that you will never be able to understand. And there is one thing you don't understand, David Mead. There is one thing that is unshakable, irrefutable, that you can never, ever cheat or get away from your crime under universal spiritual justice.

"You avoided the court system for four years. Four years! You tried repeatedly to deter my parents in their search for truth and justice. We all know about the constant and harassing phone calls that you made, the legal maneuvering and the witness tampering. David, what goes around comes around and justice will always be served. You are nothing more than a coward. You think that you're so clever, so smart, yet it's you who are too afraid to stand up and take responsibility for what you did. You are pathetic.

"The other thing that you didn't understand is that we are a strong, united family with the strengths and resources to fight this battle as long as it takes. We'll continue to fight for justice as long as you are alive. We are not finished with you yet, David Mead; we'll meet again. Every time there's a parole hearing the Stokes family will be there to see to it that you never, ever have freedom again, to see to it that you never, ever have the opportunity to kill another innocent person. We owe that to Pam."

I walked Mary back to her family and then returned to the front of the courtroom. The ladies of the Stokes family had made the points of equity so much better in sincerity and strength than I could have in anger; I only needed to make points in law. I signaled to the bailiffs that Mead held no terror for me; they could bring him back. David knew and meekly took a seat.

I addressed the lie detector: it wasn't my memory the defense was denied the presentation of a witness. They'd never named a witness, even turned down a cautionary instruction, and nothing was said about polys during close. As to the PSR, I was there after the verdict when Judge Frederick ordered the defendant to cooperate in the preparation of that document. Why should he be rewarded for disobeying the court's order? I was firmly on the record that David Mead was convicted and should be sentenced on two distinct crimes. Ironically, the defense complains there's no Utah case on point: since they intend to appeal, if David is sentenced on both counts there will be.

"We feel that he should be sentenced consecutively. We

think that prison, because of the nature of the crime itself, regardless of the defendant's background, is appropriate in a homicide. In fact, I think that it's statutorily required. And we say that these should be served consecutively, Your Honor, for two reasons, the first of which is that the defendant did have the opportunity to withdraw, after the Hendrix plan fell apart on him. He did not, though, and there should be, for people who have the opportunity to withdraw from a serious or violent crime, an additional price if they continue to go forward. Secondly, we all pat ourselves on the back a lot about how we serve out harsh penalties and, therefore, deter people. And I think that we can make an argument for deterrence, particularly in a planned and premeditated crime like this, a crime like this, which Mary Stokes referred to as a cold-blooded crime of calculation. Those people who calculate what their gain is going to be ought to be made to take into account the downside, because those calculating ones are the ones who may be deterred by harsh sentencing."

"Thank you, Mr. Lemcke. Is there anything else, Mr. Mauro?"

"No, Your Honor, I don't want to reiterate and repeat the prior arguments we made about whether or not there's a greater or lesser relationship or whether they're separate offenses. I think that I've preserved the record on that. Other than that, we'll submit it, Your Honor."

After a wave of the judicial hand, the shackled defendant was assisted to his feet. He moved to the podium with much less gusto than he took the stage earlier. The gallery leaned forward to hear each and every word.

"All right, there being no legal reason why I should not impose sentence, I will do so at this time. Mr. Mead, it is the judgment and sentence of this court that you serve the term provided by law in the Utah State Prison for the first degree felony crime of murder, the term of five years to life. It is also the order of this court that you serve the term provided by law in the Utah State Prison as to the second degree felony crime of solicitation of murder of one to fifteen years and that those terms are to be served consecutively and not concurrently. I will, moreover, order that you pay restitution at this time of the funds that you derived from the life insurance policy on your victim. You are to repay those funds as restitution, all the funds that you obtained in that regard, and, moreover, that you pay a fine in the amount of $10,000, for the murder and solicitation crimes that the jury found you guilty of."

His Honor leaned forward and slowly and directly spoke to David Earl Mead, who had no humor left in his face. "It is my view, Mr. Mead, having heard the evidence in this case, that you are indeed the calculating and cold-blooded planner of this murder, that indeed, you are a clear and present danger of serious, violent behavior, if you were released from prison, and that's why I impose the maximum available to me. This was, in my estimation, a heinous crime in that you took advantage of someone who trusted and apparently loved you. She was indeed a vulnerable victim and in a calculated fashion you planned her demise and carried out this murder knowingly and intentionally and you have shown, since the first day of trial, a total lack of remorse and/or acceptance of responsibility.

"I therefore think, Mr. Mead, that the best place for you is in prison. An order of commitment will issue forthwith. As I am bound to do, I will grant you twenty-seven days' credit towards your ultimate sentence."

Without further ceremony David, who never looked back, was escorted through the heavy, gray steel door that welcomed him into his future.

Judge Frederick returned to Rich's Motion to Withdraw, said he'd grant it at this point, gave me a week to object, but my only problem was not wanting it granted before imposition of sentence. With the commitment, the court lost jurisdiction to the board and the issue was moot, so I wouldn't object. The motion was granted, Rich was to prepare the order and *State v. Mead* was adjourned.

It was, as it should be, the family's moment in the spotlight. My few observations that morning paled in comparison to the eloquence of the Stokes women, and David probably did David more damage during sentencing than I did. I just stood in the background, drank in the morning sunlight that for a moment streamed between broken clouds to the glass wall and let everyone know Pam was to be remembered in a Mass.

By the time I walked up the front steps of the Cathedral of the Madeleine, where Monsignor Francis Mannion baptized me into the Catholic faith just two weeks earlier, it had started snowing those big snowflakes that swirl slowly down in Bing Crosby films. The TV folks were setting up and Monsignor Francis wondered about cameras I'd never explained. I didn't know who would show up, but soon the Stokeses, Pastor Davis, Jill and friends started coming in, brushing snowflakes from shoulders and hair. Without any notice, Monsignor Mannion gave a homily on loss, justice, redemption and remembrance that lifted all spirits. A detective cried. From the pulpit came the prayer intentions for the Church, the community and those in need of prayer and we responded, "Lord, hear our prayer."

"And we pray for those who have gone to their rest, in the hope of rising again, bring them into the light of your presence, especially Pamela Camille Stokes, who we remember in a special way in this Mass. For this, we pray."

"Lord, hear our prayer." I just wanted to give Pam back to her family.

We stood, held hands and sang the Lord's Prayer. Francis held wide his arms. "Lord Jesus Christ, you said to your apostles, 'I leave you Peace; my Peace I give you.' Look not on our sins, but on the faith of your Church and grant us the peace and unity of your kingdom, where you live forever and forever."

"Amen."

"The Peace of the Lord be with you, always."

"And also with you."

"Let us offer each other the sign of Peace."

We turned to one another, shook hands and hugged. And finally, four years after my entry into this drama, after so many long hours and days of giving my attentions to the man who took Pam's life, I could finally turn those attentions to the woman who gave Pam life. I could look her in the eye, take her hand and say, and wish, and pray, out loud, "Christ's Peace, Sinie Stokes."

Epilogue

Ron Yengich took David Mead's appeal to the Utah Supreme Court. I guess David's family found the money somehow. This case was very hurtful to them. In a way, they too were a victim family. The appeal to the Utah Supreme Court contained nine allegations of error and two "pour-over" allegations. The evidence wasn't sufficient to support a conviction and all the small errors, even if individually not sufficient for reversal, were "cumulative" error requiring it. Ron put together the "Defendant and Appellant's" paperwork, including a prolonged exchange over whether or not Judge Frederick allowed Rich to call a polygraph expert on rebuttal, that went back and forth till the Supremes heard oral arguments on February 6, 2001, then took the case "under advisement." Marian Decker from the Utah Attorney General's Office headed up the team of Assistant AGs, including Tom Brunker, who carried the State's side as "Plaintiff and Appellee." I helped their crew "Moot" the case to prepare Marian for argument and sat next to her during the hearing in the old, dignified Supreme Court Chambers in the state capital.

David's family was there, as nervous as I was but honest enough to show it. Both sides did well enough that I stayed on edge until July 10, when my desktop computer beeped to indicate new e-mail. *State of Utah v. David Earl Mead* was one of three cases whose URLs appeared in the blue letters of an Internet link, "Newly Posted Opinions—Utah Appellate Courts." I flinched before clicking on it. Not to say that I wasn't confident in the case or in Marian's good work, but this was a big chunk of my life and the past and future peace of Pam's family, for whom I'd fought so hard, in the hands of strangers. Mercifully the opening paragraph of the fourteen page opinion was short and to the point: "A jury convicted David Mead of murder, a first degree felony, in violation of section 76-5-203 of the Utah Code, and criminal solicitation, a second degree felony, <u>see</u> Utah Code Ann. (section) 76-4-204 (1995), Utah Code Ann. (section) 76-5-203(2) (Supp. 1998), in violation of section 76-4-203. Mead appeals his convictions, alleging numerous errors at trial. We affirm."

It was over. After reading the entire opinion and re-reading several parts of it, I learned the court felt His Honor Frederick probably should have allowed more follow-up questioning of the jurors, error but not reversible error. The opinion considered the allegations, found no other errors and went on, "Having concluded the only error committed below was the trial court's failure to allow follow-up questions during *voir dire*, we do not address Mead's contention that the jury verdict should be reversed due to cumulative error. We conclude that there was sufficient competent evidence as to each element of the crime charged for the fact finder to find, beyond a reasonable doubt, that the defendant committed the crime. Accordingly, Mead has provided us no reason to second-guess the jury's determination. <u>Durrant</u>, Justice. Chief Justice Howe, Associate Chief Justice Russon, Justice Durham and Justice Wilkins concur in Justice Durrant's Opinion."

There was another round of phone calls to make. Anne was delighted, as were the folks at the Bureau, the medical examiner office and the airline for which Pam had worked. Then I made the most important of my calls. When I reached the Stokeses I avoided suspense: "I've got good news." Afterwards, Jill, Meesh and I employed appropriate beverages in celebration and filled Stormy, friend, in on details of the fishpond case unavailable to Stormy, witness.

Today the Lemcke family prospers with blessings too numerous to count. Our daughter Amy graduated from college and is climbing a corporate ladder in the Midwest. Our son Dan wound up in college down in Texas, studying computers and learning the origins of his dad's sometimes drawl, and looks to graduate a year from this spring. Our other daughter Sara heads off this fall to another of my origins and enrolls in a Chicago area school, leaving my loving and lovely wife Nance and I empty nesters.

Salt Lake City elected a new mayor in 1999. Chief of Police Ruben Ortega retired to another state between the election and the inauguration. Jill Candland's lawsuit against Chief Ortega and the PD was quietly settled out of court and placed under seal, but it's no secret she received her choice of assignments till she finished out her twenty years and retired in late 2002. She chose the FBI Inter-Agency Olympic Joint Terrorism Task Force and did her part helping get us through a marvelous Winter Olympiad. Everybody says her golf clubs sure look good in the back of that new luxury SUV as she drives off to her country club.

Dave Yocom got re-elected in 2002, but hints it'll probably be his last term. My assistant Michelle took a far better offer in terms of money, assignment and potential to advance. She has her bachelor's degree and a home under construction on a hillside.

Stormy has come into new and better circumstance. She, Jill and Dr. Maureen Frikke, who won a personal battle with cancer, came to last year's Cathedral Choir School Spring Auction. I've lost track of Winnie, but I wish her well and try to remember her in my prayers. It's Winnetka Walls's turn to have good things and nice people come her way.

Ron Boyce fell suddenly ill last fall, and passed away a few weeks later. The last time I saw him was at his "Spring Legal Update" for criminal law practitioners where he came across *State v Mead* a few times and, each time, stopped and made a point of saying what a good win and a tough case it was. This wasn't something that Ron did and, coming in front of my professional peers from a man we personally and professionally respected as much as Ron, that may be the greatest professional compliment of my career.

The cruel mistress of narcotics addiction claimed Jack Hendrix. In a weak moment, he sought out a fix and perhaps his body lost its tolerance; it killed him. In an additional insult heaped on Jack's family, his wallet was stolen and his body went unidentified and unclaimed for several days while his family had nothing but uncertainty. Prayers are needed here as well.

Roger Tinsley made it to Hollywood and I smile when I see his name in the credits. Anne Sulton moved to the East Coast where she's teaching, practicing law and sending her own beautiful kids off to college. I keep in touch with her and with the Stokeses and hope that they are at peace. Some of the nicest people I'll ever meet, even through such terrible circumstance, they're often in my thoughts and prayers. So many times I think about Pam, child of Garfield and Sinie, child of God, my sister I was never privileged to meet, and wonder what she would have been like as a neighbor, co-worker or friend. The Stokeses bonded with Pastor Davis over these events and these years. His congregation at Calvary Baptist recently dedicated a brand new church where God will be wonderfully praised for years to come. I will always value his counsel and comfort.

The Board of Pardons has set a date to consider whether or not David Earl Mead should be given a still later date to be placed on parole or be required to spend his natural life behind bars, October 1, 2016. I hope to be there, but if my appearance isn't possible I'd like to set forth the reasons why I believe that David Mead should be given natural life.

How does that square with Catholic belief that God requires forgiveness for trespasses directed against each of us? I forgive David Earl Mead for any trespass he has, in his thoughts, words, plans or deeds directed toward me. I wish David a peaceful heart in regard to his impressions of me and my thoughts towards him, but clearly I am not the only, nor the first, person from whom David needs to seek forgiveness. I'm way down that list, but maybe, just maybe, I can be a start.

I seek David's permanent incarceration out of policy, not pique. Not only is natural life an appropriate penalty to impose for the wrong done to the secular community I serve, it is the appropriate length of time to safeguard my community from whatever evil might come from people who have committed evil deeds like David Mead. Forgiveness for the past is one thing, trust for the future quite another.

For those down the road who would make a calculated

risk/reward assessment about committing crime, we ought to make them factor into their balance a risk that is very great, indeed. For those who might coldly fix a price on the life of another, they ought to take notice that society can and will set a harsh price on their freedom. Someone who can pretend for evil purpose to be a perfect husband, or a perfect anything, over an extended period of time should learn that even an extended period of appearing the perfect prisoner will be viewed with jaundiced eye by a board that's not pretending.

Those who announce a list of people upon whom they will exact revenge ought to be denied the opportunity. Finally, to answer that inevitable advocate who someday will appear before the board and make the argument that Pam's death, by being struck over the head and then drowned, was not of an especially heinous, cruel or shocking nature, let me remind the board that David Earl Mead employed the cruelest weapon of all, love.

ACKNOWLEDGMENTS

The author would like to acknowledge the support and encouragement he has received from: First and foremost his own family, Nancy, Amy, Dan and Sara; Garfield and Sinie Stokes, their family, Anne Sulton, Stormy and other people I was privileged to meet over these events; The irreplaceable Michelle, Salt Lake District Attorney David E. Yocom and my other friends and co-workers in his office; My friends and co-workers in the Salt Lake defense bar, courts and press; The unflinching Detective Jill Candland, the personnel of the Salt Lake Police Department and those other local, state and federal officers and officials whose company I've long been blessed to enjoy; Too many others dear to me to name. Finally, my publisher Dr. Joan Dunphy for recognizing that somewhere under the pile of goobledygook a first-time author sent her, there was a story worth telling.

ABOUT THE AUTHOR

Howard R. Lemcke has served as a prosecutor in Utah for the past twenty-two years and has tried several hundred cases, including more than sixty homicides. He says this was his most fascinating case. He currently serves as co–vice chair of the Utah State Bar Criminal Law Association. He lives with his family in Salt Lake City, Utah.

Don't miss the page-turning suspense, intriguing characters, and unstoppable action that keep readers coming back for more from these bestselling authors...

Tom Clancy
Robin Cook
Patricia Cornwell
Catherine Coulter
Clive Cussler
Dean Koontz
John Sandford

Your favorite thrillers and suspense novels come from Berkley.

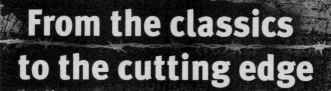